P9-DDG-809

NOTES ON A KILLING

**LOVE, LIES, AND MURDER
IN A SMALL NEW HAMPSHIRE TOWN**

Kevin Flynn and Rebecca Lavoie

BERKLEY BOOKS, NEW YORK

THE BERKLEY PUBLISHING GROUP
Published by the Penguin Group
Penguin Group (USA) Inc.
375 Hudson Street, New York, New York 10014, USA

USA / Canada / UK / Ireland / Australia / New Zealand / India / South Africa / China

Penguin Books Ltd., Registered Offices: 80 Strand, London WC2R 0RL, England
For more information about the Penguin Group, visit penguin.com.

NOTES ON A KILLING

A Berkley Book / published by arrangement with the authors

For information, address: The Berkley Publishing Group,
a division of Penguin Group (USA) Inc.,
375 Hudson Street, New York, New York 10014.

ISBN: 978-0-425-25876-7

PUBLISHING HISTORY
Berkley premium edition / April 2013

PRINTED IN THE UNITED STATES OF AMERICA

10 9 8 7 6 5 4 3 2

Cover photos: *Home at Night* © Cappi Thompson; *Vintage Composition Book* © Hank Frentz;
Pencil Texture © Ra Studio.
Cover design by Jane Hammer.

ALWAYS LEARNING   PEARSON

To Paul Falco: 3/2/05.
—KF

To the friends I've tried to save,
and those who have taught me you can only save yourself.
—RL

Acknowledgments

There are many people we would like to thank for their assistance in gathering the facts and sharing their perceptions so we may tell the most accurate story possible.

Thanks to the New Hampshire Attorney General's Office and the many people there who helped facilitate the research. They include Jeff Strelzin, Lucy Carrillo, and Jennifer Hunt. Thanks also to Nancy Lawrence and Lee-Anne Deveny at the Sullivan County Superior Court, and Annie Zinkin and Lauren Scott at the New Hamsphire Supreme Court.

Thank you to the many people who shared their memories with us or otherwise helped contribute to this book. They include Russell Lamson, Kirsten Wilson, Jonathan Purick, Judy Long, Joanne Dufour, Jim Swan, Steve Duggan, Terri Casey, John Encarnacao, Shawn Skahan, Will Delker, Annmarie Timmons, Sandy Merritt, and Mark Sisti.

The work of investigating a homicide is handled by many law enforcement officers. In some scenes in this book, the names of those people have been omitted to simplify the narrative flow. This decision was merely editorial and does not diminish the work of those individuals or our respect for their achievements. These officers include Trooper Stephen Lee, Officer Matthew McClay, Trooper John LaPointe, Trooper Scott Ellis, Sergeant Paul Hunt, Sergeant Craig Robertson, Lieutenant Jerome Maslan, and Major Barry Hunter.

The authors also wish to thank our agent, Sharlene Martin, and her staff at Martin Literary Management for continuing to support our work.

Lastly, we'd like to show our appreciation for the relationship we have with The Berkley Publishing Group and its wonderful staff, including Joan Matthews, Adrienne Avila, and Gary Mailman. Highest among them is the indomitable Shannon Jamieson Vazquez, our editor and friend, who smoothes the rough corners and makes each story better than the last.

Prologue

It had been another cold night in the foothills of New Hampshire. The men had been in and out of the elements all day, fighting the chill of the New England winter, but it seemed their bones would never be warm again. During the winter some of them lived like nomads in Chryslers—following snow-bandaged byways by day, their only shelter from the harsh elements frosted windows and heated front seats. The extra effort of trudging to and from their cars through fresh, deep snow had bent their knees and backs in unnatural ways, but even at the late hour their bodies did not complain. The men were all large and strong. They were not physically tired, but their mental fatigue was growing. Searching does that to a cop.

After daylight disappeared in the late afternoon, the

night in the woods felt timeless. Only their stomachs could tell them how long it had been since the sun went down.

For too long, they waited at the turnoff from the two-lane highway at the mouth of an unpaved road hidden beneath a foot of newly fallen snow. It took what seemed like an eternity for a plow to arrive and cleave a path through the woods suitable for their souped-up sedans. They watched helplessly while the truck and its blade turned off the smoothed road and bushwhacked its way into the woods, swallowed by the night. Several minutes later, the rattle of every loose bolt on the truck announced itself before the headlights retraced the trail it had created. The plow's driver didn't stop to ask if his work was satisfactory; he simply merged with the main road and continued his nightly rounds in the storm.

Transmissions were engaged and the cruisers rolled at cautious speeds, making first tracks over the packed, virgin path. Heaters were blowing full blast, and the swaying motion of the cars' suspension systems over the trail could easily have rocked a grown man to sleep.

The locals knew where they could find the turnoff to this trail, but the road wasn't on most maps. The town itself, Lempster, didn't appear on any map of New Hampshire that didn't have a conscientious level of detail. The town lay among the trees in West-Central New Hampshire, twenty miles in all directions from a highway of any significance. The closest full-service town was Newport—ten miles due north on a map but frustratingly farther away because of the ponds, mountains, and wetlands that necessitate the tortuous ribbons of the state highway system. As was too often said in New England, "You can't get there from here."

If they weren't stationed at the local barracks in Keene, twenty-five miles away, few members of the New Hampshire State Police would know the way to Lempster. Now, a whole team of those troopers was rumbling down this off-the-grid road in an off-the-beaten-path town searching for a missing woman.

Their headlights were almost useless, as they reflected nothing but the white static of the swirling blizzard a foot in front of them. They had to trust that the frozen trench carrying them deeper and deeper into the woods would bring them to their destination. As impossible as it was to consider the unkempt corridor they were traveling a "main road," the plowed path veered left at a side street while the rest of the buried artery continued straight into the night. They followed this new road until they came to the turnaround the plow had made for itself.

New Hampshire State Police Trooper John Encarnacao was among the four officials who parked and waded through the drifts to get to the front door of the last house on Quimby Farm Road. The front stoop had already been shoveled, so Encarnacao knocked and received no answer. They tersely peered through windows, examined the ground for footprints in the snow. They called aloud for the missing woman. No response.

Encarnacao walked around back, pressing on doors

and windows, looking for a way in. He and another trooper found entrance through a storm window and, after an awkward tumble into the house, moved from room to room searching for signs of their missing person.

Inside, the house was small, more like a cabin than anything else. The living room connected with an open-concept kitchen under a cathedral ceiling that captured high the warmth thrown off by a kerosene heater and a pair of woodstoves. The walls were wood paneled, the floors covered with throw rugs. Overall the place was a mess, with books and clothes and cast-off possessions everywhere. Mixed in with a leather armchair and an upholstered sofa was a rattan table and chair set that was better suited for a deck or patio. The walls were adorned with several paintings of zebras, the black-and-white motif repeated in a cheap lamp and other decorations. A shelf held about a dozen old Nancy Drew books, their familiar yellow spines faded yellow chiffon. On the passageway arch leading to the hallway was a framed placard urging all to LIVE WELL, LAUGH OFTEN, LOVE MUCH.

The house remained still but for the machinations of the two troopers. Doors opened and closed dejectedly; footfalls rapped and squeaked in pivots. Each man listened for the other to shout out something encouraging from his end of the building, or even to yell out something discouraging—a trace of blood or a discarded personal item, but the men remained largely silent.

The troopers stepped outside into the blizzard. The latest bands of snow were already erasing their incoming tire tracks. How long until they would need to call the plow back to rescue them? There was another hour or two of passable travel, perhaps, until the snowpack was higher than the cruisers' drivetrains. There was width enough for only one vehicle in the driveway, and getting stuck would plug the narrow channel out to the road.

Despite the accumulating snow, there was one small section of the backyard that had dimpled in the drifts. It was a fire pit.

Encarnacao, snow up to his shins, kicked his way to the pit. The remains of paper and branches covered the outer layer. The covering of new wood seemed less like it was meant for fueling the fire, more for concealing it from prying eyes. There was no active flame and the top layer was gray with ash, but some embers still cooked below. Stuck in the ground near the pit was a large stick. It was five feet long and several inches thick. The bottom half was charred black and the end worn to a point. It had been left an arm's length away as if it had been used to stoke the fire.

The trooper kneeled carefully by the fire and pulled the branches off one by one. He examined each burned kindle with his flashlight before setting it aside. Snow continued to fall on the back of his neck, and powder collected on his shoulders. Wind gusts of ten to twenty miles per hour were blowing flakes into his face and eyes. It was not a task he relished doing for long.

Encarnacao had uncovered only a few layers when something caught his eye. It was a piece unlike the other bits of firewood in the pit. He reached in and pulled out an item the size of a thumbnail. Encarnacao turned it over under the beam of his Maglite like a jeweler might examine a rare gem.

What the hell?

The investigator was sure what he was holding between his fingers was a bone.

PART ONE

Goshen

A lake is the landscape's most beautiful and
expressive feature. It is Earth's eye; looking into
which the beholder measures the depth of his
own nature.

—HENRY DAVID THOREAU, *WALDEN*

ONE

Telephone

Sandra Merritt struggled to bring the dogs under control. It was early in the morning, about 7:30 a.m. on February 23, 2005, and it was the noisiest part of her day at the Animal Inn. It was feeding time and yelps of all pitches were tolling through the air as she dragged bags of food into the kennel, where dogs whose owners had gone on vacations paced impatiently, their collars clanking against the fencing of the pens. Pavlov's bell was nothing compared to the crash of kibble into a tin bowl, causing a cascade of tongue slobber and tail wagging.

The canine chaos was grating to most people, but Sandy had grown to accept and absorb the energy put off by the dogs. A single woman, she'd woken up that morning alone. Before rising and taking her pills, she meditated:

Grant me the serenity to accept the things I cannot change; the courage to change the things I can; and the wisdom to know the difference.

Sandy Merritt was forty-four years old. She was a pear-shaped, mousy woman with unkempt dark hair covering her face and eyeglasses. Nonetheless, hers was the face that launched a thousand salvos in an emotional tug-of-war involving nearly all of her friends. It had started with an illicit romance, but many had witnessed how ugly it had become. Most had risen up as her protectors, as her champions. It was impossible to believe someone could still get hurt in a mess that had already hurt so many.

Sandy lived in Newport, a Western New Hampshire town of fewer than five thousand people on the banks of the Sugar River. The seat of Sullivan County, Newport's most prominent feature was its broad Main Street with turn-of-the-century brick buildings, many of which had been restored to their former glory. A scattering of rural villages, none that boasted the modern conveniences of its eight-pump gas station or national franchise brand coffee shop, surrounded Newport. It was an oasis for locals and mid-trip tourists alike.

Sandy's family had a little bit of money. There was a wide swath of farmland they owned at the end of a dead-end street. Sandy lived in an apartment added on to the main farmhouse, which was owned by her brother. The addition had been intended for their grandparents before they died. Now Sandy lived alone in this sectioned-off structure with her dog, Moisha. She cherished the quiet of the farm.

Sandy had always been an animal person. For years, she'd made ends meet by walking dogs and working as a pet sitter. Sandy would pass around a business card with her information to townsfolk and friends. It wasn't uncommon for people to see Sandy around town, clutching the reigns of a pack of mismatched dogs, the way a child might grab the tethers of a pack of uncooperative balloons.

Her life had changed dramatically over that last year. She had been in a car crash that resulted in much self-reflection. It also brought her to Alcoholics Anonymous. She had tried to quit drinking before and had failed. This time, though, she was fully committed to the program and was staying sober. She had the support of good friends. But she still regretted starting a new romantic relationship while she was trying to get back on the wagon. It had been a bad idea from the start.

The bays of the dogs at the Animal Inn continued until Sandy quieted the pack one bowl of food at a time. She felt like she was running a bit behind. Last night's snowstorm had left another two inches on her car and the roads, and the world was running in the slow motion that always came after a storm. Dogs don't care about inclement weather, however. They just want to be fed and have no problem barking until someone puts some kibble in front of them. The noise echoed so sharply off the walls that Sandy almost didn't hear the office phone ring.

"Sandy? This is Pen."

Sandy smiled at the sound of her friend's voice. Edith Meyer, known to all as "Pen," had been one of her most ardent supporters over the past four months, ever since Sandy had decided to break off her relationship with her boyfriend. The early morning call was a surprise, as Sandy was sure Pen knew morning was her busiest time at work. She would have to politely nudge Pen off the phone so she could finish doing her job. But what Pen said next erased all notions of hanging up from Sandy's mind.

"Sandy," Pen said, "I want you to reconsider your relationship with him."

Sandy shook her head in disbelief. Pen was mistaken. She was done with him. He was a married man.

He had lied to her, manipulated her, downright terrorized her. Everyone knew Sandy was fragile. She had her own demons—didn't they all? She had found herself in bad relationships over and over again, an infuriating pattern of self-soothing. He was a mistake, and she finally knew that. Of all the guys she'd had unhealthy relationships with, he was unquestionably the worst. But Pen must have heard something around town. She must be under the impression she had taken him back.

"I can now see how it could have been a mistake," Pen said. Before Sandy could correct her, tell her that her feelings hadn't changed, her friend continued. "I want you to go to the courthouse and remove the restraining order."

Sandy was confused. Was Pen suggesting she actually get back together with him?

"You know he's facing a two-thousand-dollar fine. I never meant for it to go this far," Pen said. "Call him at Jim's house and tell him that you'll testify for him in court and tell the judge how it was a mistake."

"Pen, are you sure?" Sandy couldn't contain the bewilderment in her voice. "What do you mean that *you* 'never meant for it to go this far'?"

"I'll leave a letter for the Court to explain how I pushed you because I was jealous of you and him." Pen's voice sounded flat, resigned.

"Sandy, I'm so sorry for my part in all this. I never planned on this. I know he truly loves you and I did my best to remove him from your life. I know he loves you and that is his only crime."

The dogs were barking louder now, a conditioned response to the delay in their scheduled feeding. Someone—the boss, probably—was bound to investigate and find Sandy on the phone neglecting her duties. Sandy covered her open ear with the palm of her hand, partly to block out the noise and partly to keep her head from spinning away from her. She couldn't believe what she was hearing. Then Pen said she was going to send Sandy a letter, which would outline all the ways she had manipulated her friend.

"I'm sorry I used you to make him hurt. It wasn't personal. I just wanted someone to love me that way. Please, Sandy, I knew from the start you two should be together. Let's forget what happened."

Forgetting what happened would be a tall task. She

and Pen had spent months trying to keep her former lover at arm's length. She was indebted to virtually every other person she knew for their part in keeping her safe. They had hidden her in their homes, and they had broken the anonymity of their Twelve Step program to testify on her behalf. But despite pleas and warnings and even legal threats, her ex-boyfriend continued to pursue her heart. It wasn't charming; it was stalking. Forgetting that would be hard to do.

Pen then said she had another surprise. She was leaving town and going to Mexico and South America. "I never told you of the affair I had with this pilot . . ."

"Pilot? What are you talking about?" Sandy knew Pen's boyfriend, Jonathan Purick, and he wasn't a pilot.

"He wants me to travel the world with him. I called him after my divorce but I never thought he would come to rescue me." Pen was breathless now. She said she was going to let Sandy's ex-boyfriend house-sit while she was gone. "If the two of you move in together—as you should—you can rent the house out and move my garden to your place."

Move in together? That was the last thing Sandy wanted to do. And what was this talk about Pen leaving the home and garden she'd lavished so much attention on?

"Sandy, you're truly a friend. I only want the best for you." Pen's voice began to crack. "Know this: Go after him the way I had you stay away from him. Think of *aloneness* like a drink"—signaling to her something she should mortally avoid—"and stick to him like glue. I know you can take care of yourself, but let him be your Prince Charming and take care of you."

Sandy was deeply confused by this bizarre phone call. "Pen, this is all a bit much. Why don't we have lunch and talk about this? I can call you sometime between noon and one o'clock."

"Keep him happy. Keep him out of jail." Then Pen told her to keep their conversation secret from her own boyfriend, Jonathan, and to have no contact with him. She finished by saying she had given her beloved sheepdog, Fluff—whom Pen had in the past admitted to loving like a child—to Sandy's ex.

In the turmoil of those ten minutes, Sandy couldn't remember how the call ended or who said good-bye to whom. There was something about a "chain saw accident" that didn't make any sense. For a frozen moment, she stood among the howling dogs with the phone receiver still in her hand, unable to put it back in the cradle. *What was that call all about?*

Sandy couldn't ignore the animals any longer and finally resumed the morning feeding. She made a mental note to call Pen in the afternoon so she could find out why it was her friend had had such a sudden and shocking change of heart. But she was never able to reach Pen that afternoon, nor that evening.

In fact, no one ever heard from Edith "Pen" Meyer again.

TWO

Pen

Cloth is as dependent on its maker for strength, texture, and quality as a story is to its writer, or a drama to its actors. The threads that bind together, horizontal and vertical, determine everything from purpose to finish, color to coarseness. The weaver, much like the storyteller, is God to the cloth, present even before its birth, choosing its makeup and planning its purpose. Throughout time and all over the world, women have played this role, working looms that construct the fabric of home and body, flag and sail, prayer carpet and shroud.

Today, most of the world's textiles aren't touched by the hands of human weavers, and instead are produced by mechanized looms housed in gray factories where remote villages once stood. But the women who've held on to the loom are forever bound, not only to their ancient craft, but to one another, throughout time and place, woven inextricably together by their shared power of creation.

The woman of Goshen, New Hampshire, that people knew as Pen Meyer cut a striking portrait. Petite, slender, and tan, Pen couldn't be described as anything other than stunning. Her long, once-brown hair had finally been allowed to turn silver, and her frame, though slight, bore the muscles of a woman who made a habit of hiking and swimming several times a day.

Pen's eyes were slate gray, her clothing well made, laid back, and always oversized, which those close to her often saw as a disguise of sorts, a way for the slight woman to appear as large as her spirit. Her arms jangled with the sound of her signature silver bangles, which she wore constantly, whether dressed for a benefit or skinny-dipping behind her house in Gunnison Lake, affectionately dubbed the "Goshen Ocean." The bracelets were distinctive, collected over many years of travel. The most striking were the wide silver cuffs she wore on each wrist, one carved with a buffalo, a reminder of a trip taken to the Southwest with her daughter.

Pen had the carriage and reputation of someone who lived well below her means. She drove a modest, but perfectly maintained, Honda CR-V. Her home wasn't large, but beautifully constructed with an eye for detail and an ideal site on the sloping shores of the lake.

An avid gardener, Pen went "back to the earth" before it was fashionable to do so, believing that everyone stood on equal ground, especially when they were barefoot. This belief manifested itself again and again throughout her life, her environmental causes, and even her weaving. She believed that the pieces she made shouldn't be reserved for the galleries occupied by elite craftspeople, but should instead be considered useful. She sold them at the same farmer's markets where her neighbors shopped for fresh vegetables and homemade candles.

That's not to say, however, that Pen wasn't equally at home dealing with entrepreneurs and politicians. She was, simply, talented at people, and related to almost everyone; especially those she sensed needed more help than they knew how to ask for.

Pen was known for many things around her town, but none more so than her constant companion: a furry English sheepdog she'd named Annise Hissop. He got his formal dog name from the purple perennial herb that grew wild in New Hampshire, but Pen had a thing for nicknames and always called the dog "Fluff." Maybe it was because of an expensive training course they took, but Pen and Fluff were inseparable. Fluff went everywhere with Pen, from the grocery store, to family gatherings, to the auto mechanic. If the weather wasn't too extreme, Fluff would wait in the CR-V. The farmer's market was not dog-friendly, so in the summer Pen would sneak Fluff into her booth and hide him beneath the bolts of fiber and fabric. He accompanied her on all of her outdoor adventures, too, a constant companion as she swam, hiked, and canoed in the Goshen Ocean. Those who knew Pen would be hard-pressed to think of a time she'd been anywhere without the dog, and she wasn't embarrassed to admit that she loved him like a child.

As a young girl, Pen might not have imagined she'd land in such a peaceful and pastoral place, or that she'd grow up to a life largely lived without the suffocating trappings of old money. Edith Meyer was born into a big family in Boston on July 4, 1949. She was given her mother's name and it didn't take her mother long to realize the folly of having two Ediths in the house. She began calling her "Penny," short for Independence Day. This was the nickname that stuck, and was eventually shortened to "Pen."

Having eleven children wasn't a hardship for the Meyers, at least not financially. They were a family with means in the rare way that direct descendants of the *Mayflower* often are. Her father was a wealthy Boston industrialist, but the family had homes all over, including tony Rhode Island.

Later in her life, Pen would describe her childhood as one defined by her fear of her stifling and patriarchal father, whose old-fashioned values extended to the harsh and draconian discipline of his free-spirited daughter. She described her family relations as strained. Despite the plethora of siblings to choose from, Pen was not close to most of her brothers and sisters. Whether she knew it or not, Pen was looking for a life that was different than this.

As a teenager, Pen attended the Pingree School in South Hamilton, Massachusetts, a progressive, all-girls day school founded in 1961 in the family mansion of Charles Pingree. After graduation, she moved to New London, New Hampshire, to attend Colby-Sawyer Junior College (now Colby-Sawyer College), where she graduated with a liberal arts degree in 1970. Shortly after graduation, she married the boy she'd met there, Colin Campbell, ensuring that she'd never have to return to her family's sphere of influence. The couple eventually had three children, Justin, Kira, and Hayley.

The traditional trappings of marriage and motherhood never constrained Pen from pursuing causes ranging from women's rights and the environment, to new passions and creative pursuits. After settling with Colin in Wilmot, New Hampshire, Pen befriended another housewife named Julie Morse, and the friends decided to learn to weave. It was a skill that Pen took to quickly, mastering it to the point where she was able to turn it into her livelihood. (A modest livelihood was all she required; though indifferent to her family, she was not indifferent to her trust fund.) Pen earned a reputation among New Hampshire's artisan community for her ability to infuse radiant color and masterful technique in even the most practical items, such as place mats, napkins, and table runners.

In 1985, Pen and Colin were divorced, and she moved back to New London, where she filled her schedule with part-time work as a gardener and flower arranger at a local farm stand. She worked for one season at a historic farm and life preservation museum, where she dove into her projects with so much passion that ultimately she was terminated for her strong opinions about how the estate should be landscaped. Throughout this time, Pen maintained a friendly relationship with her ex-husband, and made many friends, all of whom saw her as the devil-may-care artist who didn't mind being seen at the local food market browned and bare-shouldered, still dirty from digging in the dirt of someone's garden.

Pen enjoyed to walk and hike, having worn bare the soles of many a pair of shoes. In the winter, Pen would take long nighttime walks in her neighborhood, stopping to make stealthy, silent snow angels in the yard of a neighbor in order to surprise the young children who lived there when they woke up in the morning. After each snowfall Pen would return and carve another secret angel, much to the squealing delight of the children.

One Christmas, Pen asked to come in and look at the family's tree that she could see from the street. "Follow me," Pen said to the children. She led them to the living room and the massive tree trimmed in the window. Pen got down on the floor and lay on her back underneath the tree. She drew the children and then the adults to follow her example. Soon the whole family was beneath the evergreen, their legs sticking out like spokes from the center, admiring the lights and decorations.

"Gives one a different perspective on things, doesn't it?" she said.

Many years later, that neighbor would write a letter to

the editor, remembering Pen as having been an angel that touched her family, often reminding her that they should all live their lives with dignity and worth, and to pass those affirmations along to their children.

Pen Meyer may have been an angel to some, but she was no saint. In fact, she was all too human. Pen had a secret shame: She had been sexually abused as a child. The pain drove her to seek ways to soothe herself. Pen drank. She was a very discreet drinker. Few if any of her close friends or family suspected she had a problem with alcohol. Not that woman with the sun-kissed skin and the dirty hands. That wasn't part of her persona.

In the mid-1990s, Pen had a nervous breakdown and was hospitalized. Friends say the incident finally forced her to face her demons. After a few failed attempts, Pen gave up drinking for good and joined AA. She also began the emotional healing process related to her molestation. In many ways, Pen became an overachiever when it came to recovery. She made herself an advocate for women looking for sobriety or trying to get over an emotional trauma. It was a turning point in her life.

In 2001, with her two oldest kids grown and living on their own, her youngest still under wing, Pen married again, to a landscaper from Goshen named Richard Rankin. The marriage was ill-fated from the start, as

Richard proved himself to be too jealous and controlling of the freewheeling Pen. Richard drank too much and was verbally abusive toward his wife. When they separated less than three years later, Pen purchased a house on rural Center Road in Goshen, where she settled in with Fluff, and began renovating in earnest.

To those in Pen's circle, her home on the Goshen Ocean was an extension of her spirit, the center of her new life surrounded by a new family. Pen remained close to her children, but when it came to her own family, close relationships were rare. And those ran deep.

Out of her ten siblings, she was closest with Jessie, a sister thirteen years her junior. As kids, Pen played a mothering role to Jessie, often looking out for her, teaching her how to get dressed, walking her through puberty, and famously teaching her baby sister how to throw a perfect football spiral. While Jessie attended college in Vermont, she'd often hop on the Green Mountain Trailways bus to New Hampshire, and spend weekends at Pen's house with Colin Campbell, helping to care for her nieces and nephew and her sister's many animals. Even after Pen and Campbell split, they agreed that Jessie, who was always so good with their children, should remain the guardian should anything happen to them.

Pen's relationships with those she cared about only intensified once she moved to Center Road in Goshen, free of the constraints of anything but her own timetable, her garden, and her weaving. It was the first home she owned by herself, the first place she could design her very own garden in her own way, plant whatever she wanted, anywhere she wanted.

The house instilled in Pen a grave sense of place and responsibility. Even as she hired out the plowing of her driveway, she'd be the first one in the neighborhood outside on snowy mornings, hand shoveling her porch steps and the path to her door, and then, climbing to the roof to clear the snow's weight off it. Jessie, now living three hours away in Rhode Island with her own husband and children, would chide Pen about her worry over the house, as it sometimes meant Pen would cancel a visit for fear something might happen to the house while she was gone.

The dream house was not set parallel with the road. It was set at an angle to ensure the view from the back would be an unobstructed view of the lake. The property had a pair of sloping grass hills that led to the water, and hiking trails intersected her land. Pen built a stone path leading to the shoreline. Each time she would walk around the Goshen Ocean, she would find a flat rock and carry it home. Her friends and her children would also bring her rocks they'd picked up along the way. Pen would lay them out so people could walk across them and she planted thyme between them. She received rocks on Mother's Day and as birthday presents. Her daughter Kira once lugged from Vermont a beautiful—but enormous—flat stone she came across on a hike. She and her husband nearly broke their backs—and their Honda Accord—yanking the smooth stone from a brook.

Pen created beautiful rooms for her children in her

home, adding skylights and colorful paint to a large bedroom reserved for when her youngest daughter, Hayley, would visit. She never purchased a couch, preferring instead to entertain guests at the large, rough-hewn farm table in her kitchen. She set aside an entire room for weaving, creating the first dedicated studio she was ever able to work in. The house was Pen's sanctuary, her sacred space. Jessie would later describe it as "tranquil, beautiful, homey and a little on the funky side too." Just like Pen.

From even a small distance away, the fabric of Pen Meyer's life seemed to have finally found its purpose and strength as she built her life on Center Road. She seemed to feel it had, too, with strength left over even for all-in dedication to environmental causes and the tiring work of supporting her friends in the community and in AA. But if that fabric had a weakness, it may have been Pen's confidence that her real life had only just begun, and her unwillingness to concede any part of it, even if it meant putting herself too far out on the line.

As Pen Meyer made her way in Goshen, those who knew her watched the woman grow in strength and in determination. Beautiful, tan, earth-loving Pen was everywhere, and always seemed to be welcoming others inside her home, inviting them to add their own threads to her story.

Politically outspoken, she stood on the sides of roadways, holding signs that screamed her belief in what was right. She shed her clothes without shame, diving into frigid autumn waters as if to hold on desperately to the disappearing summer season. She sought out the wounded, and tended to their deepest scars, even if they hadn't yet acknowledged they bore them. And she boldly faced what she may have feared most, the uncontrollable force of a man unwilling to cede any control to a woman, especially one so incapable of falling in line with his dangerous manipulations.

It was this last act of bravery that may have revealed the hidden weakness in the fabric of Pen's newly crafted and colorful existence. If Pen herself had left frayed threads unattended in her armor, it was the man who hated her for what she was, beautiful and brave, that tore at them, breaking the interwoven bonds she'd so meticulously created. And when those bonds began to give way, it wasn't long before all of it was destroyed, ripped to unrecognizable shreds.

Despite her design, Pen Meyer's new life wasn't destined to live up to its promise. Not when the man decided to pull at that hidden fray, tearing apart a life that had taken many turns, woven many stories, but had, at least seemingly, finally emerged fully formed, with divine finish, and invaluable purpose.

THREE

Missing

Joanne Dufour stared out the window of her rural New Hampshire home, peered at her wristwatch, then back out the window. It was 9:35 a.m. Her ride was late.

Joanne had a dentist appointment, but few dentists open practices in tiny hamlets such as Goshen, New Hampshire. They do so in places with active business communities, where there are plenty of residents who have dental insurance, fishing where the fish are. That means residents of Goshen have to commute for cleanings and checkups, and for all manner of medical care.

This was the trade-off of living in a small New England town, even one as progressive as Goshen. In exchange for the view and the privacy and all the undeveloped land, you give up the idea of a neighborhood doctor or dentist.

There's no trash pickup or pizza delivery, either. No cable TV. Or full-service grocery store. Or full-time fire department. In a small town such as Goshen, you have to do for yourself, or get in the car for a lengthy ride.

There certainly isn't a taxi service, either. People like Joanne rely on friends for rides. And Joanne Dufour had no closer friend than Pen Meyer. Pen was her regular lift to the store and to her appointments. Pen was also Joanne's ride to their most important shared errands of the week—Alcoholics Anonymous meetings.

Joanne was born in East Hartford, Connecticut, and had moved north to New Hampshire as a young woman. She married and had two children, a boy and girl, who were now teenagers. Joanne was divorced, trying to make it on her own for the first time in her life, and had turned to Pen for guidance and inspiration. The pair had become fast friends in recovery and saw each other frequently outside of meetings.

With Pen, Joanne felt she could share her anxieties about being a single parent in her forties. Pen, who'd been divorced twice and had three adult children, could relate to her worries about making it without a man in the house. Joanne found Pen easy to talk to. But then again, everyone found Pen easy to talk to.

Joanne, who had no car, would walk to her breakfast shift at McDonald's before the sun rose. Pen would surprise her on the road, unexpectedly pulling up behind her on cold mornings and urging Joanne to let her drive her to work. She gently encouraged Joanne to apply for a better job in a local office as an executive assistant. The encouragement from Pen was all she needed. Joanne got the job. It came with a decent salary and benefits, including dental insurance.

Joanne called Pen's home to remind her about the appointment. When the machine clicked on, she left a message. When Pen's CR-V still didn't pull up in front of her home, Joanne called again. Pen had called the night before to double-check the time, so Joanne was sure she didn't just forget.

I hope she wasn't in an accident, she thought. Black ice was an almost constant threat on New Hampshire roads in February.

Joanne still needed a ride to the dentist. She began calling other friends, other people from the program. No one had heard from Pen that morning. Although relatively little time had passed—she was less than an hour overdue—everyone agreed that Pen's no-show was strange. She had a reputation for punctuality, and it was unlike her to make plans if she had a previous commitment.

A male friend from AA named Peter offered to take Joanne to and from her appointment. When she got home in the early afternoon, there was no message from Pen and the thermometer still hadn't crossed the 30° mark.

If she had been in an accident, she would have called me. She would have gone to somebody's house and called to tell me she wasn't going to make it. That's just how she is.

Joanne wasn't one to overreact, but to have the entire morning pass without Pen trying to reach her was unsettling. The woman made some more phone calls. She didn't have his number, but she asked mutual friends to get a message to Pen's boyfriend, Jonathan.

That afternoon, Jonathan Purick got a call at work from Peter explaining that he'd just taken Joanne Dufour into town because Pen failed to show up for the appointment. Jonathan said he'd seen Pen the night before. The two had been at an Al-Anon meeting and had talked afterward. He'd passed on an invitation to spend the night at her house and called her that morning, but she hadn't answered her phone. He'd assumed Pen was walking her dog, Fluff, around Gunnison Lake, just like she did every morning.

Peter said Joanne was upset. Jonathan couldn't shake the feeling that something wasn't right, either. He left another message on Pen's answering machine asking her to call as soon as she got in.

Jonathan had a commitment in the early evening to drive some men to an AWOL (Another Way of Life) meeting. It was another life skills support program for addicts similar to AA. Jonathan decided he'd drive to Pen's home as soon as it was over.

It was a string of bad relationships and failed marriages that had led Jonathan Purick to Northern New England. "Alcohol does strange things to you," he would later say. "My problem was getting married a lot."

He had grown up in New Canaan, Connecticut, the son of a man who drank too much. His father died young of lung cancer, but Jonathan said it was the drinking that killed him. Just as sure as alcohol killed the drunk driver who missed the stoplight, it was the taste of whiskey that put those cigarettes to his father's lips. There's no doubt in Jonathan's mind on that score.

As a young man growing up in the 1960s, Jonathan never felt comfortable in his own skin. He didn't know what he wanted to do, but he sure as hell didn't want to go to Vietnam. He enrolled in September 1965 in one of the only colleges that would take him: Transylvania University in Lexington, Kentucky. There, he majored in girls, drinking, and playing bridge. He excelled at all three. It took four semesters for Jonathan to flunk out, and losing his 2-S deferment, he was going to be drafted into the Marines.

Beating Uncle Sam to the punch, Jonathan enlisted for three years in the Army. In high school, he had fostered an interest in photography, and—since he knew how to develop his own film—Private Purick was trained as a combat photographer. Soon Sergeant Purick was running a photo lab in Vietnam. He'd hoped an assignment in the rear would keep him out of the field, but it didn't. Just like Joker in Stanley Kubrick's movie *Full Metal Jacket*, fun-loving Jonathan would go "in-country" with his 35mm camera and see things he'd rather forget. It was in Vietnam that he first got introduced to heavy drugs. He tried heroin. He played cards. It was like Transylvania U.

all over again, or at least that's what he'd say to himself
in order to cope.

After his discharge in 1971, Jonathan spent three
decades trying to find a career that suited him. He tried to
make a living as a photographer and running a photo lab.
He took the job as far as he could and then got into sales.
He sold vacuum cleaners door-to-door, which, he often
liked to joke, "sucked." He tried his hand at computer sales
and eventually sold used cars. He never equated his drinking
with his professional problems, nor his personal ones. He
had been married four times. He dismissed the failures of
those relationships to the failures of others, not himself.

Jonathan had landed a job selling new Lincolns and
Mercuries on New Hampshire's seacoast. New cars sold
well, and luxury cars sold even better. He was the dealership's top salesman for several months. Yet they still let
him go. They told him he wasn't the right fit, the right
personality for the job. Again, it didn't occur to him that
his drinking might be the true cause of his problem.

By the mid-1990s, Jonathan was making $5.50 an
hour at a warehouse in Central New Hampshire. His
fourth wife wanted him out of the house. He had lost his
car, along with everything else. With nothing but a pack
of cigarettes left in his pocket, he sat down for some deep
soul searching. *What is going on here? Why am I where I
am?* He couldn't blame his funk on the job or his wife or
even the cigarette burning between his fingers.

It's the drinking. The revelation had taken years.

The road to recovery is neither a straight path nor a

fast one. Jonathan's inspiration for sobriety had been, of all people, his adult son. The younger Purick had gone to rehab and was in a Twelve Step program. Because he had grown up in an alcoholic home, Jonathan thought he could relate (the irony being that—at the time—he couldn't see he'd also created an alcoholic home for his son). Jonathan began to attend Al-Anon meetings, a support group for families of alcoholics and addicts. He thought he was there to work out his feelings about his father and his son, not to deal with his own issues. His Al-Anon sponsor brought him to an AA meeting, but again Jonathan saw it only as a sociological field trip—an investigation of demons his son battled, but not him.

On December 23, 1995, Jonathan and his son spoke long-distance. The father was mildly resisting the attempts of his son and daughter-in-law to get him to visit them in North Carolina for Christmas. Jonathan's excuses were weak: "I have this . . . I have that . . ." Part of him didn't want to intrude on their holiday; part of him was still unable to articulate that his soul was broken and preventing him from getting too close. Despite rebuffing the invitation, his son persisted.

"I can't come down," Jonathan said. "I promised my sponsor I would go to my meeting . . ."

Jonathan was referring to his Al-Anon meeting, which remained a passive, clinical interaction for him. But on the other end of the phone, his son was suddenly energized.

"You're going to a meeting?" Then he covered the receiver and turned to his wife. "Dad is going to AA." The couple exploded with joy and encouragement. Passing the phone between them, they praised Jonathan. *We always knew you could benefit from a Twelve Step program,* they said. They were so happy at the thought of Jonathan going to an AA meeting, so relieved at the thought of him getting sober, that he didn't have the heart to correct them.

Buoyed by the emotional wave that was carrying him ashore, Jonathan got in his car and drove from New England to North Carolina. On Christmas Eve, with his son by his side, Jonathan Purick attended his first Alcoholics Anonymous meeting as a true participant. As he introduced himself and spoke freely about his drinking, tears of relief rolled down his face. He had taken the "First Step." He admitted he had a problem he couldn't control. Now he was willing to turn himself over to "The Program"—to a "Higher Power"—to make his life manageable again. He left the meeting with a white chip, symbolizing his desire to stop drinking for one day.

Jonathan Purick had been working on his sobriety for almost ten years. Now clean and sober, he had dedicated himself to helping others find serenity. He attended meetings regularly, both AA and Al-Anon, and became an enthusiastic sponsor for those new to the program. His path crossed with all types, people who were bankers and lawyers, school nurses and construction workers. Some came to meetings with sharp haircuts and aftershave on their cheeks. Others were stone-cold sober but still dressed like they'd stumbled out of the Bowery. Some got lit on premium vodka and some on Sterno, but they all had the gene of addiction in common.

They had the brains of addicts, and their compulsive behavior wasn't limited to drinking. They spent money foolishly and shopped compulsively. They soothed themselves with food. They had sex with multiple partners to ease their pain. Just about every "-oholic" label mainstream society placed on those who misbehaved was in clinical presence among their numbers.

In a roomful of flawed people—some who were working through their struggles, some who had risen above them—it was not surprising that Pen Meyer would stand out to Jonathan. He first met Pen at an Al-Anon meeting in Newport, New Hampshire. He'd noticed her thin frame from across the room and was immediately struck by her slate blue eyes. Her poise was also remarkable, and the way she interacted with the other members of the meeting made it impossible for him *not* to fall in love with her.

He had been out of his last long-term relationship for many months, but was he truly ready to start something new? For more than a year, he fought his feelings for Pen. He had the willpower for sobriety, but found himself powerless to resist her.

At first, they would spend time together after the conclusion of the meetings and would talk about the life lessons preached earlier. When the weather turned cold, they'd sit in Pen's car with Fluff lying patiently in the backseat. The talks were heavy, cathartic. Pen had been attending Al-Anon because her second husband was a problem drinker. She needed to figure out her role in his drinking, in his life. Pen had decided she was going to ask for a divorce.

When it was clear she was emotionally severed from her husband and when his courage was at its peak, Jonathan asked Pen out on a date. "I'd like to do something with you," he said. "I'd like to take you to a concert."

She looked at him sideways. "I *probably* would date you," she said. "But I would have to be divorced first." Jonathan's initial disappointment was replaced by an appreciation for Pen's integrity. *She is going to remain true to her vows,* he thought.

Pen's divorce from Richard Rankin was finalized on September 15, 2004. After nearly a year of wooing, her relationship with Jonathan Purick finally began.

Jonathan was not used to living a life of public advocacy. His work with fellow addicts was, as one might expect, largely anonymous. Pen Meyer's passion for social justice demanded the labor-intensive work of showing up, holding signs, knocking on doors, and confronting people. If he wanted to spend time with her, he was going to have to tag along. And just like Fluff, he did.

Pen's latest cause concerned the ski resort on the mountain that cast its peaked shadow over Goshen. Mount Sunapee loomed above the lake of the same name, a word meaning "Lake of the Wild Goose" in Algonquian.

The lake's crystal water and accessible, yet rural location had attracted upscale residents for decades, including Aerosmith's Steven Tyler, but its shores were also dotted with old family cottages, or "camps," that remained in the hands of those who could still afford to shoulder their hefty tax burdens.

Mount Sunapee was owned by the state, and when plans for a tourist tramway to the summit evaporated after World War II, officials installed a modest chairlift. As the sport of alpine skiing blossomed in North America, adventurers brought their skis up the chairlift and cut the first downhill paths through the wilderness.

From humble beginnings such endeavors grow. Over the next several decades more lifts and trails sprouted along Mount Sunapee. Artificial snow fell for the first time in the 1980s. Sunapee was making money for the state, but it struggled to compete with the luxury resorts throughout New Hampshire and Northern New England, despite a well-earned reputation for having some of the best ski conditions in the region. The resort's growth was controlled, although some conservationists wished the mountain had been altogether left alone.

By the late 1990s, the upgrades and maintenance to the mountain were financially burdening the state; the ski park had operated at a loss for dozens of years. In a grand stroke, New Hampshire leased Mount Sunapee to a private corporation. Though Sunapee remained public land, the new operators had a vision of expansion and modernization.

Earlier in 2004, the operators of Mount Sunapee asked the state to lease them an additional 176 acres to connect the resort to a swath of undeveloped land they had purchased. They envisioned new trails down the western bowl of the mountain on which people could ski to the doorsteps of new luxury town houses. These new mountain homes would be within the town footprint of Goshen.

Faster than you could say "urban sprawl," Pen and her neighbors were up in arms about the prospect of 250 new housing units in the unspoiled community of 800 people. "This would completely change the character of Goshen," Pen complained publicly. "Before long, we'll have strip malls and gas stations and burger joints all to accommodate this unsustainable growth."

Driving through the massive traffic circle along Route 103 in Newport, one can either pull into the ski resort entrance or turn into Sunapee State Park, which contains a fine-sand beach on Lake Sunapee and dozens of hiking trails. The grassy island in the middle of this roundabout was where Edith Pen Meyer and her dog were found one Saturday in late October 2004, holding a sign in each hand and waving them to passersby. One sign said, SAVE GOSHEN; the other said, PROTECT OUR PUBLIC LANDS. She emphasized the point with tiny thrusts of her placards, her silver jewelry jangling with every movement.

"No condos on Sunapee!" Pen yelled at passing cars.

"Woof," barked Fluff, punctuating his owner's pleas.

Jonathan had tagged along with Pen and her dog to the protest. He noticed that the other townsfolk who were her friends—the ones who didn't know her from their mutual AA circle—greeted her warmly. Pen may not have been the leader of the opposition, but she embodied the soul of it. Cars and trucks spun through the rotary with a mix of reactions. Some blew their horns, some stuck out their middle fingers. Most drivers were going just fast enough that they had to crook their necks to catch all of what was happening on the median. Watching Pen's activism up close, sensing her passion, Jonathan felt bad for any condo developers that may have driven by.

After the demonstration, the Friends of Sunapee (as the grassroots insurgency had dubbed itself) held a coffee reception at a community building on the mountain. It likely irked the corporate lessees to no end that the gadflies could celebrate their opposition *to* the resort *on* the resort, but such are the loopholes of private-public land operation.

Jonathan entered the room of strangers planning to lie low until Pen gave him his cue that they could leave. He was patient, but this wasn't really his scene. Pen, however, was lit up. She stood in the doorway and scanned the room. There had been some new faces at the protest and Pen was hunting for them.

Pen's eyes locked on a young woman across the room with a paper cup in her hand. Jonathan could tell Pen was sizing her up. But for what? He watched her face as it grew intense.

"That woman there," Pen said discreetly to Jonathan, "is an abuse survivor."

He glanced at the woman Pen was talking about. "How would you know that?"

"I just know."

Pen left Jonathan at the door and walked up directly to the woman. Jonathan had an urge to call out and stop her, or advise some kind of caution, but the impulse disappeared as soon as he realized that Pen Meyer was going to do what she wanted to do, as she always did.

Pen introduced herself with a handshake, and after pleasantries were exchanged, she got right to the nut of it. After just a few minutes, Jonathan overheard the woman telling Pen her deepest emotional secrets. He walked around the community room, keeping a respectful distance from the psychological operation going on. He drank the coffee and nodded to others. On his second pass by Pen and the woman, he could see tears in both of their eyes. Pen was holding the woman's hand.

Jonathan continued making small talk, learning more about the perils of expansion on Sunapee. Each time he looked over at Pen, she was in deep concentration, nodding her head and drawing more of the woman's story forth.

As the hour came to a close, the protesters zipped up their jackets and filed out. From the corner of his eye, Jonathan could see Pen and the woman embrace and finally untether. Following Pen out the door, he looked back at the woman drinking the last of her cold coffee.

She's been healed, he thought. *Not completely, of course. But she is so much better off than before she met Pen.*

"How did you do that?" he asked her on the way out.

Pen just shrugged and smiled at him, taking his hand for the walk to the car.

Pen told Jonathan when she was about nine years old, she was attacked by a relative and beaten to the point where she passed out. When she awoke, she was told that the family dog had intervened and jumped on her assailant. They said the dog might have saved her life. For Jonathan, it explained in part where Pen's affinity for victims came from. It also explained her deep affection for dogs such as Fluff.

That night, Pen and Jonathan sat at the farm table in her kitchen. Fluff would occasionally wander in and check on them, then would pad away and go about his business.

"I'm fifty-five and I'm just getting to be with you," Pen said. "We should have met sooner."

Considering all the living and learning that had happened before, all the dragons they each had to slay, Jonathan just shook his head. "We couldn't have."

She agreed. She might not have liked the twenty-five-year-old Jonathan Purick, or even the forty-five-year-old Jonathan Purick, and vice versa. Everything in their lives had directed them to this moment. This version of themselves was who they wanted to be, but it had been a hard journey getting here.

"Come closer," she said. Jonathan scooched his chair in her direction. Pen leaned in and kissed him. The one kiss seemed to last forever. She put her arms around his shoulders. The cool metal of her bangles rested against his cheeks and were momentarily silent. Jonathan responded by putting his hands on her back and pulling her tighter. He could feel her tiny frame, how delicate her bones seemed to be. The kiss didn't end as much as it simply dissolved. They opened their eyes and looked at each other.

"Wow," Jonathan commented.

"Wow," she agreed. "I think I'm ready."

Jonathan grinned. He thought he knew what she meant, but he wanted clarification. "Ready for what?"

"I'm ready for you to spend the night," she said.

Pen took his hand and led him to the bedroom. The room was immaculate, but didn't show signs she'd prepared for his stay. Everything felt spontaneous, natural.

The next morning, the sun rose above Mount Sunapee and its yellow light dappled off Lake Gunnison. The warblers had already flown south, but a few sparrows and juncos loitered behind and sang their morning songs. Pen woke Jonathan up with a kiss, then curled into him like a cat. The tiny tinkle of Pen's bracelets had the sweet sound of wind chimes dampened by warm flesh.

"I feel wonderful," Pen said. "That's the first time in my life that I've slept with a man and slept all the way through the night."

A lover's ego could not be stroked by higher praise.

According to Jonathan, he luxuriated in the compliment. It wasn't until weeks later that he considered what the statement truly meant. It wasn't about him at all. He realized that Pen, like him, also had spent her adult life uncomfortable in her own skin, unable to open up to another person. She feared her own vulnerability and worried that whomever she was with would pull the rug out from under her. Pen had said as much, but Jonathan was too wrapped up in his own victory lap to have registered it.

When he talked to her about it afterward, Pen said, "I've always been terrified."

Now, a mere twelve weeks after that romantic night, Jonathan Purick was faced with a mystery. Why wasn't Pen answering her telephone? It was Wednesday evening, and the AWOL meeting he had spent so much time preparing for was over. Jonathan had to give a ride home to two of the men who'd attended. He was heading south from Newport back into Goshen.

"Do you guys mind if I stop by my girlfriend's house?" he asked. "I have to check something out."

His truck pulled up in front of the home around 9:30 p.m. A light was on. *That's a good sign, isn't it?* He had one of the remotes to Pen's garage door. When he clicked it open, he saw her CR-V was parked inside. Still, he asked the passengers to stay in the vehicle. If he went inside and found Pen sick or injured—or worse—he didn't want her exposed like that.

Jonathan pulled the house key Pen had given him from his pocket. It had been a gift from her, an advance on their plan to move in together when spring finally came. The latch clicked free of the strike plate and the front door opened.

"Pen?" There was no answer. He called again, but still, no one replied. The hairs on Jonathan's neck stood up. His heart was in his throat. He hadn't felt this way since he was in Vietnam. Something was making his body go on high alert.

He made his way to the bedroom, then the bathroom. *Did she slip and fall?* He looked around and the house seemed to be in relatively good shape. The bed was unmade. The smell of drying paint was in the air. There were dirty dishes and pots in the sink. There was a towel on the floor in the bathroom and some laundry strewn about. Otherwise, there wasn't any sign of her.

Jonathan stood over Pen's answering machine and watched the light blinking red. He pressed Play and heard a number of calls from Joanne Dufour asking for Pen. *Of course, Joanne would have called out of concern. It wasn't like Pen to blow off giving her a ride.* Then he heard another woman's voice.

"Pen, it's me, Sandy. Call me, I'm having lunch now. I want to talk to you more about the bombshell you dropped on me this morning."

Bombshell? What could Pen have said to Sandy that was a "bombshell"?

The next set of messages on the machine were from him. He heard the worry in his own voice.

There was a tiny set of *click-clack*s and a faint jingle coming from the other room. Fluff walked in to greet him. The furry sheepdog gazed up at Jonathan with human eyes, and then looked around him. It was as if the dog were hoping Pen would walk in behind him.

Jonathan stopped calling for Pen. *None of this adds up*, he thought. *Pen only has the one car. And she certainly wouldn't go anywhere without her dog.*

He felt like he was back in a combat zone. He was going nutty. He could hear the blood rush into his ears, just like it did when he was in combat. Every turn of his head was greeted with a sense of vertigo. The realization washed over him all at once. If she didn't leave in her own car, she left with someone else.

Jonathan had to make it to the door, had to get out. There were two unsuspecting men outside in his truck. They knew nothing of what was happening; and they—and he—were defenseless. With lead feet, he tromped across the room, reaching for the doorknob. He was suddenly overwhelmed by the fear that *someone else* was in the house with him.

He threw himself outside into the cold night. The wind slapped his face and helped clear his head. *Pen is gone*, he thought. *And I know who took her.*

FOUR

Ken

Kenneth Carpenter was born the middle brother of three in August 1951 in the Western Massachusetts city of Greenfield. His family moved around a little bit, following his father to different jobs. When he was a toddler, the Carpenters moved to Florida, but found themselves back in the unforgiving weather of New England soon after.

Carpenter came of age in Chelmsford, Massachusetts, a half hour outside of Boston. His cousin Allen Long, who was mostly neglected by his own parents, hung around with Carpenter. The boys drank their first beers together. They sat down in the grass on the hill behind Long's house. They each pulled a ring tab off, then dropped it into the frothy can of beer. The six-pack probably cost about 99 cents, but they never discussed how

Carpenter got it. It was cold and bitter, but it tasted good after they got used to it. They sat on the hill drinking, watching the sun go down on Chelmsford, not knowing there was something in their makeup that would bewitch them to alcohol. They were fifteen years old.

Ken Carpenter's parents, Alfred "Bud" and Bernice "Bernie" Carpenter, bought the Chelmsford Twin Drive-in theater shortly after they moved to Massachusetts. It was a popular destination for families and groups of teens wanting to watch such fare as *The Love Bug*, *Yellow Submarine*, or *2001: A Space Odyssey*. The family also owned a second drive-in in nearby Tyngsboro. That theater gradually moved away from showing popular hits to showing adult movies. The shows had names such as *Fraulein Doktor*, *How to Seduce a Playboy*, and *I, A Woman (Part I)*.

Films for Ladies and Gentlemen above the age of 21, the newspaper ads would explain. Now through Sunday, 2 Adult Features, No One Under 18 Admitted, I.D. Required. "Starlet" X X X (so adult one X isn't enough) Co-hit "The Big Bounce." Both businesses seemed to do well, but had very different clientele.

A drive-in movie theater wasn't such a bad family asset for a teenager to boast about. Ken could see plenty of films. He could help himself to concessions (when the adults weren't looking). When his friends were old enough to drive, he could sneak them into the theater for the latest James Bond flick. The aura of a family-owned business gave classmates (most of them the offspring of mill workers and other blue-collar laborers) the perception that Ken Carpenter had money. He didn't.

Carpenter had an easy way about him. He moved between different cliques at school with ease, though he was never very popular himself. He was more reserved, perhaps shy. Other kids called him "Jeb" (the origin of the nickname was lost to the ages). Just as other boys in the 60s were just starting to, Carpenter wore his hair long, swept over his forehead and parted to the left. His clothes were modern. He looked pretty much like any other kid at Chelmsford High School except for his piercing yellow eyes.

Where he stood out was on the football field. Carpenter played linebacker and offensive guard for the Chelmsford Lions. The young man was growing into his six-foot stature and had a solid build. He quickly made a name for himself on the varsity team for his thunderous hits and vicious tackles. When he was on defense, Carpenter would crash into a ball carrier at full tilt.

"That's the way to do it," the coaches would praise from the sidelines, hoping all would follow the example set by Ken. "That's the way to hit a man!"

In 1969, Ken Carpenter was named co-captain of the Chelmsford Lions. The honor was undoubtedly deserved. For his hardnosed play, the local sports writers had dubbed him one of the best players in the Merrimack Valley Conference. His famous explosive tackles were the subject of many an inside joke in the school yearbook. "Sure I liked hitting guys," Carpenter said years later.

"Who doesn't?" Expressed thirty-five years later, at least some of his high school teammates were uncomfortable with Carpenter's affinity for the bone-crushing hits. It seemed the kid liked the violence of football too much.

Carpenter spent most of his adult life in Massachusetts. He'd married and divorced twice and had one son, bouncing around from one odd job to another. He had worked in construction and had repaired race cars, but had no defined career to speak of, something he talked about with unexpected pride.

The one thing he had been particularly good at was sobriety. Ken Carpenter stopped drinking on December 13, 1981. The Alcoholics Anonymous white chip he got for going to his first meeting meant a lot to him. Right away, he threw himself into working the Twelve Steps and dedicated the time to do the readings and reflections. His sponsor was impressed by his attitude, the way he "worked the program." Others noticed it, too. He was thoughtful about his addiction; he respected the power it held over him. His quiet dedication to sobriety made him highly charismatic to others in the program. After a few years of being clean, he offered himself up at meetings as someone who could be a sponsor to other men.

Carpenter had a magnetism that only seemed to manifest itself at AA meetings. He wasn't an unattractive man; he had a soulful face and drew a passing resemblance to Sean Connery. But he always wore his hair long, even when it had gone from black to gray, and would tie it up into a thin, ropelike ponytail. His beard was thick and often scraggly. But to men and women who'd hit rock bottom, who were admitting for the first time in their lives that they were powerless to control themselves, Ken Carpenter was a commanding figure. People listened to him, especially women.

No longer part of the bar scene, Carpenter would meet women at his only regular social event: AA meetings. Carpenter could scan the room and get an instant read on the female members. He could sense a woman's vulnerability the way animals sensed wounded prey. He would find an excuse to talk to that woman during a break or after the meeting. He seemed to have all the answers, which was attractive to a susceptible woman. It excited him to play that role, and he did it again and again.

Carpenter was stone-cold sober, but he still had the mind and predilections of an addict. He no longer got a rush from booze. Instead, he got a rush from these all-too-human interactions. The chemicals in his brain were triggered when he would approach a woman and play his game. He had declared himself helpless against alcohol, but didn't have the same misgivings about his own libido. Sex didn't give him a hangover the next morning.

After almost twenty years of hound-dogging at AA meetings, Carpenter finally found love. He started attending meetings in Nashua, New Hampshire, a small city that straddled the Massachusetts line. Carpenter met an eye-catching blonde there. Everyone called Cynthia Harvey "Harv." She was in her forties, attractively built, and well dressed.

Like many people in recovery, Harv wanted to give back to those who struggled with the same issues. She wanted to go back to school to become a nurse. Harv was also deeply religious. She went to church regularly and socialized within the congregation. The aspect of the AA program that dealt with spirituality, with surrendering to a Higher Power, was comforting to her.

Carpenter and Harv started dating in July 2000, and he soon moved into her place in Nashua. To outsiders, they seemed like a mismatched pair. Carpenter carried the persona of an aging and unkempt baby boomer. He wore comfortable clothes and rode a motorcycle in the warm weather. Carpenter was not as spiritual as Harv, but he didn't protest when she encouraged him to attend church or become friends with the pastor. He went through the motions for Harv's sake, perhaps hoping it would become more comfortable as he went along. There was a saying in the program: *Fake it 'til you make it.*

Carpenter and Harv eventually moved from the relatively urban landscape of Nashua to the backwoods of Sullivan County. They found a cottage tucked among the trees of Lempster, New Hampshire. The home was less than an hour from Harv's nursing school, and Dartmouth-Hitchcock Medical Center, one of the nation's most renowned hospitals, was just a short drive away. Harv got a job working second shift at the Sullivan County Nursing Home as a nursing assistant. The hours allowed her to continue attending school in the daytime.

Finding work was harder for Carpenter. He believed his construction experience would help him find steady employment. He got hired as a public works employee for the town of Newport, but the director let him go after the probationary period. He told Carpenter he "wasn't getting the job done." He spent some time as a driver for a concrete and gravel company, and also stocked shelves at Walmart. None of the work was steady, nor was it lucrative. Carpenter told his older brother, Dale, that he wasn't comfortable relying on Harv to be the breadwinner. His employment prospects were putting stress on his relationship.

Carpenter would purchase pieces of heavy machinery— skidders, backhoes, bulldozers—to either resell or use on jobs he'd get on the side. The machinery wasn't cheap and would appear and vanish from their property without warning, much to Harv's consternation.

There were a couple different locations in their new community where AA meetings were held: church base- ments and community rooms being the majority of them. The most popular site to attend a meeting was at Millie's Place in Newport, New Hampshire. It was a clubhouse, an establishment just for the purpose of holding meetings. Millie's had a nondescript façade among the other store- fronts in a strip mall on the John Stark Highway. It was a place members felt like they owned.

Carpenter attended several regular AA meetings in the

Newport area, including those at Millie's. As usual, other recovering alcoholics were inspired by the way Carpenter approached the program. It wasn't long before he was sponsoring members here as well. Harv also attended meetings at Millie's, but owing to her school and work schedules, she often went to different meetings than Carpenter did. Their relationship wasn't a secret to members. They socialized with other couples in the program, but not everyone who came and went in the anonymous group drew the connection between the scruffy Carpenter and the pretty, religious Harv.

Among the couples they met at Millie's were Nicholas and Dot Monahan.* They were all about the same age and fell into the kind of friendship that sober couples often seek with one another. The Monahans—Dot in particular—were taken by how openly affectionate Carpenter and Harv were.

"You two are so lovey-dovey," she'd tease, catching them in a kiss or spotting a hand resting tenderly on a shoulder. Carpenter was resistant to talk of marriage, despite the gentle goading from Nicholas and Dot. That's why Carpenter's proposal to Harv was such a happy surprise to the Monahans. They instantly accepted the invitation to be best man and matron of honor at the services penciled in for early 2003.

The Monahans first thought the relationship might be troubled on one winter evening before the wedding. The

---

* Denotes pseudonyms.

couple was late to the Monahans' home for a visit. When their pickup truck pulled in, Harv popped out, running into the house and into Dot's arms. She was sobbing uncontrollably. Carpenter, in the meantime, sat in the truck with the engine running, his arms folded across his chest.

"Harv, what happened?"

She explained that she and Carpenter began to quarrel over some trivial thing on the drive over. Carpenter began to get really heated about it, more so than the tiny issue would call for. He pulled the truck over, slammed on the breaks, and got out. Carpenter began walking back home on the frost-covered road. Harv shouted to him, begged for him to get back into the pickup. Either beaten down by her pleas or beaten up by the cold night, Carpenter jumped back into the cab and drove them silently the rest of the way.

"I didn't know he could get so angry about nothing," Harv confided through the tears. "I'm not sure I should marry him."

But Ken Carpenter and Cynthia Harvey did go through with the nuptials. They were married on Sunday of Presidents' Day weekend, 2003. The ceremony was held at Millie's with the Monahans standing up for the couple. After the vows, all the guests walked to the other end of the shopping plaza and ate Chinese food. Later, the party moved back to the newlyweds' cabin on Quimby Farm Road.

"Ken, what the hell is that?" the bride blurted out.

There was a new piece of mechanical equipment in the yard. She had no idea when it had arrived or how her husband would have paid for it. "I can't believe you'd upset me on my wedding day," she said, holding back tears.

The incident got smoothed over, but a few months after the wedding, a postcard arrived for Carpenter at their Lempster home. It was postmarked from Maine and signed by a woman named "Cindy" who wanted Carpenter to know she was moving to Sullivan County. Harv got the mail first and confronted her husband about it.

"Who is Cindy? Why is she writing you to tell you she's moving?" Carpenter brushed it off. Cindy was someone he barely remembered from a meeting somewhere and wasn't someone he'd slept with. Harv wasn't so sure; she confided in Dot Monahan that she wouldn't know why a woman would be writing letters to Carpenter if they weren't involved with each other.

Financially, their union was in trouble. The many months of sporadic employment and balloon payments for quasi-operational construction equipment dragged their bank balance into the red. Carpenter got a part-time job as a greeter at Walmart. Harv urged him to find a permanent position, but he countered that no one was hiring. If he wasn't going to meetings, Harv could find her husband in front of the TV watching his favorite shows. They were all police procedurals: *Law and Order*, *Cold Case*, and *CSI*.

* * *

Carpenter was a regular at the 7:00 p.m. meeting at Millie's. Harv worked nights on Monday, Wednesday, Thursday, and every other weekend at the nursing home and wouldn't be home until close to midnight. Carpenter felt at liberty to mingle after the meeting, grab a coffee or a plate of Chinese food with others.

On January 23, 2004, a new face turned up at Millie's. The woman's name was Sandra Merritt. Sandy, as she liked to be called, said she was trying to get back on the wagon. She had attempted getting sober before, but had failed. The group at Millie's welcomed her as a "newbie" and offered her the necessary support.

Carpenter, who'd yet to celebrate his first anniversary with Harv, was attracted to something in Sandy. The woman didn't only suffer from alcoholism. She also suffered from depression. There was something indescribably sad about the way she talked about her life. Her sadness colored her whole demeanor. The way she talked about her problems echoed for Carpenter. He had recently begun seeing a psychiatrist and had been taking some antidepressants. There was something about a woman who had both of his challenges, alcoholism and depression, which intrigued him.

Sandy was not an attractive woman. She had none of Harv's sense of style, and with long bangs that shielded most of her face, she projected the image of a woman who didn't want to be noticed.

Dating among AA members is discouraged, but not forbidden. It could hardly be unexpected given the fact the people bare so much of themselves, and rely so desperately on one another for their own sense of serenity and sanity. Few outsiders know what it means to "hit rock bottom" and work every day at recovery. The appreciation of a lover who understands that struggle is a powerfully attractive thing. Romances blossom at Alcoholics Anonymous all the time. AA members often say that if you pay close enough attention at any regular meeting, plotlines to rival soap operas will emerge.

There is one strict rule about dating for recovering alcoholics, however: *Do not date anyone within their first year of recovery.* Some even refer to it as "the thirteenth step." It's generally accepted that a newbie needs at least that much time to adjust to recovery before putting the energy into a relationship. The newbie still has the brain of an addict, and sex is just another drug. No use getting hooked on one drug while trying to kick another.

Carpenter knew "the thirteenth step," but rationalized it away. Sandy may have been a newbie at Millie's, but it wasn't the first time she'd picked up a white chip. She was familiar with the program. All she needed was an experienced hand to help her with her sobriety.

"It's hard, staying clean," he told her after the meeting. "It's humbling."

"I haven't had a drink in . . ." Sandy's furrowed brow indicated she was working out the number of days.

"I have twenty-plus years of sobriety. There is no secret

solution, no magic trick. You surrender to your higher power and take every day at a time."

"I will try that."

Carpenter offered to be Sandy's sponsor. While men and women could fraternize in AA, Sandy knew that men were forbidden from sponsoring women. Still, there was an easy comfort between them. Sandy enjoyed his sense of humor and his undeniable charisma. There was a mutual attraction. Sandy asked about the wedding ring on his finger.

"My marriage is over. I know that now. I'm going to be asking my wife for a divorce."

Sandy just nodded. She didn't want to spoil such a profoundly cheerless statement with a smile.

Their affair began soon after that night.

Despite his declared intentions, Carpenter did not ask Harv for a divorce. The marriage was unquestionably rocky. Not seeing his wife on work nights did not make things easier. He wasn't convinced leaving Harv was going to solve his problems. It certainly wasn't going to help his financial situation any. With his wife at nursing school by day and her job at night, Carpenter was free to carry on the affair undetected.

Carpenter had led Sandy to believe his relationship with Harv was openly acrimonious, that it could end at any time. Sandy also understood that Carpenter's wife was providing a roof, three meals, and a bed—all critical to his sobriety. She understood why he chose to stay in the loveless marriage. It would be suicide for him to leave. So Sandy tacitly blessed Carpenter's decision to carry on his sham marriage.

Harv, meantime, was certainly *not* under the impression that her marriage was over. It was far from perfect, but she believed her husband was committed to their relationship. She certainly wasn't aware he had a mistress. In short, Carpenter was playing them both.

Sandy's apartment on her brother's 420-acre Newport farm was an addition built on to the main farmhouse, but it provided just enough seclusion from her brother's family. Despite his land wealth, Greg Merritt was not a working farmer. There were a couple of cows, some chickens, but he wasn't trying to make a go at living off the land. Merritt was a small business owner who ran a plumbing and heating operation. Though his sister lived on his property, he didn't poke around in her life.

Ken Carpenter and Sandy Merritt went out to dinner, saw movies together, but it was in this apartment where much of the affair took place. Carpenter would wait until Harv left for work, then make the trip to Sandy's place. The evenings were theirs. They would eat, watch television, and make love. It became a regular routine.

The lovers had a favorite TV show to watch together. They couldn't get enough of *CSI: Crime Scene Investigation* on CBS. Harv worked Thursday nights, so Carpenter was at his mistress's house each week when the crime drama would come on. Harv also worked Monday nights, so the couple could watch the *CSI: Miami* spin-off too. Carpenter loved settling into the quiet of sitting before the TV and being with Sandy. It didn't feel like they were passively watching a show; it felt like they were doing something intimate together. *CSI* felt like *their thing*. Even during the summer reruns, Carpenter looked forward to spending the time watching *CSI* with his secret girlfriend, the peepers' calls chiming in through the open windows.

Sometime between 10:00 and 11:00 p.m.—after spending an hour studying Hollywood forensics—Carpenter would slink out, drive back to his secluded cabin, and wait for his wife. He'd let out the dogs, straighten out the cabin, and go on as if he'd been home all the time. Harv seemed none the wiser.

One afternoon while he worked at Walmart, both Harv and Sandy entered the store at the same time. Carpenter ducked out of sight, moving from one department to the next. His co-workers immediately caught on and watched the melodrama unfold—Carpenter spinning on his heels as one of the women would round a corner or appear from an aisle end cap. Both of the women were asking employees where Ken Carpenter was. He begged a co-worker to lie for him and tell them that he'd already left.

During the summer of 2004, after the affair had entered its sixth month, Carpenter approached Greg Merritt while he was working on the farm. Sandy's brother never received a formal introduction to Carpenter, but he had seen him coming over in either his tan pickup truck or his Jeep. He'd also spotted Carpenter working in Walmart, although he didn't make an effort to introduce himself. Greg Merritt had no idea his sister's boyfriend was a married man.

"Can I talk to you for a minute?" Carpenter asked. Merritt put down his tools. "You and your family have a beautiful piece of land here."

"Thank you."

"I was wondering if you'd be willing to sell me a small portion of land on the far side of the property. I was thinking Sandy and I would build a little house out there. I have some money coming to me after the sale of my old business. So I'm hoping you would sell me a few acres."

Not in a million years, Greg Merritt thought. "I'd have to think about it," he said.

"It's not in the immediate future. I'm still waiting on my money," Carpenter assured him. "But I am quite serious about my offer."

Greg Merritt wouldn't see Carpenter again until after the relationship went bad.

At Millie's Place, Ken Carpenter and Sandy Merritt kept their relationship on the down low. They didn't always attend the same meetings, but if they both came to the 7:00 p.m., they'd keep their interactions to a minimum. They wouldn't enter together or leave at the same time. They never sat next to each other. Afterward, Sandy would mingle with the other women and Carpenter would keep his distance. The subterfuge worked; no one in the group suspected the affair.

Sandy chatted with the women members after the AA meetings and soon became friends with Pen Meyer. Pen's preternatural ability to identify women who were suffering and talk to them in a way that seemed soothing led her to Sandy. If the two crossed paths at meetings when Carpenter wasn't there, Sandy would take Pen up on any offers for coffee or to come shopping with her afterward.

Pen urged Sandy to come by her place and hike around the Goshen Ocean with her. She joined Pen and Fluff and learned the many trails to take around the lake. There was more than one right-of-way to access the water or the trails, but Pen insisted Sandy walk through her property, even if she wasn't home.

One morning in November 2004, Sandy pulled up with Ken Carpenter in her car. The two of them passed between the trees on Pen's land before disappearing from view of the waterfront home. The couple made their way along the trails hand in hand. At one point, they crossed paths with what they thought might be a beaver. Upon closer inspection, they learn the brown animal was a porcupine. Carpenter was tickled. He had never seen a porcupine growing up as a "flatlander" (the name the New Hampshire foothills people disparagingly give to Massachusetts residents). He offered the animal half his apple, which it seemed to enjoy. After spending some time giggling over it, and sure it wasn't going to skewer him,

Carpenter watched the porcupine waddle off into the woods.

The smile vanished from Carpenter's face when they completed the loop around the Goshen Ocean and came across Pen and Fluff in her backyard. His hand instinctively let go of Sandy's. Ken Carpenter and Pen Meyer had had little previous interaction outside of Millie's. He knew she was going through a divorce, but didn't know much else. The bulk of his relationship with Sandy had been spent behind the doors of her Newport apartment and he clearly wasn't comfortable yet with the thought of being seen together with his mistress.

Sandy Merritt and Ken Carpenter left Pen Meyer's home with a wave and a sincere thank-you. She urged them to come back and enjoy the trails anytime.

Pen Meyer had already known the nature of Sandy and Ken's relationship. In the summer of 2004, Sandy confided in her about the affair. Pen was finishing up her divorce from Richard Rankin and was attracted to—but physically celibate with—Jonathan Purick. Despite her allegiance to the institution of marriage, Pen was nonjudgmental about Sandy's role as the other woman.

"Could he be leading me on?" Sandy asked. "What is his relationship with Harv really like?"

Pen didn't have an answer. Carpenter and Harv did not attend the same AA meetings and she never recalled seeing them together.

Pen was not concerned about the infidelity as much as she was with an AA newcomer being in an ongoing sexual relationship with another member. Pen didn't outright urge Sandy to break it off with Carpenter, just to be careful.

The affair continued, mainly within the confines of Sandy's apartment. Although they were keeping the relationship a secret, Carpenter didn't play it as if it were a "no strings attached" affair. He frequently called Sandy at work. He was always checking in, and began to display a jealous streak.

Though she was fully aware that Ken Carpenter was still married to Cynthia Harvey, Sandy was still under the impression that Harv was not part of his life. It was more than just a willing naïveté on her part; Carpenter told her they were no longer speaking and were avoiding each other. But there were contradictions in his story—he said he and Harv had a marriage on paper only, but told Sandy that no, she couldn't visit his house in Lempster.

Sandy pressed the point with him. "You said you were unhappy with Harv and you were going to leave her. Why do you stay?"

Carpenter was ill at ease with this new line of inquiry. He had been extremely comfortable with the nature of his love life. Nothing would be gained from rocking the boat. He wanted Sandy in his life but didn't want to leave his wife.

"I've got no steady job, no way to support us. And I'm on her health insurance."

He used this last point with Sandy in sharp effect. Carpenter was on medication for depression and had been seeing a therapist regularly. He could never afford these benefits out-of-pocket. Sandy, who sought the same kind of treatment, could not argue against the importance of this care any more than she could argue against him going to AA. For now, the discussion was over.

In October 2004, Carpenter had lost his job at Walmart for shoplifting. The loss prevention officer, Terri Casey, had suspected him of stealing from the store for some time. She followed him around the store, taking mundane household items off the shelves, stuffing them in shopping bags, and loading up a cart. Harv was home sick, so he took some orange juice and Nyquil. When he pushed the carriage out of the store and to his car, Casey confronted him in the parking lot.

Carpenter was smooth at first, still very sure of himself. "This never happened," he said. He opened a bag of potato chips and offered to share them with his accuser. "I'm walking to my car and I will pay you tomorrow."

Casey was firm with him, ordering him back inside. Carpenter gazed up and down at the busty blonde and asked if she wanted to have sex. "No strings attached," he said, sweetening the offer.

She thought Carpenter was doing all he could to keep

his temper. He started to pump his fists and the veins on his head were popping out. Casey knew Carpenter got wound up quickly, but she found him easy to cool down, too. She said she'd lose her job if he didn't come back inside with the stolen goods. Carpenter agreeably pushed the carriage back inside and was fired the next day.

Ken Carpenter couldn't keep his affair with Sandy a secret forever. Before a 7:00 meeting in October 2004 at Millie's, Carpenter let it slip to fellow member Jim Swan. They were sitting next to each other, drinking black coffee and waiting for the proceedings to begin.

"That's my girl," he said, gesturing toward Sandy, who had just entered the room.

"I'm going to ask her how her dog is doing," Jim said, remembering something she had shared recently with the group.

"Aw, Moisha's fine," Carpenter said about the dog. "You're not going to ask her out, are you?"

Jim Swan was a bear of a man. He also has a personality as big as his girth, ready to crack a joke or fling an insult at the drop of a hat. "Why would you ask that?"

"You're a single guy," Carpenter reasoned and didn't follow up with any other comment.

After the meeting, Jim pulled his friend aside. "Am I missing something here?" he asked. "About you and Sandy?"

Carpenter quietly told him that he was having an affair, that his marriage with Harv was tenuous, and that he wanted to build a home on a parcel of Greg Merritt's farmland.

"How do you really feel about Sandy?"

"I love her very much," Carpenter said.

The two men drifted out of Millie's and into the parking lot, where they continued to talk. Until now, Carpenter hadn't told anyone about the affair or his feelings for his mistress. He told Jim that he was considering leaving his wife.

"Look," Jim said, "I have a big house. I live all alone. I'm single. If you need a place to stay for a couple of weeks, until you can find an apartment and move on with your life, you're welcome to stay with me."

Carpenter shook his hand and said he'd think about it.

On Sunday evening, November 14, 2004, Nicholas and Dot Monahan threw a housewarming party at their new home in Lempster. It was actually a "house blessing," an alcohol-free potluck affair that nodded toward the Monahans' embracing of the spiritual side of AA. The home looked beautiful, bathed in soft yellow light throughout. Everything had been adorned with the touches of colonial décor that so suited the property.

A house "blessing" was just the kind of thing that Pen Meyer would have rolled her eyes at. She would have skipped the gathering altogether were it not for Jonathan. The two had been dating for about a month, and this would be one of their first appearances as a couple.

"Fine," Pen relented. "I'll hold my tongue about any 'God' stuff."

Jonathan just laughed and slid his hand into hers. They were dressed up for a change. Pen's jewelry selection was largely the same, except for a pearl necklace that she wore only on special occasions.

"Why is it when I'm with you," Jonathan asked, "I feel like one plus one equals ten? Like we're greater than the sum of our parts?"

Pen simply smiled. "It's the first mature relationship we've ever had."

"You bring out the best in me," he said fawningly. "You're my Pen."

"*Your* Pen?" she asked. "Makes it sound like you own a swan."

He looked at her curiously, then she explained that a female swan was also called a "pen."

"What's a male swan called?" he asked.

"A cob."

Jonathan shook his head, as if some great discussion had just been settled. "That's it. I'm Pen's cob."

The two stepped out of the cold wind and entered the Monahans' home with gifts in hand. Nicholas Monahan was a gracious host, taking coats and playing domestic tour guide. He led Pen and Jonathan toward the kitchen and the chatter of many happy voices.

"It's Pen and Jonathan!" Dot Monahan's exuberance announced that the party could truly begin. Pen was taken aback at being "outed" so openly and caught her breath, as if she were about to go underwater. She reached for Jonathan's hand and found it. But the looks from the other couples gathered at the party didn't sting. Pen met their eyes and relaxed. She and her cob were welcomed.

As she moved through the room basking in the good feelings, Pen suddenly stopped. Her vision tracked the one face in the home that didn't appear pleased to see her. It was Ken Carpenter. Hanging on his arm was his wife, Cynthia Harvey. There was no denying the body language between the two of them. They were a married couple, not estranged, not in a bond of convenience. Carpenter's face betrayed his surprise to see Sandy's confidante there, the woman who had greeted the secret lovers after their hike around the Goshen Ocean. He was supposed to accompany Sandy for Thanksgiving dinner at Pen's house in about a week, and here he was, acting very much like nothing was wrong with his marriage.

Harv, whose attention was directed at other friends in the circle, was oblivious to any conflict brewing in her husband. She leaned on him, and not the way an estranged wife would. She wore him comfortably. Pen's eyes narrowed ever so slightly as the full realization swept over her. Carpenter was just stringing Sandy along, and Harv was utterly clueless.

The tides of chitchat pulled guests to and fro. Some followed the hosts on tours of the new home. Others explored solo or in groups, mixing partners into never-before cast combinations. Ken Carpenter worked deliberately to get himself alone with Pen Meyer.

"Please," he said, finally cornering her in a dimly lit hallway. "Don't tell Sandy you saw me here with Harv."

Pen matched his hushed-yet-intense tone. "I'm not going to lie for you, Ken."

"Please. You're just going to hurt her."

"You're hurting both your wife *and* Sandy."

"Only if you tell them."

Pen wagged a finger in Carpenter's face, her bangles clinking as they slid down her skinny arms. "Remember the Fifth Step: 'Admit to ourselves and another human being the exact nature of our wrongs.' You need to see what you're doing and how it's affecting you and those around you. And remember the Ninth Step: 'Make direct amends.' You need to handle this yourself."

"There's another saying in the program," Carpenter replied. "'Sweep your own side of the street.'" It was an alcoholic's way of telling another to mind her own business.

"You can do whatever you want to your wife," Pen said, "but I won't let you hurt my friend."

Pen turned on her heel and stormed away from Carpenter. She found that most of the group had resettled in the kitchen, picking at hot food and sipping club soda. Pen couldn't bring herself to look at Harv or interact with her. She knew she'd somehow betray herself. Harv would later say she thought Pen was being a snob by ignoring her.

Carpenter slipped away from the others and shuttered himself in the living room in front of the television. The

Patriots were playing the late game against Buffalo, giving him the cover he needed to withdraw. In the kitchen, the party went on. The men would occasionally peek in on the football game, ensure themselves that the Pats still had control of the lead, and then rejoin the crowd. Only Ken Carpenter refused to come back to the party. He stared at the TV, listening to the thunderous tackles on each play. Snap after snap, tackle after tackle, drawing him into a trance. Carpenter wouldn't leave the living room until Pen Meyer left the party.

FIVE

Home

Around the kitchen table of Todd and Rosie Cheatham,* the silence said more than the reports of misgivings from Goshen. The couple spoke with Jonathan Purick about the strangeness of Pen Meyer's daylong absence. Todd was one of the two men Jonathan had been chauffeuring home from the AWOL meeting on February twenty-third. After dropping off the third man in the truck, Todd invited Jonathan inside his house.

"I just can't believe she would get up and go without her dog," Jonathan told the couple. "Something is wrong. And I have a feeling that Ken Carpenter is behind it."

Rosie Cheatham knew Pen from other social circles

---

* Denotes pseudonym.

outside of AA. She agreed. If Pen took Fluff to farmer's markets, to protest demonstrations, on hikes and trips to the garden, and even to her AA meetings, she was not likely to leave the dog alone all day and night. "There's more snow coming, too," she said, underscoring the urgency.

"Anything unusual about the inside of the house? Like signs of a break-in or something?" Todd asked.

"No. Nothing." Then Jonathan added. "Someone had been painting, though."

Rosie snapped her fingers. "That was my sister. Pen hired her to paint one of the bedrooms." The woman reached for the phone and dialed from memory. After greeting her sister, she asked, "Was Pen home when you were painting today?"

Jonathan and Todd watched with clenched breath for some sign of confirmation. Rosie just shook her head. "She says the house was empty except for the dog all day."

"What do you *really* think happened to her?" Todd asked.

Jonathan fidgeted. "I don't want to say."

The three of them sat silently around the kitchen table. Rosie tried to drive the conversation forward. "Should someone call the police? Or do they wait forty-eight hours until they start doing anything?"

Jonathan shrugged his shoulders. The police would probably give him the brush-off.

"You should call her ex-husbands," Rosie said.

Jonathan didn't want to do that, but he knew whatever

discomfort it might bring would be short-lived, and he was starting to feel desperate. Rosie helped him look up the numbers.

Jonathan had not previously met either of Pen's ex-husbands. His first call was to Richard Rankin, the man Pen had divorced less than six months earlier. The phone at Rankin's house rang and rang. *That's odd*, Jonathan thought. *It's ten o'clock in the evening and he's not home.* There were a million unknown social obligations and perfectly good reasons for Rankin to be out of the house, but Jonathan was still troubled by it. Pen was missing and her abusive ex-husband was unaccounted for.

Next, he called Colin Campbell, the father of Pen's three adult children. Again, Jonathan had had no previous contact with Campbell and felt no ill will toward him. Campbell was vice-president at a local bank and a respected man in the community. When Jonathan introduced himself on the phone, Campbell was courteous. As he described the situation, Campbell remained cool.

"Well, that doesn't seem like her," was all he offered. His voice betrayed no panic or underlying suspicion.

"This is what we'll do. You call the kids. See if anyone has heard from her or knows anything. I'll go back to her place and wait for her there."

When he hung up, the Cheathams were staring at him. Jonathan told them that he was going back to Pen's house, where he would call the police and wait for them there. He pulled his winter coat back on, and as he closed the door behind him, Rosie said a small prayer.

When he entered Pen's home for the second time that night, Jonathan Purick was flush with an entirely different sensation. His body was electric, but this time he wasn't on high alert. This time the energy was sour, angry. He later described it like a force of nature, snapping him out of his denial. He knew Pen was gone, and he knew who had taken her.

Jonathan picked up the phone and dialed the seven digits it took to get a hold of the local police dispatch center. The call had to be routed from one sleepy town to the next. None of the nine-to-five police departments in Sullivan County were staffed, and the region was patrolled after dark by the New Hampshire State Police. At 10:48 p.m., dispatcher David Tucker finally took the call.

"I'm at my girlfriend's house on Center Road in Goshen and she's been missing all day," Jonathan began calmly. "No one has seen her. Her car is still here and her dog is still here. It's really bizarre."

Tucker took down the info. The closest state trooper was in the next county backing up a trooper making an arrest. The trooper was at least thirty minutes away on snowpacked roadways, even with his blue lights running. He was supposed to transport the prisoner to a local lockup, but Tucker radioed to him and sent him to Goshen instead.

*   *   *

Jonathan Purick paced a furious path across the floor of Pen Meyer's kitchen. Pen had been missing all day, and if she wasn't incapacitated in a hospital, he was sure Kenneth Carpenter had had some hand in it. *How could I have been so blind?* he thought. *I warned Pen. I warned her.*

He tapped his foot on the floor, bounced his knees nervously up and down. He walked to the bay window over the kitchen sink. Night had stolen the view of the lake. All he could see were his own worried eyes looking back at him from the panes. He felt like he needed to do something more than just wait for a state trooper.

Jonathan turned his attention to the telephone sitting on a little table. Pen's eyeglasses case was next to the receiver. Before he realized he was even doing it, he was dialing the phone. The number he was punching in was Ken Carpenter's.

With each electronic burr on the other end, Jonathan's grip on the handset got tighter. It continued to ring, but no one was picking up. The answering machine clicked on. Jonathan was unsure what to say, whether to leave a message as important as this one.

"This is Jonathan," he said forcefully. "Pen's missing. I know you know what's going on. You have to get back to me."

The silence that returned to the room was uneasy. Fluff sauntered into the kitchen still searching for his master. Jonathan returned to pacing. He picked up the phone again and called Carpenter's house. He wasn't going to wait for Ken to listen to the message. He called again, and called again. He didn't leave any more messages.

Jonathan finally sat down at the kitchen table and tried to clear his head. What else could he do? *Sandy Merritt left a message on Pen's answering machine. She said Pen had hit her with a "bombshell" this morning. What was that all about?*

"Jonathan, where's Pen?" Sandy asked when he rang her up.

"No one has seen her all day," he said. He quickly ran through the events of his evening, and told her that he was calling from Pen's empty home. "You talked to her this morning. You left a message saying she dropped a bombshell on you."

"It was so odd," she said. "Pen called right as I got into work. I couldn't hear her well because the dogs were all barking and wanting to be fed. Then out of the blue, she says I should drop the restraining order against Ken and get back together with him."

Jonathan was flabbergasted. "What? Sandy, she wouldn't say that."

"She told me that Ken had some kind of accident with the chain saw and he had some sort of change of attitude. Pen said I should go straight to the courthouse and drop the criminal complaint—which I didn't do. And then she said I should move in with him."

"Sandy, she would never say that."

"But that's what she said."

"Pen would never say that." Jonathan clenched his teeth and drew a hard breath. "Don't you see, Sandy? He had her. He *had* her!"

NHSP Trooper Marcus Harring arrived at the Center Road home in Goshen at 11:24 p.m. He found Jonathan Purick standing in the driveway, talking on a cordless telephone. The trooper stepped out of his warm cruiser wearing the forest green coat and tan pants of the New Hampshire State Police. He put his Smokey Bear–style campaign hat on, its brim pressed in a neat circle. Purick acknowledged the trooper, but kept yakking away on the phone for at least a full minute before covering the mouthpiece.

"I'm talking with Pen's friend, Sandy. She got a strange call from her this morning." Jonathan tried to summarize the conversation and explain the significance of it, but kept stumbling. "Here, why don't you just talk to her?"

He handed Trooper Harring the phone and Sandy picked up the conversation right where it had left off. She explained that Pen's about-face on the subject of her ex-boyfriend was hard to fathom and Pen had never abandoned her home and dog in such an abrupt manner before. Harring passed the phone back to Jonathan.

"Do you mind if I take a look around?" he asked Jonathan. The two of them walked to the front door, where they were greeted by Fluff.

"Don't worry," Jonathan said. "He's friendly."

The two moved past the sheepdog and into the home. The trooper agreed that there didn't seem to be any obvious signs of foul play. By all accounts it looked like an ordinary house.

"Where does Ms. Meyer work?" he asked.

"She's a weaver. She works at home. Her weaving room is right over here."

Jonathan showed Pen's workspace to the trooper. On the other side of a multipane glass and wood door was an ancient-looking foot-operated loom. The room was filled with looms of various sizes and neat stacks of fiber materials. The weaving room was attached to the dining room. While passing through, Harring noticed an orange winter coat draped over the back of a chair.

The two men sat in the kitchen and Harring took notes. He wanted to know if Pen had any medical issues, if she was depressed and likely to harm herself. Jonathan rejected both of those possibilities. The trooper wanted to know more about Ken Carpenter and why he would be angry with Pen.

"He thinks Pen is the reason Sandy broke off her affair with him."

Harring asked if Jonathan knew how to get in touch with Carpenter and he gave the trooper the telephone number. Harring went over to the house phone and called. Just as it did for Jonathan, the line on the other end rang four times and turned on the answering machine. Harring identified himself as a state trooper and asked Carpenter to call the barracks in Keene.

At quarter to midnight, Harring's police radio squeaked. The dispatcher was sending him to a 10-61—a domestic dispute—in progress in the town of Unity. It was a fifteen-minute drive in good weather.

"I have to go. I have to take this," Harring said. "But I will be back in touch with you later tonight."

"I'm not going anywhere. I'm going to spend the night right here."

Before leaving, Harring asked if he could check out the detached garage. He noted that Pen's CR-V was still there with no luggage in the car. He did not like where this story was going.

Not long after the state police trooper left, the phone in Pen's kitchen rang. Jonathan scooped up the handset, unsure of who might be calling. Was it Pen? Or was it Ken Carpenter?

"Hello?"

It was Cynthia Harvey. And she sounded pissed. "Jonathan, why the hell do you keep calling my house? I don't want to be involved in any of this shit."

"I'm sorry, Harv, but Pen is gone. Vanished. And your husband has been implicated."

Through the phone, it sounded like Harv had been knocked back by the word "implicated." It was powerful and had the weight of a formal accusation backed up by solid evidence. If it sounded like it was the police and not

Jonathan who had "implicated" Carpenter, she couldn't have cared less.

"You need to leave us alone," an exasperated Harv ordered. "We're going through our own stuff."

"I'm sorry you're going through your 'own stuff,' but she's missing and your husband knows where she is," he replied. "This ain't normal, Harv. This ain't normal."

Harv hung up the line with a resounding *ka-clunk*.

Jonathan paced some more, stared out the window some more. Was there nothing he could do but wait? He petted the dog, wishing Fluff could tell him something about what had happened earlier that day.

The phone rang another violent electronic peel. He ran to the small table in the middle of the room and scooped up the handset.

"Hello?"

"Jonathan? Is that you?" It was the voice of Ken Carpenter.

"Yeah, it's me."

"Why are you calling my wife's house and trying to upset her?" Jonathan inferred from his phrasing that Carpenter was not at his home in Lempster and was calling from somewhere else.

"I was looking for you. Pen is missing and you know what's happening."

"I don't appreciate you mentioning my name to the police," Carpenter said. "They've already been here."

"Good," Jonathan shot back. "I'm surprised they haven't already arrested you."

"Quit calling me and accusing me of things."

Ever since the house blessing, the confrontations between Carpenter and Pen had been escalating. "Oh, give me a break. You two have been going at it for so long. And now she's missing and I want her back."

They exchanged more angry words before hanging up. Jonathan's heart was racing now. He had no way to know if the police had really been to see Carpenter—wherever he was—as he had claimed. He certainly didn't believe Carpenter wasn't involved in Pen's disappearance.

Jonathan called Todd Cheatham and asked him to come over to Pen's house. He agreed to spend the night there with his friend. When he arrived and Jonathan let him in, the nervous boyfriend took a couple of looks into the darkness behind them, just to make sure they were alone.

"Aren't you afraid of Ken Carpenter?" Todd asked.

Jonathan shrugged. *Afraid?* he seemed to answer, *not really.* But would that stop Carpenter from looking for him if he were out settling scores? Jonathan realized he was vulnerable. "I don't own a gun," he said.

Because there was no sofa, the two men slept on the kitchen floor. It occurred to Jonathan he could sleep in Pen's bed. He had—with her—on many occasions. But for a reason he didn't want to speak aloud, he knew he shouldn't disturb it. The bed should remain empty until Pen returned.

Jonathan and Todd were awoken on Thursday, February 24, by rapid knocks on the door. Jonathan squinted at his wristwatch as he picked himself off the floor and staggered to the door. It was 8:00 in the morning. When he pulled the door open, he was greeted by one of the largest men he'd ever seen. Trooper Jayson Almstrom was a hulk of a man, his thick arms straining the seams of his New Hampshire State Police uniform. Jonathan stepped all the way aside, and Almstrom entered the house. He was followed by an NHSP sergeant and three people that Jonathan recognized. They were two of Pen's three children and her first husband.

Trooper Almstrom had been briefed about the Meyer case earlier that morning by Trooper Harring, who explained what had happened the day before. While he was driving to that domestic disturbance, Harring learned the dispatcher got a call from Carpenter's wife, who had offered up a phone number where Ken could be found. They called him, but Carpenter said he didn't have any idea where Pen Meyer might be.

Harring also spoke to Kira Campbell, one of Pen's two daughters. She gave the trooper some more insight into Pen's daily routine. Kira told him her mother was a creature of habit and extremely regimented. She was an avid walker and she always took her dog with her. Harring asked Kira to meet with investigators at the Goshen home first thing in the morning.

Now they were in the kitchen with Jonathan Purick, absently staring into the corners of the rooms looking for signs of Pen. There was a perceived coldness in the room when Pen's children and ex-husband entered the house. They showed no sign of pleasure in seeing Jonathan among Pen's belongings, nor did they acknowledge his feelings of worry for the missing woman. Pen's relatives were a tight bunch, and Jonathan Purick was feeling very much on the outside of their concern.

Trooper Almstrom was joined by his sergeant, David Griffin. They did their own search of the home. They saw that Pen's snowshoes were in the garage, dry and untouched. Afterward, they tried to separate the different people in the house so they could ask some more questions.

Pen's son, Justin Campbell, was older than his two sisters. He acted very much like the oldest child would: taking a lead role and protecting the others in his family. He told the troopers that his mother had a strict routine: walking in the morning and snowshoeing in the afternoon. Fluff was always by her side for these outings. He said Pen's recent divorce from Richard Rankin had not been amicable. One of the troubling secrets unearthed by Pen about her husband was that he ran an adult-oriented website for a group called The Bearded Clam Society. While not outright pornographic, Pen found the frat-boy flavor of the group demeaning to women. It was but one of many positions on which the divorced couple didn't see eye to eye.

Kira Campbell told the police that she found Jonathan Purick to be obnoxious. She thought his actions—like sitting watch in her mother's house and accusing people over the phone—were out of control. Kira explained to the troopers that she and Pen had an argument about her relationship with Jonathan around Christmas. She didn't spend the holidays with Pen and they hadn't spoken since then. Now she faced a terrible thought: *Was that argument my final conversation with my mother?*

Colin Campbell, the children's father, confirmed much of what Justin and Kira told the authorities. Although they had been divorced since their kids were young, Colin and Pen had remained close. He said they spoke on the phone every week or so.

The family members all knew that Pen went to regular Alcoholics Anonymous meetings, but none of them knew exactly why she went or why she had identified herself as an alcoholic. They said Pen never appeared to have a drinking problem, so her participation in nearly daily meetings was a puzzle to them. They told authorities they suspected that Pen's nurturing soul brought her to AA, not for herself, but to assist those less fortunate than her. And in Sullivan County, there were few people who were not less fortunate than trust-fund fiber artist Pen Meyer.

* * *

Sergeant Griffin and Trooper Almstrom questioned Jonathan separately from the others. The boyfriend who had fretted his waking hours the previous night with nothing to do gave the troopers a handwritten page of notes about the investigation, which even included the case number he'd gotten from the dispatcher.

case number 05-002066
Edith Meyer Centre Rd Goshen
missing since 900 hrs 022305
last phone contact 740 hrs 022305
with Sandy Merritt of Newport

The notes went on to explain why Ken Carpenter might be involved and detailed the call between Jonathan and Sandy. The investigators collected Jonathan's notes—not because they were terribly insightful, but because his zeal to direct them to Carpenter was unusual.

They then asked whether Pen might have dementia or a similar disorder. Jonathan said no. Had she been depressed or wanted to harm herself? "Of course not," he replied.

"Is she on any medication that you know of?"

"Pen doesn't believe in medication," he said. "I'd be surprised if you even find a Tylenol in the house."

A roar passed overhead. Jonathan recognized the noise as a helicopter. The troopers told him that the search for

Pen was well under way. After Jonathan's call to the police, authorities had spent the night checking local hospitals to see if Pen had been admitted there. Around 3:00 a.m., state police issued a BOLO—Be On the Look Out—for Pen Meyer based on Jonathan's physical description. Patrolmen in both New Hampshire and Vermont were checking every rest stop and scenic pullover for her. At that moment, more than a dozen searchers were gathering to comb the snow-covered woods and trails around Goshen and Lake Gunnison.

During a lull in the questioning, Almstrom stood alongside Jonathan with his colossal arms folded across his chest. The formidable trooper suddenly snapped his entire body around and virtually straddled the man he had been casually talking to.

"Where is she? Do you know where she is?" Almstrom roared.

Jonathan was impressed by the move. The trooper was horribly intimidating, and the startling confrontation would surely have forced guarded words from his mouth. *Of course I'm a suspect*, he thought. *I'm the boyfriend and she's missing.*

"I don't know where she is," he said evenly.

"Can you account for your whereabouts yesterday?"

"My birthday was Sunday and my driver's license had expired. In the morning I drove to Concord to get it renewed before I went to work."

"So you were driving around with an expired license?"

It seemed like such a silly thing to admit to a state

trooper, especially considering he had practically accused him of a felony a half minute earlier. Jonathan just laughed his answer. "Well, yeah."

Griffin and Almstrom conferred with each other. They weren't getting the feeling Jonathan was hiding anything, and his concern for his missing girlfriend seemed sincere. They told Jonathan they were going to do a twenty-yard perimeter search and look around the house for footprints before leaving.

"All right, you're going to have to leave the house now," Sergeant Griffin told him. "This is now a crime scene."

SIX

Interloper

Sandy Merritt confronted Ken Carpenter about his marriage in her apartment three days after the Monahans' housewarming party. It was Wednesday night, November 17, 2004, and Carpenter came to the familiar hideaway as he always had when Harv was working the night shift. He'd come over on Monday, half expecting to find Sandy with Pen and prepared for a confrontation. But that night Sandy had seemed none the wiser and they watched *CSI: Miami*, as always.

But if Carpenter thought Sandy would never hear about the housewarming party, that he would just keep coming to her home and continuing their affair, then he was fooling himself. This night, Sandy had clearly been told the story. She called off the relationship, telling

Carpenter she could not take the lying or the attempts to control her anymore.

"You can believe Pen if you want," was his defense, seemingly confident in theory that Sandy would doubt the veracity of the claim. None of what Sandy's friend said was true, he declared. Sandy ordered him to leave and he did.

Ken Carpenter could easily have walked away from this failed relationship. Although she was angry, Sandy hadn't threatened to tell Harv about their eleven-month affair. He was free to continue his convenient marriage and reap the benefits of a fully employed wife. Strangely, Carpenter did not appear to be grateful for that small favor. He either felt confident enough about his sway over Harv, or cared so little about losing her it didn't matter. When confronted by Pen at the Monahans' party, it was after all Sandy's ignorance and not Harv's that he begged to save. And Pen was the one whom Carpenter blamed for spilling the beans to Sandy and ruining their relationship.

The next evening was Thursday, and Harv left for work at the nursing home as she always did. Carpenter stayed home, and at 9:00 watched *CSI—their* show—alone. It wasn't the same. Carpenter was determined to get Sandy back.

That night he called Sandy's home. "I just want to talk—as friends."

"We are not friends!" she said firmly. "Don't call me here again."

On Friday, November 18, Carpenter turned up

unannounced at Sandy's place in Newport. "Sandy, we can straighten this out."

"Don't come here again!" She shooed him off the farm.

The phone calls didn't stop. Carpenter rang up Sandy's employer, the Animal Inn, and tried to talk with her there. She told him she didn't want to see him and to stop calling. He called her back again and again, calling her at home over the weekend despite her pleas to be left alone.

On Monday, November 21, 2004, Sandy came home and found a message from Carpenter on her answering machine. "I want to know if you'd like to go to Thanksgiving dinner with me. I figure we could go as friends . . ."

Sandy immediately dialed Carpenter's number. She had forgotten they had discussed going to Pen's home on Thanksgiving before the breakup. Now she was cursing herself for ever mentioning it to him. "I don't know why you're telling people that we're friends because we are not!" She slammed the phone down.

The next day, Sandy started carrying in her pocket the telephone number of the local police department. She was beginning to be afraid Carpenter would show up at her workplace and make trouble.

Pen made a traditional turkey for Thanksgiving. She hosted a small party at her home on the Goshen Ocean. Jonathan Purick was there. Pen's daughter Kira came with her husband, Aaron. Pen also invited Sandy Merritt. She came with a tall man with dark curly hair named Ronnie,* with whom she had attended school as a child, and who only recently had starting attending AA meetings. Pen graciously welcomed him to the table and set about to learn more of their new acquaintance.

Ronnie seemed like a nice enough guy. He had good manners and a light sense of humor, making him the ideal dinner guest. Sandy and Ronnie didn't act like a couple, and it was a clear from the outset that they weren't on a date, but Sandy seemed much brighter than she had in some time.

Pen told Jonathan she was relieved that Sandy had broken up with Carpenter. "It was the wrong kind of relationship for her to be in," she told him privately. She was openly concerned about his attempts to contact Sandy.

Jonathan couldn't help catching disapproving looks from Kira Campbell. Pen was wearing a dress, a fashion selection previously out of character for her. At one point, Jonathan placed a hand in Pen's lap, which she lovingly covered with her own. Jonathan thought he saw Kira telegraph something in her eyes to her husband. Jonathan never knew Pen in any of her previous iterations and had to take her at her word about her claims of a newfound serenity. Could others who'd known her longer be seeing

---

* Denotes pseudonym.

something new in Pen, too? Judging by her coldness to him, Jonathan believed Kira did not care for this new version of her mother and held him responsible for the perceived change.

November 26, the Friday after Thanksgiving, was a busy day at Millie's Place. Most members of the AA group had the day off work and were able to catch the daytime meeting. Willpower can be tested in a daylong slog with annoying in-laws and unguarded cocktails. Getting together with those in the program the day after a holiday was an important tool in recommitting to working the Twelve Steps.

There were many familiar faces at the early meeting. Pen gave her friend Joanne a ride to Millie's. Jonathan met them there. Ronnie was in the group and so was Ken Carpenter. Neither Sandy nor Harv was at this meeting. Jonathan sensed it was a good opportunity to talk man-to-man with Carpenter. As the session broke up, Jonathan cornered him in the back of the room.

"Number one: You're a married man. If your wife doesn't know about this, then you shouldn't be doing it," he began. "Number two: You know you can't be hitting on a newcomer in the program. That's a big no-no. That's verboten."

Carpenter's reaction wasn't angry, just unapologetic. "I really care about Sandy. I really do."

He spoke as if there had simply been some big misunderstanding that could be easily rectified if only he could speak to his beloved girlfriend.

"Ken, you have to stop calling her and bothering her."

Having said all they could to each other, Carpenter turned to leave the clubhouse. On his way out, Carpenter stopped to make some small talk with Ronnie.

"How was your Thanksgiving?" he casually asked the newbie as they went through the door.

Jonathan walked the length of the strip mall to catch up with Pen and Joanne. They were standing in front of the video store with some other women talking about their holidays. Joanne was smoking a cigarette. She knew the smoke bothered Pen, so she stood far enough away to keep it out of her face. Suddenly, they heard the rising whine of a car engine coming closer. They all turned to see a tan Jeep—Carpenter's Jeep—bearing down on them.

The Wrangler stopped short with a squeal of rubber on the frozen asphalt. The door swung open and Carpenter jumped out.

"My personal business is none of your business!" he said, waving a finger at Pen. All of them stood in a frozen tableau, watching the man with the flaring yellow eyes scream at Pen.

"You don't get to tell me how to live my life or tell others, either!"

Pen opened her mouth to answer. Carpenter took another step closer and forced the words on Pen's lips back down her throat.

"And you revoke my invitation to dinner? I was supposed to go to Thanksgiving dinner with Sandy!"

Pen's face blanched. "I didn't know Sandy had invited you to dinner."

"No, that would have just messed up your plans for setting Sandy up with Ronnie! And what's all this about how I'm not supposed to be involved with a newcomer? And what are you doing at Thanksgiving? You're fixing her up with a newcomer!"

It clicked with Jonathan that Carpenter had been fine until he ran into Ronnie. When they chatted after the meeting, Carpenter had to have learned that Ronnie took his place at the table and that had stoked his jealously. Jonathan started racking his brain for a way to calm the situation.

"Why don't you let me explain that, Ken?" Jonathan took a couple of steps to his right, trying to draw Carpenter's attention away from Pen and the group of smokers. But Carpenter continued to rant in Pen's face with no sign of quitting.

"What you are is a bunch of hypocrites! You need to sweep your own side of the street, goddammit." Carpenter stomped back into his Jeep and slammed the door. The Wrangler spun its wheels and flew out of the parking lot.

Pen stood there shaking, her eyes never leaving the vehicle charging down the secondary highway. Joanne Dufour, her forgotten cigarette burned to ash, blurted out, "What the hell was that all about?"

* * *

In the days following the confrontation, things did not cool off. Carpenter became even more determined to talk to Sandy, to get her to see the error of her ways. He had always had a powerful sway over the woman. He just needed to get her alone, to talk to her without anyone else interfering and confusing her.

Carpenter's desperation for Sandy grew in direct proportion to his animosity toward Pen. Not only had Pen been the one who had disrespected him by telling Sandy his secret, she was also the one playing matchmaker to replace him in Sandy's heart. He couldn't understand what motivated Pen to be an interloper.

She is jealous of what we have, Carpenter wrote in a notebook, obsessively trying to work through his feelings. *Pen is a lesbian,* he scrawled.

On November 28, Sandy went to Millie's Place and scanned the parking lot for any of Carpenter's vehicles before going into the meeting. He didn't come into Millie's until the meeting was under way and Sandy couldn't get up and leave without making a big scene. Carpenter was really engaged in that meeting. When it was his turn to share, he talked about forgiveness.

As soon as the meeting broke up, Sandy was out the door in a flash. Carpenter chased out after her.

"Sandy, let's talk."

"Leave me alone."

"But we can work this out."

She continued to walk away from him, never missing a stride. "Leave me alone."

"Sandy, I love you . . ."

"It's over. Leave me alone."

Carpenter would not relent. He continued to assail her with his loud devotion until she got in her car and started the engine.

On the night of November 29, Sandy ignored two phone calls from Carpenter. Then the knocking came on the door.

"Sandy! Let me in. We can talk about this!"

The woman was paralyzed with fear. *Should I call the police?* It would take several minutes for a response. Instead Sandy called her brother in the main farmhouse. She told him her ex-boyfriend was rapping on the door.

"Do you want me to come up and talk to him?"

"Yes. Please."

Greg Merritt threw on a warm coat and turned on the porch light before walking out. As he made his way around the home toward the apartment, he saw Carpenter's Jeep head down the driveway and flee the property. Sandy invited her brother inside. She explained the whole mess to him and about Carpenter's bad behavior of the past two weeks.

While they sat there hashing out the troubling details, Sandy's phone rang again.

"It's him. I know it's him."

"Do you want me to take the call?"

Greg Merritt picked up the phone and waited for the

caller to ask for his sister. With no other pleasantries, Merritt told Carpenter that he was not to call this number, not to come on this property, and not to harass Sandy again. He hung up, not bothering for confirmation that Ken had got the message.

"Tomorrow," he said to his sister, "we go to the police."

On November 30, 2004, Ken Carpenter received a phone call from an officer at the Newport Police Department. He told Carpenter that Sandy Merritt did not want any more contact with him. Carpenter appeared contrite.

"I feel badly for having put Ms. Merritt in this situation. Can I call her to apologize?"

"No," the cop said. "No telephone calls. No visits." He said Sandy requested he stay at least one thousand feet away from her.

Carpenter would later claim that he asked the cop if he could write her a letter, and although it appears to contradict the spirit of the message he was delivering, the cop said letters would be fine. At least it was that clear-cut in Carpenter's mind.

Less than a week later, Greg Merritt was starting his day before dawn as he usually did. He was puttering around the old colonial when he spotted a pair of distinctive rectangular headlights bobbing slowly down the main road. Merritt went to the window to get a closer look. He saw a Jeep—its headlights now off—slowly driving the path around the farmhouse toward the back apartment.

Merritt hustled around to the back door, the most direct line to the apartment, grabbing a coat and shuffling into his boots. As soon as the morning air struck his bare face, the Jeep was driving away from the property. The vehicle's lights were still off.

Merritt walked over to the apartment door to see if the lock had been disturbed. On the front step, he found a bouquet of fresh flowers left for his sister.

Ken Carpenter's behavior was starting to worry Pen Meyer, too. She didn't appreciate his yelling and swearing in her face. The behavior had all been ostensibly about Sandy, but the anger was pointed squarely her way. Pen had been a victim for most of her life, and she wasn't going to abide by it any longer.

Pen contacted the Goshen Police Department. The entire force consisted of a chief and a part-time officer. Pen knew that Carpenter had not been given any clear boundaries. There had been no consequences for his actions. He could go on bullying Sandy, Jonathan, or anyone else he wanted to at Millie's Place.

"I want to make you aware of a situation," she told the officer. He listened and agreed to reach out to Carpenter and deliver the message.

On the fifth of December, an exhausted Sandy left work at the Animal Inn in Grantham. The psychological battle she had found herself locked in left her physically fatigued and now she was fighting off a nasty cold. She was seeing the ghost of Ken Carpenter in every shadow she passed. After going to the police the previous week, she initially felt relief. In fact, it was the first time in two weeks she had slept through the night. If the advice and threats of her family and friends weren't working, Sandy thought that police would have been enough to scare him straight. Then the flowers had arrived. For Sandy, keeping an even keel was a lifelong struggle.

As she got to her car, she noticed something on the windshield. There was a letter left under the windshield wiper. *Ken was here*, she thought. Sandy grabbed the letter and locked herself in the car as she tore it open and began reading.

"You did say to write, as opposed to stopping by, remember?" It was Carpenter's handwriting. Sandy felt exposed out in the parking lot, so she drove straight home before reading the rest of the letter.

She clutched the edges of the lined paper, her knuckles going white, and scanned its message as fast as she could. At first, Carpenter meandered through several thoughts. He wrote how he sat next to Jim Swan at a recent AA meeting. Jim, who in Carpenter's letter is somehow unaware of his affair with Sandy, began telling him how Sandy wanted friends to visit her while she nursed a broken heart from an unnamed lover.

"She invited me over to watch *CSI*," Jim reportedly told Carpenter. This made the ex-lover physically shake and become sick to his stomach. How could Sandy share *CSI—their show*—with someone else? On the page, Carpenter begged God to remove his pain and help him not think of hurting himself.

Carpenter couldn't help airing his latest grievances against Pen. He'd even written out the script of how he imagined Pen must have discussed the matter with the police. In this passage the "police" asked the interloper if Carpenter had threatened her, had struck her, had ever lost control with her—all questions this "Pen" answered no to. In this melodrama, even "Pen" strengthened Carpenter's claim that he was a righteous, unfairly accused lover. She reported that Carpenter tried to apologize to Sandy and wore his heart on his sleeve whenever he saw her at Millie's.

"His eyes fill up when she walks in the room. He stares at her," said the fake dialogue attributed to "Pen." Later in the letter, Carpenter sarcastically referred to Pen as Sandy's "savior," then struck a line through this word and apologized in the margin.

The letter went on for several more pages. In it, Carpenter continued to wax poetic about his love for Sandy. He scolded her for bringing the police into the situation, because she had broken the anonymity of AA by dragging outsiders in. He used the same anonymity rational to complain about Sandy's brother giving him a warning to back off. Within the same paragraph, he granted Sandy forgiveness for this indiscretion because, "After all, I was going to be his brother-in-law some day."

Carpenter listed all the transgressions that had led Sandy away from him. But despite whom she'd ratted him out to, whom Sandy brought to Thanksgiving, or whom she watched *CSI* with, Carpenter saved his ire for one person in particular. He ranted about "the insanity of . . . you allowing Pen to run your life." Carpenter said Pen had made her involvement personal and scolded Sandy for allowing her to be her friend.

He closed the letter with another appeal for them to sit down together. He proposed using Father Ed, a local pastor and brother of an AA member whom Carpenter was sponsoring, as an intermediary. In the postscript, Carpenter inserted one last, tantalizing bit of information.

"My new doctor is talking about borderline personality disorder. Know anything about it?"

The next day, Carpenter returned to the Merritts' property around midday, when everyone was out of the house. He crept to the door of Sandy's apartment with a letter to slip under the crack. Even a modest New England home is weatherproofed to a better degree than to allow a gap the width of a sealed envelope, so he had to leave the note in a plastic bag on the doorknob.

On the other side, Carpenter heard the barks of Moisha, Sandy's dog. "Not yet," he whispered through the door. "I'm not coming home yet, boy."

Sandy also bared her teeth when she discovered the letter.

Again, Carpenter opened with chitchat before launching a salvo of emotional declarations for Sandy. After a few paragraphs the passion petered out, and he started casually discussing his latest odd jobs (clearing brush, welding in a shop, boiling tree sap for maple sugaring). When he had no more small talk to write about, his anger at Pen again came to the surface.

He continued his motif of assigning Pen dialogue that revealed her selfishness and exonerated him. "I, Pen," he wrote, "first don't think it fair someone would love someone else, not me, Pen, that way." He painted Pen as jealous of the love Sandy received, the attention paid to her, and that she wished Carpenter were chasing her instead. He called her "The Great Pen," a selfish force of nature. Carpenter closed the letter by begging Sandy to talk to him and reason this out.

Sandy Merritt was good and scared now. Ken Carpenter wasn't going to stop. As she drove to work the next morning, she passed Carpenter coming up her driveway. She pulled her car around him and drove straight to the Animal Inn without stopping. Later she met with some friends after an AA meeting at Millie's to discuss her options. They agreed that Sandy needed to feel safe, and that she needed to feel safe at Millie's Place if she was going to be successful in maintaining her sobriety. They urged her to seek a restraining order. The fear of arrest might be the only thing left to end the stalking.

In New Hampshire, violating a domestic violence petition is a criminal matter, but *seeking* a domestic violence petition is a civil one. No prosecutor was going to make Sandy's case for her. If she could not hire her own lawyer, she would have to stand up before a judge herself and convince him. Pen, Jonathan, and fellow group member Fred Evans all offered to go and speak on her behalf.

Sandy went home and gathered all the letters Carpenter had delivered to her. On Thursday, December 8, 2004, she then consulted with an AmeriCorps legal advocate, who helped Sandy file the paperwork. In this case, the system worked quickly. The Newport District Court issued a temporary restraining order that day. A full hearing on continuing the order for one year would be held four days later, that Monday.

On Friday, December 9, 2004, Fred Evans was home entertaining his brother, known affectionately as Father Ed, the same person Ken Carpenter had suggested should play mediator between him and Sandy. Ed Evans was a calming influence for the members of Millie's Place, as he always made himself available for spiritual counseling.

Fred Evans had lived many lives in his seventy-three years. Fred had been a security officer for the Central Intelligence Agency. His exploits in the CIA were always shrouded in mystery, so to those who knew him, they seemed even more dangerous and daring than they could have possibly been. But if Fred had sent one signal that the real life of a spy mirrored that of James Bond, it would have been that whole martini thing, because the retired CIA officer was a recovering alcoholic.

Fred had flown to New Hampshire from the Mid-Atlantic states to visit his brother on September 10, 2001. The next day the world changed, and Fred thought New Hampshire seemed like the ideal place to stay put. His blood pressure was high; his health was declining. He'd had a heart attack in 1999. New England would be an excellent place to retire. He moved into his brother's home in Sunapee and, after a year, purchased his own place in Newport.

Fred was active at Millie's Place. He'd later become an assistant manager there—a largely ceremonial title that included taking responsibility for cleaning up and brewing coffee. When he needed a sponsor, he approached Ken Carpenter. There was a twenty-year age difference between them, but Carpenter had a significant amount of time sober. Fred also thought Carpenter had "street smarts." He talked a good program in meetings. Carpenter agreed to take Fred on, and by 2004, he had been his sponsor for several years.

It wasn't unusual for Fred to open his home to others in the program. While he entertained his brother in the basement, Richard Dow was in the living room watching Fox News. Dow was a disabled Vietnam veteran with only about six months of sobriety. Before Fred extended the offer, Dow had been homeless.

Dow looked away from the talking heads debating President Bush's new nominee for Secretary of Veterans

Affairs. He saw Carpenter's tan Jeep rush up the driveway. It was dusk. The vehicle had its headlights on and it was coming in hot. Dow got up from his seat and yelled down the stairs to Fred.

"Ken is in the driveway. He seems upset. He's coming in the house."

Dow hobbled over to the breezeway door and opened it slightly to let the guest in. Carpenter shoved the door the rest of the way open and brushed past Dow.

"Is Fred here?" he growled.

"Come on in," Dow said sarcastically, closing the door that had been shoved open in his face. "He's here."

Carpenter was clearly agitated. He was moving quickly, visibly twitching. The slow shuffle of Fred Evans coming up the stairs got louder until he reached the top and walked to the kitchen to greet his sponsor.

"What the fuck is going on? I thought this shit was over!" Carpenter yelled at Fred. "I just talked to her yesterday and everything was fine. I thought this shit was behind us."

"What are you talking about, Ken?"

Carpenter took a business card out of his pocket. It had a police insignia on it. "I found this in my door with a note to call! They're going to serve me papers tomorrow morning at nine! I'm going to have to be in court Monday! What do you have to do with it?"

"I didn't know she filed anything with the court." Fred was being somewhat truthful, but not completely forthcoming. Pen had been keeping Fred informed about

Carpenter's threatening behavior at Millie's. Fred had also given Sandy a ride to the police station to meet with officers and the victims advocate.

"Monday! I have to be in court this Monday! It's all out of the blue!"

Carpenter continued to rant in Fred Evans's face. His brother, Father Ed, could hear every word from the basement. Richard Dow stared at the fiery spectacle proving to be far more entertaining than Fox News.

"I don't need this," Evan pleaded with Carpenter. "My blood pressure . . . I can't be in the middle of all this." Carpenter threw his hands in the air and then stormed out.

The old CIA security officer felt threatened by Carpenter's verbal attack. He contacted the Newport Police and filed a complaint. A few days later, his doctor started him on a new blood pressure medicine, which he directly attributed to the stress of the incident.

Carpenter sat in the darkened cottage at the end of Quimby Farm Road waiting for his wife. Time was outrunning him. It was Friday night and he was due in court on Monday. If an order was issued, there would be no way to keep the secret from Harv. If the restraining order included Millie's Place, included AA meetings, she was bound to find out about it. Besides, Millie's was his home turf, the one place he felt most in control of everything, and everyone. Not to mention that he'd have to find a new place to maintain his sobriety.

Harv didn't have to work at the nursing home that evening. She had gone out with Dot Monahan and returned to find her husband sitting mournfully at the kitchen table. His eyes were watery.

"Harv," he said. "We have to talk."

SEVEN

Target

Trooper Jaye Almstrom and Sergeant David Griffin of the New Hampshire State Police wanted to pay a visit to the man Jonathan Purick was so eager to accuse the night before: Ken Carpenter.

The men had driven to Newport to the home of Jim Swan. The overnight dispatcher told them that he got a hold of Carpenter on the phone at that address. Swan worked second shift at the hospital pharmacy at Dartmouth-Hitchcock, so he was home the morning of February twenty-fourth when the troopers came calling. Swan told them that Carpenter had been staying in his guest room for a few weeks while he worked out his troubled marriage. He said Carpenter wasn't there. After a series of late-night phone calls, he'd left—presumably to his home in Lempster at the request of his wife. Griffin and Almstrom thanked him and left.

The road to Carpenter's cottage in the woods was hard to drive after a day of snow. It had not been the biggest storm (an old-fashioned nor'easter was on the radar for later in the week), but it made for slippery treading, especially in the woods on what is classified as a "Class VI" road. For everything from Classes I through V, the state maintains some level of service. Class VI roads are left to Mother Nature. They don't get paved, and they don't get plowed. In the winter they're the playgrounds of snowmobilers; in the spring, they're mostly mud and are passionately sought out by ATV owners and other motorized daredevils.

Hurd Road was Class VI. The state police cruiser bobbed over the crushed ice and compacted snow. The car turned on to Quimby Farm Road, another street in winter disrepair. They rolled on searching for the house listed as Ken Carpenter's address. As it turned out, he *did* have a police record for a restraining order a decade earlier.

On the property they were searching for, they discovered a man snowblowing a section of the land in front of the home. He was wearing a gray sweatshirt, jeans, and a black knit cap. He looked up from the rattling machine at the green state police cruiser that pulled into his driveway, then engaged the drive and went right back to throwing snow. The troopers exchanged a quick glance. When the state police visit your home out of the blue, there ought to be *some* kind of reaction.

Almstrom and Griffin got out of the car and walked over to the man. The smell of wood smoke hung in the air. The giant peace officer motioned the homeowner to cut the engine and the questioning began.

The man who'd sent those two uniformed officers to Quimby Farm Road was Detective Sergeant Russell Lamson. There were several avenues to go, and less than twenty-four hours into this investigation, Lamson already suspected this case was a "whodunit."

As they'd learned from Jonathan Purick, Ken Carpenter had a beef with Pen Meyer, but so did her ex-husband Richard Rankin. Pen was an environmental rabble-rouser who could have drawn the ire of some powerful political interests, and Lamson wondered if her public opposition to the Mount Sunapee expansion could have played a role in her disappearance. Of course, it was also possible that Pen could have gone off on her own, jumped off a bridge, shacked up with a biker, or joined the circus. And Lamson couldn't rule out that a woman who liked to walk in the woods didn't just break a leg on a branch, fall through the ice, or take a wrong turn in the snow. All of these options were on the table.

Lamson got the rundown on the missing person case during an early morning phone call to his home. The dispatcher gave him the thumbnail sketch of who the players were and what steps they'd taken overnight to locate Pen. None of the hospitals they contacted had admitted any woman identifying herself as Pen or fitting her description.

Lamson pulled a utilitarian dress suit out of the closet. Ironically, it had always been the look of the dress uniform that drew him to the New Hampshire State Police. It was the forest green of their jackets that set the NHSP apart in the sea of blue that usually identified law enforcement. Each jacket had thirteen shiny brass buttons, symbolizing New Hampshire's place as one of the original United States. The tan campaign hat made every trooper look like a Marine drill instructor. Lamson loved that uniform although now he mostly worked in plainclothes.

Russell Lamson grew up in Windham, New Hampshire, a small town near the state line with Massachusetts. He had two sisters and, as the only son, was his father's pride and joy. Russ Lamson Senior was a carpenter by trade and taught Junior everything he knew. When he got out of school, Lamson Junior went to work for his father. It was a family obligation, but one he did not mind fulfilling. He was good with his hands and enjoyed the craftsmanship. When his father passed away suddenly in 1988, the young man knew he could not keep the business going himself. Lamson decided to pursue the career in law enforcement he had always dreamed of.

Lamson's first job out of the police academy was for

the Barrington, New Hampshire, Police Department. It was a small community of about six thousand people not far from New Hampshire's brief coastline. When Lamson patrolled Barrington, the job mostly entailed catching speeders, petty burglars, and drunk drivers. When the opportunity to join the NHSP arose in 1994, he leapt at it.

As a road trooper, Lamson found himself doing a lot of the same kind of small-town policing he had done in Barrington, backing up the local constabulary in the state's villages and hamlets. He worked out of Troop C in Keene, one of a half-dozen barracks around New Hampshire. Troop C covered the southwest corner of the state, a rolling green wedge dotted with church-steepled village squares tucked between Vermont and Massachusetts. He moved his family to Sullivan County, not just to be closer to the work but because he liked the area.

Lamson was tall, clean-cut, with red hair and fair, freckled skin. He held himself with the poise of a military man. His specialty was firearms training, and he knew just about all one could know about guns and rifles. He recast his own ammunition from empty shells and black powder in his home office, a room he refinished with the carpentry skills that had never left him. Lamson's reputation in the department was as a clever, meticulous man, a quality that helped him stand out in the field of law enforcement.

In 1998, Lamson became a plainclothes detective at Troop C. He investigated every kind of felony—short of homicide—that occurred in his region. He helped get convictions for sexual assaults, armed robberies, and an attempted murder-for-hire plot. In 2000, he transferred to the state police's Major Crimes Unit in Concord. There, Detective Lamson worked on murder cases, kidnappings, and other complex investigations. He learned about forensics and advanced crime scene techniques. In 2002, Lamson was promoted to detective sergeant. The bump-up included a new assignment: to return to Troop C and run its small detective bureau.

Now, in February 2005, Lamson was in charge of two other detectives as the lead investigator on the Pen Meyer case. Lamson kept a sheet of assignments, a to-do list that kept getting longer and longer. The morning after Pen's disappearance, he assigned some troopers and his detectives to go door-to-door and question the neighbors about Pen. Based on the information gathered by Sergeant Griffin and Trooper Almstrom, Lamson had to track down Jonathan Purick's alibi: that he was getting his license renewed at the time Pen vanished.

Lamson was told that Pen had an extended family out of state and that they were very wealthy. They had a home on the West Indian island of Antigua, and it was possible that Pen was out of the country. In the meantime, Fish and Game rescuers were combing the trails around Goshen looking for a stranded hiker. Lamson ordered bloodhounds to the scene to help out. He also got the NHSP helicopter to buzz the woods and lake and take pictures from the air.

It didn't take long to verify that Jonathan's license had indeed been renewed the day before and that he went to work in the afternoon just like he said he had. Lamson still wanted to talk more with Pen's boyfriend. The note-taking and finger-pointing were out of the ordinary, but nothing else about the guy made Lamson overly suspicious.

Lamson continued calling the number for Richard Rankin, Pen's ex, but he wasn't answering his phone. This, and his unsavory website, were red flags to the sergeant. All indications pointed to fresh wounds from a recent divorce. Lamson wondered if Pen could be with Rankin that very moment at some unknown location.

Pen's children were able to give authorities the name and phone number of one of the missing woman's sisters. Lamson called Jessie Meyer-Eisendrath in Matunuck, Rhode Island.

"The first thing I said when Justin told me she was missing was 'Where is the dog?' " she told the investigator. Jessie knew that her sister wouldn't willingly go anywhere without Fluff.

Jessie said Pen was not close to the family, except for herself and their sister Daphne. Jessie feared that her family's wealth could have made Pen a target for profit-motivated kidnappers. Lamson said no ransom demands had been made. Jessie said her elderly parents were currently at their second home in Antigua. She promised to call the rest of her siblings and would report back to Lamson if someone heard from Pen.

Nothing was adding up. What Lamson really couldn't get his head around was the phone call Pen had allegedly made before disappearing. If she had been such an advocate for her friend Sandy, why would she suddenly change her tune about Kenneth Carpenter? And why was she in such a rush to do so, to call first thing on a snowy morning? Lamson called Griffin and Almstrom and asked them to find Carpenter and question him. Carpenter was still considered a "soft target," but authorities had to feel him out and see how he fit into this picture. Which was how Trooper Almstrom and Sergeant Griffin found themselves in Carpenter's front yard on February 24, 2005.

Ken Carpenter obeyed the request of Trooper Almstrom to switch off his snowblower. The three men stood out in the cold at the end of the driveway. A path for cars had already been dug between the house and the road. Carpenter was in the middle of clearing another patch near a camper and some logs off to the side.

"I know why you're here," Carpenter said to the troopers. "I'm pissed that Jonathan Purick would mention me to you and drag me into this."

Almstrom was surprised by Carpenter's instant agitation. His gripe seemed to be with Jonathan, so he tried to steer things back to Pen. "Look, the family is really concerned. They just want to know her whereabouts. I'm sure you can appreciate that."

Carpenter calmed down. He didn't raise his voice for the rest of the interview.

"How do you know Pen?"

"Through a mutual acquaintance."

"Who's that?"

"Sandy Merritt. We met at AA meetings."

"How would you describe your relationship with Pen?"

"We're just acquaintances," he said, then he added, "We both enjoy the same flavor of Life Saver."

"When was the last time you saw Pen?" Almstrom asked, ignoring Carpenter's strange aside.

"About two weeks ago. It was at an AA meeting. She was there with her friend Joanne, who works at McDonald's."

"Do you have any idea where Pen is?"

Carpenter just shrugged. "With Sandy, I guess."

Despite the rocky welcome, their "soft target" was rather nonchalant and cooperative. He wasn't acting like a man with something to hide.

"Can you tell us about your whereabouts yesterday? What you were up to?"

Carpenter had to reflect on the question for a moment. Then he told them that, after having breakfast, he'd gone out snowshoeing first thing in the morning.

"I went on the course at the Newport Golf Club. I was done by about seven thirty. Then I went back to Jim Swan's house."

Carpenter confessed to having marital problems and cited them as the reason for living at Jim's house.

"I changed my clothes and drove to Claremont for a nine thirty appointment with my psychiatrist. But when I got up there, I realized I didn't want to go to the appointment so I skipped it." Carpenter paused and said he really couldn't remember what he did the rest of the day.

The troopers pushed back a little harder, urging him to think what he had done. Carpenter insisted he was blanking out on what he had done after 9:30. But he did remember he met with a logger that afternoon named Alan Thurston, who had come to clear some trees. He also said he burned brush the rest of the day.

Sergeant Griffin took a turn at Carpenter. He decided to play one of the few cards they'd been holding.

"We have information that you followed Ms. Meyer home one night after an AA meeting. Why did you do that?"

Carpenter's eyes darted back and forth between the two of them.

"I wanted to know how Sandy was doing. Sandy had a restraining order on me. So I followed Pen home, and when she got out of her car, I asked how Sandy was. Pen told me, you know, that there was a restraining order and I wasn't supposed to be talking to her. So I left."

"Were you going there to hit on her or something?" Griffin asked.

"Oh, no no no no." Carpenter couldn't dismiss the idea fast enough. "My only reason was to find out about Sandy. I care about her deeply."

The troopers asked if they could have a look around and Carpenter didn't object. Almstrom examined the cars that had been parked on the property. There was a purple Ford Escort hatchback, a tan Jeep Wrangler, and a silver Nissan pickup truck. The trooper walked around the vehicle, peering in the windows. The hatchback—with bumper stickers that said, EASY DOES IT and WWJD—had a black bag of sand in the back, just right for helping spinning tires get some traction on iced-over roads. He spotted a pair of snowshoes in the pickup. The vehicles seemed unremarkable.

The pickup had been backed up to a snowbank, the tailgate down. There was a small thirty-gallon metal barrel on the ground between the truck and the snowbank. There was a mound of sand in the bed of the pickup and an impression in the sand. It looked as though the barrel had been resting in the truck before being offloaded. Almstrom glanced into the two-and-a-half-foot-tall container. The barrel looked like it was half filled with burned garbage.

After twenty minutes of talking, Almstrom and Griffin got back into the cruiser and made their way out of the woods. They began to compare notes on Carpenter's answers and mentally plan whom they might talk to next. Before they contacted Detective Sergeant Lamson about their next assignment, a thought flew into Almstrom's head.

"Shit," he said. "We forgot to ask him about something." Almstrom found a place to turn the patrol car around on the snowpacked road and headed back to Carpenter's house.

Carpenter was where they had left him not ten minutes earlier, still snowblowing that section of his property. This time, the man shut the machine down and greeted them calmly on their return. Again, getting out of the car, Almstrom was struck by the smell of wood smoke. He was reminded of the burn barrel near the pickup. There was a fire going somewhere on the property.

"We forgot to ask you something. Were you involved in a chain saw accident?"

Carpenter frowned and shook his head slightly. He told them he'd had a close call with a tree a couple of weeks ago. "When that happened, I nicked my boot with the chain saw. See there?"

Planting his heel in the snow, Carpenter stuck out his work boot. The steel toe had a notch that could have been gouged out by a saw. While it would have put a scare into any amateur lumberjack, it wasn't a life-threatening injury.

"Well, then, can you explain," Griffin went on, "why Pen would call up Sandy and tell her that you had been in a serious chain saw accident and that she needed to drop the restraining order and get back together with you?"

"I don't know why," Carpenter said, adding simply, "That's weird."

* * *

Before returning to Keene to debrief Sergeant Lamson, Almstrom and Griffin drove to the Newport Golf Course. In the summer, it's a rolling green playground with many scenic ponds and flora, and a tricky par 5 dogleg on the eighteenth hole. In the winter, it's a stark and barren landscape, blanketed in white.

The state police cruiser pulled up to the clubhouse. The parking lot had not been plowed since the snowfall the previous day and there were no tire tracks. The men got out and looked across the course. There were no imprints, paths, or other markings that indicated anyone had been snowshoeing there in the previous twenty-four hours. They drove around the property and up to the course's Moose Club to check out the back nine. Again, there were no disturbances in the snow on any of the access points or atop any of the fairways.

The troopers got back into the running car and put it in gear. They had important information to bring to the lead investigator in the case. Ken Carpenter had a problem with his alibi.

EIGHT

Consequence

When Dot Monahan's phone rang on Friday evening, December 9, 2004, the last person she expected to hear on the other end was Ken Carpenter. She had just dropped Cynthia Harvey off at her home in Lempster. Carpenter's voice was low and serious.

"Harv is on her way over to your house," he explained. "I just told her I had an affair. She's very upset."

Dot hung up the phone and stood by the door watching for the headlights to Harv's Ford Escort. As she thought about what Carpenter had told her, some things were starting to make sense. She'd seen Carpenter eyeing other women during AA meetings, especially the ones that Harv didn't attend. The previous summer, Carpenter had told the Monahans he wanted to move out of his

Lempster cottage to get "some space," and even asked if he could rent a room from them. They had told him no because it would be in conflict with their friendship with Harv.

When the car finally pulled in and Harv ran up to the door, Dot was waiting there with open arms for a hug. Harv's face was tear-streaked, and she burst into a fresh round of sobbing in her friend's embrace. Dot guided her into the living room, the same room Carpenter had holed up in at the housewarming a month earlier.

"Ken called me," Dot said, hoping to spare Harv the humiliation of explaining anything. But the wronged woman launched right into a fit of anger.

"He's been screwing around on me with Sandy all this time! I don't know my life at all. I don't know my own husband at all."

Dot didn't know what to say. She now believed that Harv's husband was manipulative, cunning, and disingenuous. But whether she should say these things to her friend in this darkest of moments wasn't clear. Should she spit out the truth or swallow a lie?

Harv told her that Carpenter said he had a court hearing on Monday. If his mistress won a restraining order, it could keep him out of Millie's, threatening his recovery. Dot absorbed the irony that Harv was now arguing against her husband's being barred from seeing the woman he'd been cheating on her with.

"Why *Sandy*? Why *her*?" Harv moaned. Both women acknowledged that Sandy Merritt did not look like anyone's definition of a home wrecker. They thought the woman was plain and fragile and her issues went much deeper than addiction.

"I don't get it," Harv kept repeating.

The women sat for a long time in the living room. Harv prayed for guidance with her friend. She was emotionally exhausted. It hadn't taken her long to travel the distance from anger to heartbreak.

"I just want to go home and have Ken hold me," she said. "How could Sandy have done this to me?"

Cynthia Harvey made a decision: She was going to return to her home and win her husband back. She was going to reclaim her man. She asked God for the strength to do it.

On Saturday, both Carpenter and Harv arrived at Millie's Place for an AA meeting. They sat beside each other but their eyes avoided contact. Other than Assistant Manager Fred Evans, none of the other people who were aware of their unfolding drama were there. During the meeting, Harv couldn't say much without sobbing.

"I am partly the cause of my wife's pain," Carpenter said. For using the word "partly," Harv fired a vicious glare at him, the only time she looked at him during the whole meeting. Carpenter cleared his throat and admitted he was *all* of the cause of his wife's pain.

"How could I do it?" he bemoaned. "How could I let go of one addiction only to pick up another?" He said he had been gambling and "playing around with women."

Harv continued to cry silently, unable to speak.

Carpenter said, "Why do other people have to get involved in my business and hurt my wife by meddling?" To the other members, it didn't sound like a statement of someone accepting blame, or someone who felt sorry for betraying his wife. It did, however, sound like someone who was sorry he got caught.

The next night, Sunday, December 12, Carpenter and Harv returned to Millie's Place. This meeting was typically one of the largest of the week. Pen Meyer was there, but didn't attempt to engage the struggling couple. Harv looked very much like she had the night before: Her eyes were red and she had trouble saying anything without melting into tears. She didn't socialize before the session. She sat in a chair while her husband got coffee and worked the room.

Carpenter tapped a female member on the shoulder and signaled that he wanted to have a word. Her name was Jennifer Ross,* and had been Sandy's actual sponsor since she joined AA. He knew Ross had great influence over Sandy but outside Pen's circle of social influence.

"I need you to call Sandy for me," he said. "Tell her I want her more than anything." The request made Ross sick to her stomach.

There are different formats for different kinds of

---

* Denotes pseudonym

AA meetings. There are "Big Book" meetings, in which members read from the Alcoholics Anonymous main text. There are step meetings that focus on the Twelve Steps. There are discussion meetings, in which a chairperson offers remarks on a related topic and prompts attendees to contribute. Protocols vary from group to group, but generally people speak in turn and do not engage in cross talk, response, or direct questioning of one another.

At this Sunday meeting, just hours before he was supposed to appear in district court to defend himself at the restraining order hearing and answer the stalking charge, Ken Carpenter could no longer take the pressure. He was fifth in line to speak, but when the floor was open to discussion, he spoke out of turn. He didn't even address the group with the traditional "I'm Ken and I'm an alcoholic" preamble, allowing the group to acknowledge him before speaking. He just cut to the chase.

"My life sucks and it's not getting better!" he began. "I don't know why *somebody* would tell my wife things that would only hurt her!"

Carpenter dragged out the word "somebody" and stared directly at Pen Meyer several seats over. Harv's head was down and her shoulders were heaving slightly.

"Why do people have to get involved in my personal affairs?!" he continued. "They don't know what my life is like! They don't understand me!"

Several members got up from their chairs and left the meeting, clearly uncomfortable with Carpenter's diatribe. Discussions aren't supposed to be targeted, nor get so specific and personal. AA meetings are not supposed to be "pity parties."

While Carpenter continued his rant, Pen stayed in her seat, shaking visibly.

"People need to stay out of my stuff. Some people just need to sweep their own side of the street!" he said, finishing by crossing his arms with a flourish.

Pen's usual state of warm composure snapped. She spun in her chair and faced Carpenter directly as she spoke out of turn herself.

"The principles of AA are honesty and taking responsibility for your own actions! If *people* have trouble with the honesty part of the program, then they need to start working the steps again for themselves!"

Tears fell from Harv's face to her lap as Pen went on.

"*People*," Pen went on, "may need to evaluate where they are in life, and in the program, and outside of the program!"

Pen pivoted in her seat and sat stewing. The remaining members quickly figured out a speaking order and the meeting continued, an awkward tension poisoning the oxygen in the room. When the session concluded, Jennifer Ross drifted to Pen, who stood steaming in the corner.

"I *cannot* believe how he is acting. And that he's not taking responsibility for any of his actions," Pen told her.

Outside the clubhouse, Carpenter stood with all the smokers, his body language telegraphing barely contained rage. Harv remained inside the building and was comforted by a group of sympathetic women.

*   *   *

Jennifer Ross did not deliver Carpenter's message for him, but Sandy Merritt did get another letter over the weekend before the final restraining order hearing. It read like his final plea to get Sandy to call off the proceedings.

"I want to show you a total partnership of love and trust, making myself a sitting duck, open and naked. Tell me where I stand. I need to know." He signed the letter, "Me."

Sandy, Pen, Jonathan, Jennifer Ross, and Fred Evans all attended the final hearing on Monday, December 13, 2004. Ken Carpenter, dressed neatly with his long gray hair pulled back into a ponytail, entered the courtroom with Cynthia Harvey. Harv took her place behind the table Carpenter commanded. It was an extraordinary moment for all of them. They all were coming to break their anonymity. At this moment, for example, only Pen knew Jonathan's last name. They were going to give up their anonymity in the program to testify on the public record about their relationships. *Sandra Merritt v. Ken Carpenter* was under way.

"Ms. Merritt," Judge Ed Tenney asked as she stood, "please tell the Court what the grounds are for your stalking petition."

Sandy ticked off the list of times Carpenter had accosted her since their breakup less than a month earlier.

The relentless phone calls, the unwanted letters and flowers, his ignoring the repeated pleas from her friends, family, and law enforcement. The judge took notes, making sure he got each date correct.

"Mr. Carpenter, is there anything you want to add?"

Carpenter stood. "First, I'd like to express my sincere apology to my family, in-laws, and friends. Also, I'm sorry for any disappointment or hurt I have caused my wife in this outrageous, selfish, shameful act of breaking my wife's trust in total disregard for my marriage vows."

It was more responsibility he had taken for his actions than in any of the previous AA meetings. Then, a curious statement: "I never loved the plaintiff, nor have I ever intended to leave my wife for the plaintiff."

The gathered friends shifted in the benches at the lie. They wondered what strategy Carpenter was playing now.

Carpenter told the judge that his attempts to talk to Sandy were motivated only by his desire to apologize to her. His phone messages had gone unreturned. Each time he tried to make amends in person, Sandy would run away. He said the Newport police officer told him letters didn't count as having physical contact with the plaintiff.

When the officer had later returned and told him "no letters," Carpenter said he was contrite, readily complied with the instruction, and had not written any letters to Sandy since. He implied that he had been terribly misunderstood.

"On twelve-nine, I sat down with my wife and I told

her I'd been having an affair with the plaintiff for eleven months," he said. "It wasn't an easy thing to do, but it was an honest thing and . . . and . . . and . . . and it was . . . it was tough . . . it was a tough thing to do. I had no intention of going back to the plaintiff. I came forward and I was honest with my wife. At least I would have a semblance of dignity.

"I truly believe the Court should not grant a continuance of any kind of stalking. I . . . I . . . I . . . I'm sorry. I feel I would have to be on constant vigilance where she is, thinking that she's gonna walk into a place. I believe that some plaintiffs do this in order that the defendants have to keep these plaintiffs on their minds and I don't want that. My wife has been through enough. The plaintiff has been through enough. I would like to just dismiss this and get on with our lives."

Wait, Jonathan thought. *Did he just say the restraining order was Sandy's ploy to keep him thinking about her?* He hoped the judge wouldn't see it that way.

"I have no intention"—Carpenter put his hand over his chest—"honest to God, of ever talking to the plaintiff again, ever seeing the plaintiff again, or being anywhere in the presence of the plaintiff. I cannot afford *not* to go to a meeting because the plaintiff comes in. I can't afford to lose my sobriety or feel that I'm gonna drink or use drugs because I cannot get a healthy message out of fear that the plaintiff's gonna walk in. I need to focus on the things that I need to focus on and that's getting well. I believe no good would be coming from the continuance of the order. I can give you a solemn vow. I can tell you that I'm not gonna approach the plaintiff."

"All right," Judge Tenney said, turning back to Sandy. "Do you want to respond to that?"

"If I could, I'd like to call a few friends."

The judge nodded and Sandy signaled Pen to take the witness stand. She pulled the microphone close. "My name is Edith Meyer. I live in Goshen."

Pen then spoke of the time she spoke to Carpenter before Thanksgiving and the confrontation at Millie's after.

"Both times he got really, really angry at me and felt I was an instigator when indeed I was only voicing what Sandy had asked. That he leave her alone."

Pen testified that she went to the Goshen Police to alert them. She believed Carpenter's behavior and language crossed a line.

"The police called me back," she continued. "He did acknowledge that he knew it was inappropriate and that he would leave me alone. They said if he didn't I had grounds to file a petition."

When Pen returned to the gallery, Carpenter jumped out of his chair. "Could I address that, Your Honor?"

"Yes. Go ahead."

"I never used inappropriate language with Pen," he said. "The Goshen Police told me there's a potential situation, which is what Pen told them. And I said, 'Did I ever threaten her, did I do anything?' And they said, 'Absolutely not.' 'Did I swear at her or is there anything that I did?' and they said no. And I said, 'Am I being charged with something or should I be on alert of anything?' and they said no. They don't know why she's stopped by. She just happens to be one of those people that needs a cause. And if it's not the condominiums on Sunapee Mountain—"

"All right, all right." The judge cut him off. "I'm not interested in all the other things that are going on between all of you." He asked the participants to keep their comments limited to the stalking order at hand.

In a mock grand gesture, Carpenter said with the tiniest of bows, "I apologize to Pen."

Jonathan Purick testified about the incident after Thanksgiving. Jennifer Ross said Carpenter had been showing up at her workplace trying to get messages to Sandy. Fred Evans told the court about the way Carpenter bum-rushed his way into his house and yelled at him for helping Sandy. Fred said he had later told Harv that he was dropping Carpenter as his AA sponsor.

"I love the man," Fred testified, "but he's doing stuff that's inappropriate. And I don't want to see people hurt in AA because of inappropriate conduct."

When the judge asked Carpenter if he wanted to respond to the remarks, he brushed off the thought that Fred Evans had been a facilitator in the case.

"I'm sure that Pen had something to do with the stalking order, because I know she came down to the courthouse with the plaintiff because that's part of her cause."

"Do you have any evidence, Mr. Carpenter? Any

witnesses other than your own testimony that you want to call?"

He turned to his wife, sitting stoically behind him. "Mrs. Harvey," he said.

Harv walked to the stand and told the judge she didn't know if what she had to say was relevant, but she did have a concern about the order. He encouraged her to speak.

"We go to meetings—Ken goes almost on a daily basis, several times a day. Going to meetings keeps him sober, keeps me sober. And if we were not able to go to the meetings because the possibility the plaintiff was there, that's a risk to his life. He has a life-threatening illness."

Harv argued that ever since he was told not to call, mail, or contact Sandy, her husband had complied.

"I, too," she finished, "would like to get on with our lives."

The judge sat at the bench, quietly scribbling some orders down on the documents in front of him. After several minutes, he ordered the defendant to stand.

"Mr. Carpenter," he said. "You should have done what you're asking the Court to do some time ago. You indicated your desires to simply move on, and you should have followed that advice yourself. You've disrupted Miss Merritt's life with your behavior since the breakup and obviously some other friends of yours as well."

Judge Tenney told Carpenter the stalking order would remain in place for one full year. He said Sandy could withdraw the order early if she wished. The order would expire after one year, unless Sandy petitioned the court for an extension. The order called for no communication and no in-person contact. The judge also clarified that the current order was only a civil order.

"I believe you could have been subject to a harassment charge, which is a criminal charge. That isn't the case here. This is a civil order. You're not being convicted of any criminal offenses."

Carpenter challenged the judge. "So if I go to an AA meeting and she shows up, I have to leave?"

"If you're gonna go to the same place that you've been going, and you know it's where she goes, that's going to be a violation of the restraining order," the judge countered. "You basically at this point forfeited your right, as long as this order's in effect, to go to meetings at that particular location because you know she's there."

"But ninety percent of the meetings I go to there, she's not there," he said. "Wouldn't it be easier if I had a list just telling me when not to go?"

"No."

Carpenter blinked and looked around the courtroom. He couldn't believe the breadth of the restraining order. He couldn't believe the court could keep him away from Millie's Place. He had to make the judge realize this punishment was totally unfair.

"Okay, so if my wife and I go to a restaurant to eat, I have to leave?"

"That's the penalty that occurs when somebody's got a restraining order on them." Judge Tenney was through

NOTES ON A KILLING   135

with Carpenter, his patience having been strained. "It may be inconvenient, but you should have heeded the warnings that came from everyone else long before you got before me. I don't think anybody has any sympathy for you. Certainly not the Court. You've brought this situation on yourself."

Tenney handed the order to the court clerk and left the bench. The bailiff ordered everyone to rise as the man in the black robe turned his back on the whole soap opera.

"Because she's mentally ill," Carpenter fired off, the last word he hoped to get in with both the judge and Sandy.

NINE

Interrogation

New Hampshire State Police Trooper Jaye Almstrom sat in his cruiser with the lights off, keeping an eye out for one of Ken Carpenter's three vehicles. In the car with him was Sergeant David Griffin. It was about 6:45 p.m. and they had spent all of February 24, 2005, looking for Pen Meyer. Now they sat quietly in the parking lot of the South Congregational Church in New London watching the door. They knew Carpenter attended the 7:00 AA meeting and believed he'd be coming.

Carpenter's pickup truck pulled into the lot. It was the same silver Nissan they had seen earlier that day when they visited his home in Lempster. Carpenter was alone in the cab. He was striding across the snow-shoveled walkway as the two uniformed troopers intercepted him.

"Ken," Griffin called out. "Would you mind coming with us to the Newport Police Station? We'd like to speak to you some more."

"Right now?" Carpenter blurted out. He appeared nervous and stressed out. "I really need this meeting right now."

The troopers looked at each other. They weren't there to arrest Carpenter and could only request his voluntary cooperation. The man said the AA meeting would only run about a half hour and he promised to meet them at the police station once it was done.

Earlier that same day, after they'd interviewed Carpenter at his home and checked out the golf course, Almstrom and Griffin—and about a half-dozen other investigators—continued their search for Pen. Sergeant Russ Lamson, the lead investigator, wanted the team to fill in Pen's timeline from February twenty-third.

They began by tracking down the man that Pen had hired to plow her driveway for the season. He said he hadn't noticed anything unusual when he'd driven over to clear it before dawn. He also said he'd never seen Pen without her dog at her side.

They spoke to "Pebbles" Sillars, the painter who was working in the house and the sister of Rosie Cheatham. Pebbles said she'd known Pen for about fifteen years through AA. She had recently started the painting business and Pen had hired her to do a bedroom in her

Goshen home. The quote for such a job was $300, but Pebbles had given the work to Pen as a Christmas present.

On Tuesday, February 22, 2005, Pebbles came over with her co-worker, Kathy McFarlin, and worked on the room until noon. They moved some furniture and prepped the walls, but were planning on completing the work the following day. Pen was at home with Fluff that day, doing some work around the house. Pebbles said Pen told her she had an appointment to drive someone early next morning and that she wouldn't be home when they arrived to finish the job, but would leave the door unlocked for the painters.

Pebbles said she saw Pen later that same day at an AA meeting in New London and that she had seemed in good spirits.

The following day, Wednesday, February 23, Pebbles picked up McFarlin and drove to Pen's home. When they arrived at 9:00 a.m., the door was unlocked and no one was home. The garage door was closed and Pebbles saw that the CR-V was still there. She also noticed that Pen's bed was unmade. Pebbles thought this was very peculiar, because Pen was very fastidious about making her bed every morning. It was also very unusual that Pen would have left the house without Fluff, who had been there alone when they arrived.

The two worked through to noon and took their lunch break in the kitchen. They decided to let the dog out since no one else was there to do so.

"Is it cold in here or is it just me?" McFarlin said.

Pebbles checked the woodstove. The fire had not been lit that morning and the house was getting chilly. They ate their sandwiches at the table, within earshot of the telephone answering machine. A call came in and the machine picked it up. It was a woman who asked Pen to call her about the "bombshell" she'd dropped earlier in the day. The painters went back to work, the answering machine clicking on and off throughout the afternoon.

At 4:00 p.m. when they packed up their gear, Pen still wasn't home, so the two women took Fluff for a walk before closing up everything behind them. They left one house light on in the fading dusk. Pebbles called on Wednesday night to see if Pen had gotten home and seen the painted room, but she never heard from her.

The troopers decided the next step in rebuilding the timeline should be to talk to Joanne Dufour, to whom Pen had promised a ride to the dentist. Almstrom and Griffin drove to the Newport Town Office, where Joanne worked, and spoke with her in the copy room. She explained that Pen simply hadn't shown up, and how unlike her that was. Almstrom noted that while they spoke, Joanne kept wringing her hands in worry and tears welled up in her eyes.

"Do you know anybody who would know where Pen is?"

"Ken Carpenter," she said without hesitation.

"Why do you say that?"

"Because he is a sick and dangerous person."

* * *

Russell Lamson's detective bureau at Troop C consisted of two plainclothes officers: Eric Berube and Shawn Skahan. Lamson had them drop the rest of their work and dive into the missing person case with him. The uniformed troopers on the scene had already given them enough leads to start working on.

At about 11:00 a.m. on Thursday the twenty-fourth, while troopers were just making their first contact with Ken Carpenter in Lempster, state police detectives were in Newport, questioning Sandy Merritt about the phone call she got from Pen. They talked with her at the table in her kitchen.

Troop C's Eric Berube was accompanied by two investigators from Major Crimes. The pair looked the part of big-city homicide detectives—white starched dress shirts, military haircuts, fitted suits, and dark glasses. The rookie, Berube, his own shirt-and-tie combo seeming suddenly terribly uninspired, purposely said nothing while watching how the veteran officers questioned the witness.

Sandy explained how Carpenter had been stalking her and how he blamed Pen for their breakup. She said Carpenter had long been lying to her, even about things he didn't need to. Even when Sandy confronted him about his marriage to Harv, she said, he still denied any romantic involvement with the woman who was his wife. He said that both he and Harv had been at the Monahans' housewarming party, but they had arrived separately and were not there as a couple.

"He just wasn't supportive of me. There wasn't any trust between us," Sandy complained. "I would confess intimate things and he would later throw them back in my face." She said she'd thought about breaking up with Carpenter for months before she actually did.

The detectives wanted to know more about the phone call from Pen.

"It was strange. Pen knows the morning is not a good time to call, not when I'm feeding the animals. She's called me plenty of times at work and I've never received a call before nine a.m."

Sandy said the call was 100 percent opposite from all of her friend's prior advice. Pen had always been supportive of her staying away from Ken and had stood behind her in court and elsewhere. The suggestion of dropping the restraining order and moving in with Carpenter was so abnormal, Sandy said she was bothered by it all day.

"Could you hear anything in the background?" they asked. "Did it sound like someone else was there with her?"

Sandy said she couldn't tell. "It was so loud in the room, with all the dogs barking wanting to be fed. It was hard to hear just what she was saying."

"Was there anything unusual about her voice or the way she was talking?"

Sandy just shook her head. "No. The dogs were just too loud."

* * *

New Hampshire Fish and Game had a small band of searchers combing the snowy Goshen woods looking for signs of Pen. Even with all the weird circumstances behind her disappearance, the theory of Occam's razor is never forgotten in missing person cases, that often the simplest solution is the most probable. A middle-aged woman who hiked daily in the woods left her home without her car and did not return. Odds were that Pen ran into some trouble while hiking and needed help.

Officials had used Pen's pillowcase to help the bloodhounds get her scent. The dogs were interested in the doorways of the house and its immediate perimeter, but they couldn't find a trail anywhere on the property.

The team covered more than a hundred miles on the ground around Lake Gunnison by snowmobile. There were a dozen searchers on foot with dogs running in front of them. After the first day passed with no trace of Pen, the hope of finding her unharmed in the woods plummeted.

Detectives Berube and Skahan had another interview with Pen's ex-husband Colin Campbell. He said he spoke to Pen occasionally about matters having to do with the children, but didn't see her in person very often. They'd spoken about Pen's relationship with Jonathan Purick, but Campbell said there didn't appear to be any issues worth noting. Campbell said that he, too, had been remarried since his split with Pen.

"Where was your wife yesterday?" they asked.

"Skiing in Colorado," Campbell said. "She's there with friends. I'm home alone for the time being."

"Can you tell us about what you did yesterday?" The banker said he rose early and reported to work at 8:30, just like every other morning. He worked at the office throughout the day and stopped at a local market to pick up something to eat for dinner. He relaxed at home and went to bed before getting Jonathan's call.

The detectives then tracked down the two men Jonathan had taken to the AWOL meeting. They were quizzed separately and both told the same story of how Jonathan left them in the car while he poked around inside Pen's empty house.

Canvassing Pen's neighborhood for clues proved to be hit-or-miss for investigators. Some of the homeowners on Center Road used their lakefront property as vacation houses or weekend retreats. Finding residents who were home on February 23 was a challenge. One of Pen's neighbors said he did see her and Fluff on their morning walk at 7:00 a.m., a half hour before her call to Sandy. This clue was important: It meant Pen likely got home with the dog before vanishing. Now they were waiting for records from the phone company to confirm the call to Sandy had been placed from inside Pen's house.

The troopers decided to take another shot at canvassing the neighborhood before dinnertime, when people would be home from work. A state trooper found Lucy and Andrew Seabrooke* drinking wine and beer in their kitchen at 4:30 p.m. Lucy was finished with her day shift at the Sullivan County Nursing Home, and the couple said they were celebrating their freedom now that Lucy's daughter was spending half-week visitations with her father. The state police helicopter roared by every few minutes and the couple would burst out laughing. The trooper noted in his report that both Seabrookes appeared to be intoxicated.

Lucy Seabrooke told the trooper that at 6:30 a.m., she was driving her five-year-old daughter to kindergarten. As she passed Meyer's house on the left, she noticed a car parked on the side of the road. There was a man in the driver's seat with gray hair, a gray beard, and a knit cap. Lucy initially thought it might be Derrick, an older man who lived one street over, and that he might have been having car trouble. As they rolled up to the car, however, she realized it wasn't Derrick and just kept going.

"What kind of car was it?"

"Um . . . a station wagon. That kind of car."

"What color was it?"

"Dark. Gray, I think."

The helicopter roared. Lucy giggled. Andrew told her to shut up.

---

* Denotes pseudonyms.

* * *

Armed with all this circumstantial evidence, Sergeant Lamson wanted to have another crack at Ken Carpenter. They also wanted a closer look at that Ford Escort. The color wasn't quite right, but the hatchback shape of the car could easily be confused with a station wagon.

While the investigators waited at the Newport PD for Carpenter to meet them after his 7:00 AA meeting, Lamson sent another team to quiz Harv, so they could question Mr. and Mrs. Carpenter separately.

The hulking Trooper Almstrom was paired with Detective Berube. They drove to the Sullivan County Nursing Home in Unity, New Hampshire, Almstrom filling most of the space behind the wheel of his NHSP cruiser. Harv was at work, dressed in comfortable-looking scrubs, and they found an office to speak in privately.

Harv told them Carpenter had been living at Jim Swan's house for a couple of weeks, but he still had free access to their home in Lempster. She told them he would come often to let the dogs out or to complete projects, such as clearing lumber from the lot. Harv said she left for a physical therapy appointment at 11:00 a.m. on the morning of Wednesday the twenty-third. Afterward, she went straight to work and didn't come home until midnight.

When she walked in the door of their small home, the phone was ringing. She hurried to answer it but it had stopped. That's when she played the message from

Jonathan Purick accusing her husband of some cryptic crime.

"I tried to return the call to Jonathan, but his line was busy. So then I didn't know who else to call, so I called Sandy Merritt."

Harv said that she and Sandy had not spoken to each other before then. Sandy explained that Pen was missing and Jonathan believed Carpenter knew what had happened to her.

She then called Carpenter at Jim Swan's house and asked him to come home. Harv had it in her mind that a killer might be in the area preying on women who lived alone, so she thought she'd feel safer with Ken Carpenter in her bed. He agreed to go home and turned up on the doorstep at 1:30 in the morning. He fell asleep as soon as his head hit the pillow. Harv says she tossed and turned until 2:00 a.m.

Harv said she stayed in bed until 11:00 a.m. the next morning, but Carpenter had gotten up around 6:00 a.m. to meet with the logger who was working on their property. He also had told her he wanted to clear a path to the snowmobile trailer parked off to the side of the driveway because his brother might be coming up from Massachusetts to look at it. Before Harv left for work at 2:00 p.m., Carpenter told her the police had been by to question him.

"Do you know what car your husband was driving on Wednesday?"

"My Escort," she said. "He'd been driving it for a

couple days. I don't like to drive it in the snow, so he lets me drive the Jeep when the weather is bad."

Harv also pointed out that the Nissan pickup was still at her house when she left for work Wednesday morning.

"What are you driving tonight?"

"The Escort."

"Do you mind if we take a look inside the car?"

Harv agreed and signed a consent form that Trooper Almstrom hastily drew up. He and Berube followed her to the parking lot. The right rear seat of the Escort was folded down and a large yellow piece of equipment that looked like a drivetrain was laid out flat through the backseat and hatchback. There was also a black garbage bag of sand. The investigators asked Harv about the many different-colored hair strands on the seats. She said they had a couple of dogs with different-colored coats. There was no sign of blood or violence in the vehicle.

The Escort was painted purple, but like so many other cars in Sullivan County, it was covered on all sides with a thick coat of road salt. In the right light, the wagon very easily could have passed for gray.

Ken Carpenter took a quick shower and changed his clothes at Jim Swan's house after his AA meeting, then drove to the Newport Police Department as he had promised. He was greeted by the sergeant who had appeared at his home earlier that day and by another investigator he hadn't met.

Detective Shawn Skahan was another big man in a nondescript suit. As a teen, Skahan had been on the Keene High School baseball team, and still had the hard, broad build of a catcher. In his mid-thirties, he had a tight military haircut and a no-nonsense attitude.

"You don't have to be here to talk to us," Skahan said as he began recording their conversation. "If at any point you feel like you want to leave here, feel free. No one is going to stop you."

Sergeant Griffin got Carpenter an orange Gatorade and the questioning began. He went through his Wednesday whereabouts again: snowshoeing, an afternoon meeting with the logger to schedule the next morning's work, and his evening AA meeting.

"It's not for me to point fingers and stuff, but Pen was a controversial person."

Carpenter explained how she was vocal in her opposition to the condominiums on Mount Sunapee and the concrete business that was hauling natural fill to Boston. "She has these control issues. Her and Jonathan are just, I don't know, two peas in a pod."

"And being a controversial person," Skahan picked up, "has she done anything to you personally that affected your life?"

"Pen and I didn't see eye to eye about my girlfriend. She thought it was best that I didn't date her anymore until I was out of the house and working on a divorce. I guess in hindsight it's probably the way to do it."

Carpenter then told the investigators that *he* was the

one who broke off the relationship with Sandy. He said his psychiatrist thought the affair was just another problem for him. Skahan, working off notes compiled by all the troopers looking into the disappearance, asked Carpenter for his side of the post-Thanksgiving confrontation at Millie's.

"It was a jealousy thing. I just felt left out. I felt hurt," he stated meekly. "I talked to Ronnie afterwards and he said he had known Sandy most of his life. I didn't get the whole story until a month later."

Carpenter said he now remembered where he was in the afternoon after snowshoeing. He said he had an appointment with his psychiatrist in Claremont. He claimed he drove to the office but suffered a panic attack in the parking lot, so he left. Carpenter said he gassed up at T-Bird's convenience store, then drove south to Greenfield, Massachusetts, to visit his brother, Dale. When he arrived, he discovered his brother was not home. He tried to visit his father's grave at a nearby cemetery, but the entrance had not been plowed. He turned around and drove back to Lempster to meet with the logger. It was conceivable that the whole trip could have consumed the time he had left unaccounted for.

Skahan backtracked to the morning of Wednesday the twenty-third, asking for more detail about what time he got up and when he left the home.

"It would have been about six thirty," he said. "That's when I went to the high school to snowshoe."

"Are you sure you went over to the high school?"

Carpenter had told Griffin and Almstrom that morning he'd gone to the Newport Golf Club.

"No. But yeah, I think I did."

"But you're not sure."

"No, I don't think so."

Carpenter said he might have gone snowshoeing on Tuesday, not Wednesday. He said he had ADHD, attention deficit/hyperactivity disorder, and it was hard for him to keep thoughts straight in his head. He offered to go home and write up a timeline for the police.

Based on what they heard from neighbors, Sandy, and the painters, Skahan believed that Pen vanished sometime between 7:00 and 9:00 a.m. The detective let Carpenter know he had a problem because he couldn't definitively account for his whereabouts on Wednesday morning.

"She came in contact with somebody early yesterday morning. Probably got into an argument with this person, and this person did something that they wouldn't normally do. They may have done something and felt very remorseful and guilty afterwards," Skahan offered. "It doesn't make them a bad person."

The detectives looked for any signals from Carpenter, anything that indicated he might empathize with "this person." Carpenter remained cool.

"Pen may have not been the easiest person to talk to," Skahan continued. "She may have been very opinionated and outspoken. But she was a mother and a daughter, okay? There are a lot of people concerned that she's missing. It's tough. Try to put yourself in their shoes."

Again, they scanned Carpenter's body language for anything that showed he felt guilty, showed that he understood the pain of Pen's loved ones. He betrayed nothing.

"No, I understand," he said flatly. "We prayed for her tonight at the meeting."

"Well, let me ask you this," the detective pressed. "Are you responsible for her going missing?"

"Certainly not. I haven't seen her since the AA roundup in Claremont about two weeks ago."

If Carpenter was involved, he wasn't going to volunteer anything. Skahan looked up some notes from the investigation.

"With that said," he began, "would it surprise you that someone who lives on that road told us they saw a vehicle matching your wife's vehicle at her house early yesterday morning?"

"Yeah. That would surprise me."

"Is it possible you were on her road for some reason?"

Carpenter said it wasn't.

"Maybe you slowed down by her residence? Somebody saw the car there and you just kept going?"

"I didn't go over there," Carpenter said more forcefully. "I . . . I . . . how do I prove a negative, you know? I . . . I didn't go over there."

Detective Skahan and Sergeant Griffin spent some more time getting specifics from their suspect. Griffin stepped out of the room to check with the other team at the nursing home. He wanted to confirm whether Harv backed up Carpenter's claim that he spent Wednesday night at her home.

"Have you talked to Sandy at all in the last couple of days?" Skahan asked once the other trooper left.

"Do you know what the situation is?" Carpenter asked.

"Yeah, I do. I'm not asking to get you in trouble. I'm asking you, has she reached out to you?"

"Come on! What am I going to tell you? I broke the law? No, I certainly didn't."

Griffin returned to the interview room and said that Harv's story matched Carpenter's.

"So, I guess we're all done?" Carpenter stood up, hoping to end the questioning and walk out.

"Are things going to work out for you and your wife, you think?" Griffin asked him.

"I'd like to think so."

Carpenter gathered his winter coat and was about to leave. Then he turned to Detective Skahan.

"Um, you know, just because we didn't get along," he said before walking out of the police station, "I didn't know this individual. I wouldn't do this individual any harm."

The troopers weren't so sure.

PART TWO

Malice

Tis now the very witching time of night,
When churchyards yawn and hell itself
breathes out
Contagion to this world: now could I drink hot
blood,
And do such bitter business as the day
Would quake to look on.

—WILLIAM SHAKESPEARE, *HAMLET*

TEN

Defiance

On Wednesday, December 15, 2004—two days after the stalking hearing—Ken Carpenter walked into Millie's Place for the regular 6:00 meeting. It was a big day for him. It was the twenty-third anniversary of his sobriety: an admirable achievement in the life of any recovering addict. After the meeting, he was going to collect a 23-year chip.

Fred Evans was stunned to see Carpenter there after what had gone down on Monday. He was pretty sure the judge had said that Carpenter was not supposed to come to Millie's because he knew it was a place Sandy frequented. Pen Meyer had mentioned to Fred that Sandy was planning on coming at 6:00 p.m. Carpenter took his place at the end of the table in the darkest part of the room. Fred whispered to a member he knew as "Big Mike" that there could be trouble. But because Sandy wasn't there, they didn't feel like they could tell Ken to leave.

The meeting went on as normal. The group of about twenty men and women read from an inspirational guide book entitled *Change of Belief* and shared their thoughts. Jonathan Purick and Pen Meyer arrived late to the meeting. They exchanged amazed glances when they observed Carpenter in their midst.

When Carpenter spoke, Jonathan listened more critically than he had before. He had the reputation of talking a good program, but Jonathan thought Carpenter was just regurgitating buzzwords. Sure he had sobriety, but did the man truly have serenity? He'd sworn off drinking but he was a victim to his other vices. It may not have been alcohol, but Carpenter was "drinking" his other addictions. Jonathan often liked to point out his own favorite saying from the program: *You don't drink and go to meetings.*

Afterward, Fred stood up and presented Carpenter with his AA medallion. Big Mike could have been the one to hand it to him, but Fred decided he wanted to do it. He hoped that, despite the melodrama of the past week, someday they could be friends again. Carpenter had been a good sponsor for a long time before the confrontation.

Fred greeted him in the traditional way that AA members marked the anniversary of one's sobriety. "Happy birthday, Ken." Fred then hugged him. Carpenter thanked all who were there and left the meeting without causing any commotion.

Pen and Fred learned that Sandy *did* try to come to Millie's Place for that 6:00 meeting, but she had spotted Carpenter's Jeep in the parking lot and turned around. The three of them pored over Sandy's copy of the stalking order, trying to flesh out the ambiguity in the no-contact clause.

"It doesn't specifically say 'Millie's Place' on here," Sandy fretted.

"But the judge said he couldn't come here," Pen said.

"I heard him say that, too," countered Fred. "But it's not here in the order. You know him. He's just going to keep showing up hoping that Sandy isn't there."

After a beat, Pen added, "Or hoping that she is."

The next day, Fred took Sandy back to district court to try and get the restraining order amended to specifically mention Millie's. Judge Tenney denied the request, saying it was no longer a matter for the Court. Instead the judge instructed them to contact the local police to work it out. Waiting for Sandy and Carpenter to cross paths seemed like a ticking time bomb to Fred. He went to the board of directors of Millie's Place and asked them to bar Carpenter from the premises. Fred then posted a handwritten notice saying Carpenter was no longer welcomed at the clubhouse.

When Carpenter saw the sign, he was humiliated. Both

he and Harv protested loudly, arguing the court order did not expressly forbid him from Millie's and neither should the board of directors.

Fred did not see Carpenter at Millie's Place after that. There were other places in the area where he could attend AA meetings, including a half-dozen churches and the local hospital, all of which hosted Twelve Step programs. In fact, Carpenter had been a regular at a morning meeting at the Church of the Epiphany, known to the locals as "Stone Church." Millie's Place simply had more meetings, more often, and was the most convenient to his Lempster home. It was also where he'd long held court, and where, of course, he'd met Sandy.

Fred Evans also frequented the 7:30 a.m. meeting at the Stone Church and, just like at Millie's, had taken on a leadership role there: volunteer coffee maker. One morning after Christmas, having been barred from Millie's, Ken Carpenter sulked into the Stone Church shortly after 7. While Fred measured out coffee grounds for the filters, Carpenter took a seat at the table as far from his former friend as possible. For the ex-CIA security officer, the ten minutes of hostile silence were more than he could bear. He asked the organizers of the 7:30 meeting if he could be relieved of his coffee-making duties.

After the judge hit him with the restraining order against Sandy, Harv thought Carpenter would give up on pursuing her romantic rival. She thought they could work on their marriage. But they both found it hard to move forward.

Dot Monahan saw a precipitous change in Harv's personality after the court case. When they got together, Harv no longer asked Dot about what was happening in her life. Their conversations always turned to the subject of Carpenter. Since confessing his affair, their romance had been rekindled. Dot, however, thought there was a sense of sadness in her friend's words. Some days Harv would lament where the relationship had gone. Other days she tried hard to convince Dot that things were stronger than ever.

Harv continued to grill her husband about the nature of his relationship with Sandy Merritt. She wanted to know if he was breaking the court order, if he was trying to see her. Carpenter always protested. "I have no interest in her. I don't ever want to go back to her," he'd say. Harv would nevertheless press him further on his feelings for Sandy.

"Did you love her?"

"Never," he swore.

Harv knew that her husband kept journals. Writing was, for him, a significant part of his recovery. He would write about his daily meditations and his views on staying clean and sober, and keep track of the things that proved challenging to him. She'd always encouraged everything he needed to do to work the program, but she had never previously had an interest in reading what he put down on paper. One day, Carpenter went to his drawer and pulled out a notebook.

"Why don't you read some of it," he said, "if it will help you understand."

Harv found entries in the diary that detailed encounters between her husband and Sandy. They had gone for walks in the woods together, gone to the movies, and had dinner in restaurants together. Harv was crestfallen. Carpenter never did any of these things with her.

In a further effort to mend the relationship, Carpenter came clean to his wife with a brutal honesty. He told her he "got a high" chasing after other women, that it was just like any other drug for him. He said he'd wanted to pursue Sandy Merritt from the first day he saw her—which actually had been several months before she joined Alcoholics Anonymous. Carpenter even said he had already picked out the next woman he wanted to go after: a young, sexy AA member named Sofia.* The admissions left Harv praying for the strength to see things through, and wondering if she'd made the right decision to try at all.

The Monahans continued to see Harv and Carpenter together, both socially and at meetings. Carpenter's attitude toward his relationship seesawed nearly every day, something the Monahans were often witnesses to. Dot later said there were times when he seemed truly excited about taking steps to improve his marriage; others when he was apathetic and made no effort at all. Harv confided in Dot that Carpenter had begun to ration his antidepressants.

---

* Denotes pseudonyms.

While her feelings about her husband wavered, Harv's feelings about his mistress did not. She was deeply embittered about Sandy. She frequently complained to Dot about all the little things Sandy had done to make things difficult for Carpenter. Hearing this, Dot slowly came to the realization that Carpenter was feeding his wife a diet of emotional propaganda, and that she was eating it up as an alternative to the pain he was causing her.

Harv never directly discussed Pen Meyer with Dot. She mentioned she was still sore about getting the cold shoulder from Pen during the house blessing. Harv would say that her husband was still angry at Pen for encouraging Sandy to seek the restraining order, but also conceded that Carpenter's animosity probably came from the fact that Pen had been an obstacle in his pursuit of his mistress.

On January 4, 2005, Pen attended the evening AA meeting at South Congregational Church. Carpenter was one of those in attendance. The two hadn't any interaction since their blowup at Millie's less than a month earlier. There was no repeat of that scene this night; neither acknowledged the other except in the most perfunctory way.

Pen drove home knowing she had to call a friend when she got in. It was his mother's birthday and she had made a cake to send over. The CR-V slipped under the garage door and she bounded to the house without a key. The door was almost always unlocked. Pen went inside, dialed up her friend, and had barely got the conversation going when she spurted out, "Oh my God!"

"Pen, what's the matter?" the friend on the other end of the line asked.

"The guy who's been bothering my girlfriend is in my driveway."

Pen rushed to the door. Ken Carpenter stood in her driveway, his figure silhouetted in black by the pickup truck's headlights.

"Ken, you're not supposed to be here!"

"I just want to know how Sandy is," he pleaded, his hands in the air.

"Go! There's a court order in effect! No contact!"

"I know. I know," he said. "I can't talk to her. I just want to know how she is. How is she doing?"

Pen pointed a finger back down Center Road. Carpenter nodded and got back in the truck without any further trouble.

Later that night, Carpenter called Pen's house to apologize.

"Bad idea," she said to him. "Don't call me again." He mumbled something in agreement and hung up the phone.

Jonathan Purick was upset. He urged Pen to follow Sandy's lead, to contact the police and get a restraining order. Pen resisted the urge to feel intimidated.

"I'm not accustomed to being threatened in my own home." The part of her psyche that urged her never to be victimized again was flaring up. She told Jonathan, "I can outrun him."

"You can't outrun a bullet," he countered. "You're in danger beyond your own depth."

"I don't feel this often," Pen said, "but this guy is evil."

Back in Lempster, Harv came home to find her husband deeply lost in his own mind, distracted by something.

"I couldn't do it," he told her. "I just couldn't do it."

"Do what, Ken?"

He never said.

Despite the court order, Sandy still kept running into Carpenter. On her way to work in the morning, she'd see him standing on the sidewalk next to the gas station she often used. He stood there like any other pedestrian, facing oncoming traffic, as if he were looking for someone.

It snowed much of Saturday, January 8, 2005, with more forecasted for the weekend. Late in the day, the phone rang at the kennel and Sandy grabbed it. "Animal Inn," she said.

"What time do you close for the evening?"

"Five o'clock."

"This is Kenneth Carpenter of Lempster," the frantic voice said. "My dog slipped on some snow-covered ice and hurt her paw."

Sandy was tongue-tied. "We're not a vet!" she blurted out before slamming down the phone and calling the police.

Because the Animal Inn was in Grantham, the cops in Sandy's hometown of Newport directed her to the Grantham PD. The investigating officer left several messages for Carpenter over the next few days, but he and Harv weren't home. Harv's elderly mother had taken a turn and was on her deathbed in a hospital in another part of the state.

The Grantham officer did not speak to Carpenter until Thursday the fourteenth. Carpenter insisted the phone call to the Animal Inn had been an accident. He said a single card in his Rolodex listed both the Animal Inn (the kennel) and the Animal Hospital (his dog's vet). Carpenter said he was dyslexic and mixed up the numbers and started to speak after the person on the phone said, "Animal . . ." It wasn't until the hang up that he feared he'd made a mistake. The investigator made him write up a statement.

Carpenter wrote he knew the stalking order prohibited him from contacting her, but he still wasn't 100 percent sure he called Sandy. He took responsibility for the seriousness of his mistake. "Please give Ms. Merritt my most sincere apology as to this error. I will be more careful in the future."

The Grantham officer talked it over with his sergeant, and they agreed Carpenter's phone call had not been an accident. They called him the next day and asked him to come back in. When he did, the officer told him he was going to be placed under arrest for violating the stalking order.

"You got to be kidding me." Carpenter again stated his call had been an accident. He was fingerprinted, booked, then released on $1,500 personal recognizance bail. He was charged with a class A misdemeanor, punishable by up to two years in prison.

Carpenter moved out of the house in Lempster on January 29, 2005, finally taking Jim Swan up on his earlier invitation to bunk at his home in Newport. Swan was about to leave for Germany for two weeks and needed someone to watch after his two coonhounds. Carpenter stayed in his tiny guest bedroom.

Harv had mixed feelings about her husband moving out. The death of her mother, along with her unrelenting marital troubles, had wrecked her emotionally. She decided she didn't want to know anything more about Carpenter's feelings for Sandy Merritt. Everything just led back to heartache for her. Carpenter did not tell her about his arrest for violating the restraining order, but she suspected what had happened after hearing one of the many telephone messages the Grantham Police had left on the answering machine.

Dot Monahan continued to comfort her friend. She had heard from other people at Millie's about the night Carpenter had confronted Pen in her driveway. Dot was torn about whether she should tell Harv about it, whether it would just add to her pain, but she decided that it was for the best. After relaying the tale, Harv stared blankly at her, saying nothing for a moment.

"Son of a bitch," she finally moaned. "It's always one more thing."

ELEVEN

Key

Pen Meyer had been missing since early Wednesday morning, February 23, 2005. The first twenty-four hours of the investigation provided a wealth of avenues to pursue and red herrings to fish out. The ground search in the woods would continue on Friday, February 25. The state police also enlisted the help of the media to spread word about the missing woman, but hopes of an innocent explanation for her absence were fading.

Lead investigator Sergeant Russell Lamson had two persons of interest in the case. One was Pen's ex-husband Richard Rankin. He'd had an intimate long-term relationship with Pen that ended badly. Lamson had seen many people in his career like Rankin. Friends had said he didn't take the breakup well. He was jealous and now Pen was in a new relationship with a new man, something that probably pushed all the wrong buttons.

Lamson really didn't like the fact they didn't know where Rankin was. It was a huge hole in the early investigation. Rankin wasn't at his home in Newport, and judging by the snow in the driveway and covering his pickup, he hadn't been there in some time. If someone had forced Pen to make that call to Sandy, the line about running away with a new lover wasn't just an attempt at misdirection. It was a jab at Jonathan Purick. Pen's possible kidnapper wanted to rub it in her boyfriend's face.

As unlikely as it seemed, the state police could not discount the chance that Pen had meant everything she said in that call. Lamson knew that a woman with access to cash could very easily grab her passport and fall off the map.

The second person of interest was Ken Carpenter. He had an ax to grind against Pen and his alibi about where he was on the twenty-third had plenty of holes in it. But Carpenter wasn't your textbook jilted-lover-turned-criminal-of-passion. The object of his obsession was Sandy Merritt, not Pen. Lamson had too often seen a twisted man take the position that "if I can't have you, no one will have you" and turn his madness on his former lover. Removing Pen from the picture wasn't likely to change the equation, but rationality is not a trait found in abundance among known stalkers.

Detective Eric Berube spent Friday talking to as many

people from AA as he could possibly track down. His investigative notes were filled with quotes from people with only first names or single initials. Their stories were all different versions of the same main points: Pen was well liked, she never went anywhere without her dog, and there seemed to be some tension between her and Ken Carpenter.

As the magnitude of the case grew, state police headquarters had dispatched several detectives from the Major Crimes Unit out of Concord. Among the reinforcements was Lamson's old lieutenant, Russ Conte, but Conte didn't pull rank and take over the investigation. He deferred to Sergeant Lamson as lead investigator and never made the suggestion that Major Crimes run the show. This surprised Lamson, as he knew the Major Crimes Unit didn't typically let a small barracks detective bureau like his handle a case of this complexity. Lamson never asked why, but he assumed his old colleagues back in Concord had some faith in him.

Another state agency was brought into the search for Pen Meyer: the Attorney General's Office. In the rankings of law enforcement agencies, the AG was the trump card in New Hampshire. The AG's Criminal Bureau was staffed with prosecutors who would try the case if an arrest was made. The official posture of the investigation remained "missing person," but the inclusion of the attorney general meant they'd be ready if this became a homicide.

*   *   *

Pen's son, Justin, had given police his key to his mother's home and granted them permission to search the property. On Friday, February 25, Lamson sent two men with crime scene experience, Troopers Fred Lulka and John Encarnacao, to go through the house from top to bottom. They found the house on Center Road in Goshen to be largely undisturbed, save for a set of tire tracks in the driveway made by a local TV crew.

The troopers used Justin's key and let themselves in. A relative had taken Fluff the day before, so the house was completely empty. The troopers found the slate-floored foyer filled with firewood and many pairs of Pen's shoes. To the left was a door leading to a storage room and a laundry room. The storage room contained some canvas bags filled with clothes. When Lulka and Encarnacao checked out the laundry room, they noticed there were clothes in both the washer and the dryer. The load in the washer was still wet, and now smelled faintly of mildew.

The downstairs bathroom consisted of a pedestal sink, a commode, and a built-in shower and tub. There was a towel rack mounted under an exquisite bay window looking out over the property. Hanging on the left side of the rack was a pair of women's blue jeans. The two front pockets were littered with used wrappers of Life Savers Creme Savers candy. In the right front pocket, Lulka found $700 in cash. The rear pocket had an Alcoholics Anonymous medallion. The investigators thought it odd someone would willingly run off without taking the money and they knew an AA member would keep a sobriety chip with them, like a talisman against drinking.

Also hanging on the rack was a towel with a visible bloodstain. It was a small mark, about the size of a quarter. In a single woman's bathroom there are many innocent explanations for such a stain, but the troopers took the towel anyway. Lulka recovered a latent fingerprint from the mirror and cataloged it.

There were some light-colored footprints on the floor of the living room, which Lulka captured with a gel lifter. Did they belong to an intruder—or to any of the half-dozen people who had been in the house after Pen vanished? They took the usual items that might yield DNA—toothbrushes, combs, hair from the trap in the shower—but the Goshen home offered them little else to go on.

While Lulka and Encarnacao searched Pen's house, Detective Skahan had been deployed by Lamson to check out part of Ken Carpenter's alibi. The man had said he stopped for gasoline in Claremont before driving to Greenfield, Massachusetts. He had also told troopers he came back home because he couldn't get into his brother Dale's house, and the cemetery where his father was buried hadn't been plowed.

Skahan went to T-Bird's gas station on Route 12 in Claremont and asked to look at their surveillance video from Wednesday morning. The manager cued the tape up and scanned through thirteen camera angles pointed at gas pumps, cash registers, and store entrances. Skahan asked her to stop at the part of the tape stamped 9:58 a.m. A purple Ford Escort pulled in and stopped at Pump 8. They watched the replay as a man with a gray beard and a stocking cap, scarf, and sunglasses got out of the car. He checked something in the backseat before going into the store.

The manager fiddled with the software to bring up the camera at the cash register. The man gave the clerk at $20 bill and then returned to Pump 8 to fill his tank. While he pumped the gas, the man looked into the backseat several times, but no matter what enhancement techniques the manager tried, they couldn't get a good view of what was in the back of the Escort. At 10:02 a.m., the car left T-Bird's going south on Route 12, toward Lempster or the Massachusetts state line. The gas station manager burned a copy of the surveillance tape onto a CD for Skahan to take with him.

Skahan called police in Greenfield to check on Dale Carpenter's home and the cemetery. The Greenfield Police told the detective that there was no one home at Dale Carpenter's house, and the gate to the cemetery was closed because it had yet to be plowed.

Lamson had been encouraged after his questioning of Sandy Merritt that she might help the investigation in other ways. "Let's see if she'll do some one-parties with us," he said to his detectives. A "one-party intercept" was the term for recording a telephone call (one party has to agree to the wiretap of the other party). In New Hampshire, such an action would require a grant of authority of someone from the Attorney General's Office, much in the way a search warrant must be approved by a judge. If granted, the police could attempt to call the target of their investigation any number of times for a limited period of time.

Detective Skahan and a state police detective from the Major Crimes Unit went to Sandy's Newport apartment first thing on Saturday morning, February 26. They brought some recording equipment and explained to Sandy what they wanted to do. She was apprehensive, but agreed to make the calls if it would help authorities figure out what happened to Pen. It was 10:00 a.m., and they only had authority to record the calls until 4:00 p.m.

Sandy first tried Carpenter's cell phone but got no answer. Next, Sandy dialed Jim Swan's house. Swan sounded surprised to hear her ask for Carpenter.

"He's not here right now."

"Are you expecting him back?"

"He left a note that he went to AA and he'd be back after the ten thirty meeting and was going snowshoeing."

"I'll call back."

"Do you want me have him call you . . . or . . . I mean . . ." Swan fumbled. "Remember, he's got a court order not to talk to you?"

Now Sandy was tongue-tied. "I don't think it's a violation if I call him." Swan told her to try back in an hour.

At 11:30 they again rang up Swan, who told Sandy that Carpenter still wasn't home. There was no answer on his cell phone, either. At 1:30 the investigators made a fifth attempt to reach Carpenter at Swan's place.

"I'm not his keeper, Sandy," said Swan, clearly agitated. "He's basically just a tenant here. You know, he stays in the spare room, that's all he's doing."

The detectives exchanged looks between glances at their watches. It was 2:00 p.m., and they had had no luck tracking their man down. Skahan diplomatically suggested the next call be placed to the cottage in Lempster. Sandy was breathless at the thought. She knew who was going to answer.

"Hello?" said a woman's voice on the other end of the line.

"Hi. Can I please speak to Ken?"

The woman paused. "Who is this?"

"This is Sandy."

The woman's voice got cross. "No, I don't think so," she spat out before slamming down the phone.

They waited another hour and called the Lempster home again. The rings went unanswered and Sandy was prompted by the answering machine to leave a message. Skahan, listening to the call through a set of headphones, nodded that it would be okay. There was a long beep.

"Ken, if you're there, pick up. Ken?"

It was 3:45 p.m., only fifteen minutes left on the one-party intercept. Skahan and the other detective were scratching their heads, running out of places to call. As they started spitballing ideas, a knock came to the apartment door. It was Sandy's sister-in-law. She had a cordless phone in her hand, her palm covering the mouthpiece. She said Carpenter had just called the main house to find out if Sandy was okay. Skahan did a bit of pantomime, which Sandy understood perfectly. She took the phone and told Carpenter she was going to call him back on her own line. The troopers readied the recorder and Sandy dialed.

"Hello?"

"Ken? Hi, this is Sandy."

"Honey, are you okay?"

"Not really," she said, sniffing back tears.

"Do you want to meet me?"

"I can't."

"So you're not going to have me arrested for calling you, are you?"

She sighed and assured him that wasn't her intention. She looked over the talking points the detectives had laid out for her, prompts to get Carpenter talking about the case.

"I am so worried about Pen," she said. "I can't sleep. I can hardly eat."

"Does she have another boyfriend other than Jonathan she might have taken off with?"

Skahan found it interesting Carpenter would lead with this theory. It was, after all, the story Pen allegedly had tried to plant with Sandy during their phone call. Was Carpenter checking to see if Sandy took the bait? Was he fishing for a "yes"?

"No."

"That's the only thing I was thinking. She took off for Las Vegas or California or something."

"She wouldn't just leave her dog. That dog goes everywhere with her."

"I disagree, because if they were getting on a plane and going somewhere and they were just gonna start their lives over or whatever the deal would be." Another echo of the strange phone conversation with Pen.

Skahan passed Sandy a note. She asked Carpenter about whether he'd had an accident with a chain saw. He said he had been in his yard cutting down a tree, but instead of falling free, it had gotten stuck against another tree. He said he then started to cut through the second tree when the first one fell and struck him from behind. Carpenter dropped the buzzing chain saw from his hand. The spinning teeth cut into the steel toe of his boot, but bounced away without touching his flesh.

"I almost did some serious damage. I just laid there in the snow and it's like I wanted to cry. I was just kinda realizing that life was just passing me by and it's so short. And you were the only thing that ever made me happy. I felt like such a schmuck because I love you so much and I don't know how things are going to turn out."

Is that what really happened? Skahan thought. *Could that have been the event that put him over the edge?*

"Is there anything I can do for you?" Carpenter asked Sandy.

"Tell me what happened to Pen."

Carpenter didn't have an answer for her.

"What can we do?"

"We should get back together," he said, "and then you and I should look together."

Skahan shook his head. Whether or not Carpenter was responsible for Pen's disappearance, he was definitely using the crisis to manipulate Sandy. But staying on script meant Sandy had to appear fixated on Pen's peril. For the opportunistic Casanova, this was an obvious turnoff. As long as Sandy was worried about Pen, he couldn't command her full attention.

"I really believe," he said, quickly pivoting, "that she's going to be okay and this is going to work out. That's the only way that I can continue to think positive about the whole thing. Because I know that it's all in God's hands. I'm sure she's going to be okay." Then he said, "I don't know. It's like someone who is really, really in love . . . you know . . . and kinda just do stupid things. You know what I mean?" There could be more than one way to interpret that comment.

Sandy told him she needed to take a nap and would call him back later that night. The intermission would give the detectives enough time to strategize and get permission for a second one-party intercept.

* * *

After bringing Lamson up to speed and getting cleared for the intercept, Sandy and her police handlers called Carpenter at 8:00 p.m. They had left Sandy's phone off the hook in the meantime, suspecting Carpenter would try to call her as soon as the mood struck. When he picked up the phone, the first thing he mentioned was how her line had been busy for the past few hours. Carpenter's disposition when he picked up was bright and relaxed. Instead of the desperate pleading that had laced his voice earlier in the day, his tone was now warm and familiar.

"I ran to the store to get some soda and some ice cream," he said. "I didn't know if we were gonna have pizza or what. If you wanted to get a movie or what."

"No."

"Uh . . . okay."

Did he think we were going to have a date *tonight?* She was ill just thinking about it. "Oh God no. No."

"Listen," Carpenter said. "Good news, okay?"

"What?"

"I talked to God."

Sandy rolled her eyes. "Yeah. You have a direct line."

He ignored her sarcasm. "I have a direct line. Are you sitting down? Okay? Honey?" He was apparently waiting for some indication she was eagerly anticipating his answer. "Two days, three days tops, this will all make sense. Okay? Okay?"

Sandy was dumbfounded. Skahan prompted her to keep him talking. "How?"

"I don't know, but that's the answer that I got. I just wanna take it on faith and please believe me."

"What's gonna happen in two days?"

"We'll find her," he said. "We'll find out what happened and we'll find out where she is or what's going on. Trust me, okay? This is what God told me. And you know that God doesn't lie."

"This," she said slowly, "just isn't doing it for me, Ken."

"Well, that's the best that I could do right now."

"Well."

"And that's a lot better than what you had before you called me."

"This whole thing boggles my mind."

One of the detectives stifled a cough.

"Who's there?"

"My brother." Skahan wanted to turn the heat up, so he directed Sandy to some new talking points in the notes he'd written for her. "I'm still wondering if Pen left because you guys had a fight over me."

"No, no."

"I think you scared her."

"I didn't scare her."

"Well, someone told me they saw your car on her road Wednesday morning. I still think you had a fight with her and scared her off."

Carpenter's speech then sped up, and he started

switching gears rapidly. He told Sandy he'd already talked to the police and they'd cleared him. He repeated his alibi, telling her he'd been snowshoeing. Then he doubled down on the story that Pen had probably left with a secret lover and thumbed her nose at Jonathan. Sandy dismissed all of this again, and it was clear to the officers listening in that Carpenter wasn't used to getting push back from her.

"Are you okay with your meds and stuff?" he asked.

"Yes," she answered like an exasperated teenager.

"Okay. And you know drinking is not a problem right here?"

"I'm not drinking."

Carpenter urged her to hang on, if just for another two or three days. She asked him what would happen then.

"I don't know. The answer that I was looking at is that it will all make sense. That's the only feeling that I got."

"Oh, bullshit with your feelings." She went off her script and said something that wasn't one of the talking points. "If you hurt Pen, you just end up hurting me."

"Honey, I would never hurt Pen."

"Where is she?"

"Honey, I think you're a little overtired, okay? I really do." He sounded patronizing now. "And I know you've been upset. And I know it's taken a toll on you, okay?"

"I want the truth."

"Honey, I'm telling you the truth. Please. I'm telling you."

* * *

Sergeant Lamson didn't know what to make of the phone calls. It was Sunday, February 27, and Pen had been missing for four days. Lamson and Detectives Berube and Skahan were comparing notes. Some of Carpenter's intentions were obvious to them—he was trying to take advantage of Sandy's emotional state and get back together with her. That made him a creep, but it didn't necessarily make him a murderer.

The state police were setting up shop in the Goshen Police Department, a small building at the only major intersection in town. The post office was next door and the Goshen Country Store was across the street. They could get sandwiches, coffee, and gasoline from the store, so there wasn't much motivation to go anywhere else.

Between the detectives from Troop C and the members of the Major Crimes Unit, some wondered if there had ever been this many people inside the sleepy town's police station. Goshen Police Chief Ed Andersen, the only full-time employee on the force, was a gracious host who did not feel the need to get into a turf war with the other law enforcement officers. In fact, when he had moved to Goshen to become chief, one of the first people Andersen met was Russell Lamson. The trooper had driven him around the area on his day off, helping him get a feel for the back roads and rural neighborhoods.

The department telephone had been ringing on and

off all day with inquiries from the press, tips from eager townspeople, and worries from loved ones.

"Russ," Andersen said, covering the mouthpiece of the phone after picking it up. "You're going to want to take this one."

The chief offered the phone to Lamson. "Who is it?" he asked before taking it.

"Richard Rankin."

Lamson slid behind a desk and grabbed a pen to take notes. Rankin barely started to talk before breaking down into uncontrollable sobbing. Lamson had to wait a moment to let Pen's second husband regain his composure. When he finally pulled it together, Rankin said he had been in Florida since early December and just learned of Pen's disappearance from a mutual friend. He'd immediately driven north, spending the previous night in Virginia before traveling to New Hampshire.

"Can you prove you were in Florida?" Lamson asked.

"You can check my credit card statements," he said, providing the account numbers. He then added, sniffling, that he still loved his ex-wife.

"How likely was it that Pen would just run off and not tell anyone?"

"Not likely at all." With that, Rankin burst into tears again. Lamson gave the credit card numbers to his team, but he knew they would verify the man's alibi. Lamson didn't get the feeling Rankin was involved.

That left just one person of interest.

*   *   *

The detectives bounced their theories off a new member of their team. Senior Assistant Attorney General Will Delker was the prosecutor assigned to the investigation. If Pen had been murdered, then his office would assume responsibility for the investigation. The Homicide Bureau at the NH Attorney General's Office was small, and prosecutors had found the experience of visiting a fresh crime scene and listening to extemporaneous interviews was far more valuable than viewing photographs or reading transcripts before trial months later. Delker looked soft and bookish, but he was a brilliant lawyer and extremely aggressive when it came to overseeing police work. Of all the assistant AGs they could have had, Sergeant Lamson was infinitely grateful they had Delker.

The bespectacled, bowl-haircut Delker was sitting closest to the Goshen PD phone on Sunday when it rang around 5:00 p.m. All the troopers were busy, so Delker answered the call. The prosecutor looked completely lost, and his eyes frantically scanned the room for a law enforcement officer to pass the phone to.

"This guy says he's got some information."

Detective Shawn Skahan reached over and relieved Delker of the receiver.

"This is Detective Skahan," he said, but the man on the other end of the phone had little interest in who he was.

"I dropped her off Wednesday . . ."

"Who did you drop off?"

"Pen," the caller said. "I dropped her off at the airport. She was heading down to the islands."

Skahan's eyes grew wide. "It's Carpenter!" he said to the others, a hand covering the mouthpiece.

Skahan would know. He'd spent most of the day listening to the recordings of Carpenter and Sandy and recognized his voice easily. All chattering in the office ceased as assembled officers listened to Skahan's side of the conversation.

"And she left something under the phone at the Goshen Store."

"Who is this?"

The caller said he was "a friend" and hung up.

Skahan searched the room for Chief Andersen. "Is this line recorded?"

"No, we can't record incoming calls here."

"What was that?" Lamson demanded.

"It was Carpenter trying to leave an anonymous tip. He said he dropped Pen off and she's going to the islands."

"Doesn't make sense," the lead investigator said. "She's not down there with her family."

"He said that she left something under the phone at the Goshen Store."

They all looked at one another. "That's just across the street."

"I saw Carpenter's pickup truck there an hour ago," said Chief Andersen. "I know it was him."

Lamson summoned his men and they resisted the urge to kick the door open and run across Route 10. Instead they strolled casually to the other side of the road, keeping an eye all around. They didn't know where the call had originated from or why they were being led to such a ridiculously short distance from the PD. *Is he holed up somewhere watching us now? Are we walking into an ambush?*

The caller said "the phone," and the first thing that caught Lamson's eye was the wall-mounted pay phone on the side of the building. They approached it as if it were booby-trapped. Making sure to keep his hands in his pockets, Lamson carefully got down on one knee and peered at the underside of the pay phone.

"We got something."

The mysterious object they came for remained untouched until the evidence team of Lulka and Encarnacao arrived and took photographs before meticulously removing the tape that mounted the object to the underside of the pay phone. Lamson flashed his badge at the store clerk and asked if she'd seen anyone hanging out near the phone that evening. She said she hadn't, and offered to let the state police look at the surveillance video the exterior camera had captured. It would have views of the store interior and the gas pumps, she explained, but it didn't have a clear shot of the pay phone on the side of the building.

Lamson and Skahan watched as they went back fifteen, twenty, thirty minutes, an hour. "Right there," the detective said. "Play it from there."

They watched the black-and-white frames flip forward on the monitor. Ken Carpenter, wearing a black Stetson, entered the Goshen Country Store around 4:00 p.m. He bought a newspaper and a candy bar and paid for them at the register, then left.

"Our guy was here," Lamson said. "But we can't tell if he went to the phone."

The troopers brought their recovered object back to the Goshen PD to examine it. It was a plastic bag that had been taped to the pay phone with a strip of orange duct tape. Inside the bag was a bank envelope from Laconia Savings Bank, the institution where Pen's first husband worked. They slowly opened the envelope and removed its contents: a single key.

"What's it for?"

Lamson twisted the key between gloved fingers. It had a number engraved on it: 822. He didn't like how this was adding up. "It's to a safe-deposit box."

The lead investigator in this missing person case was positive he had just become the lead investigator in a homicide.

TWELVE

Beautiful

Pen Meyer was distracted during her AA meeting at the South Congregational Church in New London on the night of Tuesday, February 22, 2005. She had plenty going on in her life, but something preternatural was tugging at her attention.

After the meeting, she socialized briefly. Pebbles Sillars, the house painter, chatted about the weather. Snow was coming overnight and was forecasted into the morning. She spoke to Joanne Dufour and double-checked the time she needed to pick her up the next morning.

Outside, standing by her CR-V, Pen leaned into Jonathan Purick and gave him a kiss.

"Happy birthday," she said.

"Thanks. I missed you this weekend."

"Baloney," she scoffed. "You had a great time without me."

"No, no," he tried to reassure the lady who protested too much. He had spent the long Presidents' Day holiday weekend at an AA retreat for men. Then he said, half to himself, "I have to get my driver's license renewed tomorrow."

Pen reached out for his hand and gave him a funny look. The relationship had been good. Despite the objection of her daughter, Pen was growing closer to Jonathan. They had talked about his moving into her home on the Goshen Ocean. They would wait for warm weather—like any seasoned New England couple would—because no one wants to be hauling boxes in the snow or spring mud.

"Did you pack a bag?" she asked, squeezing his hand. That was their code for: *Do you want to spend the night?* Jonathan shrugged, signaling that he had not.

"I'm sorry. I've got the first AWOL meeting tomorrow night and I haven't prepped for it . . ."

"No, it's okay. You worked hard to get AWOL going. You have to prepare." Her words indicated understanding, but their tone underscored her disappointment. She stood there in the night, the first flakes of snow falling on her head, holding tightly to Jonathan's hand.

"Are you okay?" he asked.

She said she was.

He kissed her on the forehead. "You're my Pen."

"And you're my cob," she said back. The swan reference had become their private joke.

Pen turned and got in the car and drove away from her boyfriend.

On Wednesday morning, February 23, 2005, Henry Calcatt* lumbered out of his home on Center Road in Goshen to clear his car of the four inches of snow that Mother Nature had again hit him with. Calcatt—like every other New England Yankee—took the precipitation personally. It was as if snow were designed only to punish him for some past sin. The disdain for the weather was what warmed his bones on February mornings in the hours before the sun could climb higher than the trees.

Calcatt dug in hard with his elbows to scrape away the crust of ice that had formed between the snow and the glass windshield. Beneath the sound of the warming car engine, a rhythmic pattern was growing in intensity. It was like the muted shuffle of jazz brushes on a drum, punctuated with a dampened *ting* on a ride cymbal. Calcatt looked downwind to see his neighbor, Pen Meyer, approaching with her dog. They were walking right down the middle of Center Road without a care in the world. The scrunch of her boots on the unplowed street and the jingle of Fluff's tags provided musical accompaniment to the bitter morning.

"Lovely morning," Calcatt said, summoning up all the sarcasm a bundled man with a plastic brush in his hand could muster.

---

* Denotes pseudonyms.

"It's beautiful!" said Pen. "I love it."

But the way *she* said it was far from sarcastic. She didn't sound like one of those New Englanders who complain about the Red Sox or black fly season. She sounded genuine. She sounded like she loved every minute of breathing in air colder than an icecube.

Calcatt nodded as Pen and Fluff marched past, and he gave a mock salute with his scraper. When he was satisfied with his work, he slipped into the car and made one reflexive shiver as the humid blast from the heater hit his face. Placing his wet gloves on the seat, he grabbed the shift with a cramped hand and rolled out of the driveway, noticing the time on his dashboard: 6:59 a.m.

Calcatt made a wide path and offered another neighborly wave as he passed Pen on his way out of the neighborhood. On the other side of the street was a vehicle (*What was it? A big car? A van? It was dark. Maybe a van.*), and he noticed in his rearview mirror that Pen was stopping to talk to the driver.

Calcatt continued on. *It's 6:59*, he thought. *Why am I going to work this early?*

Calcatt dipped around the curve on Center Road and Pen disappeared from his mirror. He was the last person—next to her killer—ever to see Pen Meyer alive.

THIRTEEN

Isolation

Sergeant Russell Lamson put the safe-deposit box key back in the bank envelope and started writing up an affidavit. He needed a search warrant for the box that the key belonged to. It was Sunday night, February 27, and Lamson wanted a judge to sign it so he could get into the bank first thing Monday morning.

Lamson requested authorization from Senior Assistant Attorney General Will Delker for another one-way intercept between Sandy Merritt and Ken Carpenter. Delker granted it and Detective Skahan took off for Newport with the recording gear.

At 8:20 p.m., Sandy's telephone rang. Skahan was already set up and recording when she answered it.

"How ya doing?" It was Carpenter.

"I'm tired, I'm . . ." Her voice trailed off.

"You sound tired." Then Carpenter reconsidered his answer and said, "Actually you sound terrific, you know that?"

"So what's up?"

"I was talking to a trooper today and they might have some kinda news tomorrow."

"What kind of news?" Sandy asked.

"I don't know. He wouldn't speculate."

"What'd he say?"

"All he said was they might release some information tomorrow. They just gotta run down this lead."

Skahan was scratching his head. He knew no one from the investigation had talked to Carpenter that day. When he prompted Sandy to ask him which trooper it was, he said that they all looked the same to him.

Sandy tried to steer things back to Pen. "Do you have anything more to add to our conversation?"

"Geesh, you were kinda out of it last night. Just overtired?"

"I'm still thinking the same things."

Carpenter again tried to ease her mind by saying information about Pen would be coming out soon. "I hope to talk to you tomorrow if I can, okay?"

"Whatever," she said.

On Monday, February 28, 2005, Lamson took his affidavits to a district court judge in Newport to get the warrants he needed. The sky was bright but colorless. The air smelled like snow was about to fall again. The news promised this storm was going to be much worse than the one on Wednesday that had hampered the beginning of their investigation. The weatherman forecast more than a foot and dangerous travel conditions throughout the night. Sergeant Lamson knew it was going to make moving investigators from place to place difficult.

Lamson took his warrant and the key to the president of the Lake Sunapee Bank. He confirmed that Pen Meyer was a customer there and did have a safe-deposit box, then pulled the access card for Box 822 and made a photocopy for the detective. There was somewhat of a pattern on the card, as Pen seemed to have accessed the box on a given date, then accessed it again a week or so later. But the box had not been opened in about a year. The signatures on the card proved the only person who had ever accessed the box was Pen Meyer.

When they opened the box, Lamson found a number of financial records. There were some savings bonds, a will, a power of attorney, and other personal documents, including the birth certificates of her three children. There was some jewelry and some silverware in the box as well.

The most important item Lamson found in the safe-deposit box was Pen Meyer's passport. It likely accounted for her pattern of accessing the box once in a while, then returning about a week later. She was probably picking up her passport for a trip, then stashing it back in the safe-deposit box when she returned home. If Pen had willingly left for the islands this time, she would have come for her passport, yet here it was.

Lamson learned that Pen had only one credit card and that she rarely used it. The card company promised to flag any new transactions on the account.

Later that day, Lamson received a fax from the security officer at the Mascoma Savings Bank, another local bank at which Pen had an account. Lamson had provided them with a search warrant on all of Pen's financial information, which they promised to retrieve. The security officer said that Pen was last at the bank on Tuesday, February 22, at 4:45 p.m. She cashed a check from AG Edwards—which handled her trust fund—for $1,000. She then deposited $300 in her account and took the remaining $700 in cash. The amount matched the $700 found in Pen's jeans pocket in her bathroom.

Detective Shawn Skahan stayed with Sandy Merritt on Monday, February 28. The placement of the key under the telephone was a peculiar move, but a calculated one. The detectives knew that Carpenter and Sandy liked to watch crime procedurals such as *CSI*. Skahan asked her if they had ever seen an episode where something similar happened. She couldn't recall.

The state police were frustrated that in the many phone calls they recorded, Carpenter had yet to say anything outright incriminating. Now that Carpenter was their number one suspect, they wanted to make the phone calls more provocative in hopes of eliciting a better response.

Sandy Merritt's will to participate in the operation was waning. She was a high-strung person anyway, naturally riddled with anxiety. She'd been wound tight ever since Pen went missing, and suspecting Pen's predicament had anything remotely to do with her was fraying her last nerve. She didn't want to do the phone calls anymore. She got sick to her stomach just talking with Carpenter. Now the police wanted her to be more accusatory, more confrontational. It just wasn't in her nature. Skahan was sympathetic, but he convinced Sandy to go through with it in order to find out what really happened to Pen.

They began by making calls to Jim Swan's house, leaving messages on the machine for Carpenter. Swan called Sandy back and told her to stop calling his house looking for Carpenter.

Around 2:00 p.m., Ken Carpenter called Sandy and reminded her that he still needed to go to court in April to face criminal charges related to the stalking order. "I called your work accidentally and I don't want to go to jail because of a mistake." Swan was also apparently ready to kick him out for contacting Sandy.

Carpenter again floated the idea that Pen was in Las Vegas with another man. Sandy rebuffed the idea and again asked Ken if he had told her everything he knew.

"Am I ever going to see you again, Sandy?"

Sandy didn't answer him, instead staring silently at the wall of her apartment.

"You're breaking my heart, Sandy." Carpenter then broke down into tears, telling Sandy she was the biggest loss of his life. When directed by her handlers, she agreed to speak to him later that day.

As Detective Skahan described what he needed Sandy to do next, she expressed her reluctance. They'd already made more than twenty phone calls—some a success, others not—and each time they dialed the phone, it took even more out of her. She was not well, but she agreed to continue on.

At 3:00 p.m., Sandy called Carpenter back. "My brother was just here and he brought the state troopers," she told him.

"Why? Honey?"

"They said you were on Pen's road and you had an argument with her."

"That's insane, I . . . I wasn't on Pen's road and I didn't have—"

Sandy cut him off. "You listen first." Carpenter shut up and complied. "They said you left the key to her box underneath the phone at the Goshen Store. And the police know you're the one who made the phone call to the police department. Something about taking Pen to the airport. The police think I'm involved. You have to tell me if she's still alive."

Carpenter did not lose his cool. "I don't know what you're talking about."

"Ken, listen. It's time for the lies to stop."

"You gotta stop this," he told her.

"Hey! State troopers! Badges! Guns! Everything! Here!"

"I know. I had 'em at my house. Okay?"

"No it's *not* okay. They don't lie."

"Oh, sure they do," he said. "They want you to."

"They think I'm involved in this in some way."

Carpenter considered this for a beat. "They think I'm involved?"

"Evidently."

Sandy could tell that the wheels in Ken Carpenter's head had begun turning.

Detective Skahan wanted to talk with Harv to see if she had anything new to share. He also wanted to share some of what they'd learned in the phone calls between her husband and Merritt. He went to the Sullivan County Nursing Home only to find she had left her shift early. She had told her supervisor she was going to the emergency room at Valley Regional Hospital in Claremont, where her husband had just been admitted.

As Skahan raced over to the hospital, the leading edge of the snowstorm was on him. He radioed the latest twist in the case to Sergeant Lamson. They called Valley Regional to find out why Carpenter had been admitted, but HIPPA privacy laws prevented the staff from telling even the state police about a patient's condition.

Skahan scanned the waiting room in the emergency department and spotted Harv waiting alone in a plastic chair. He asked if he could talk to her in private and found an empty break room for the interview.

Harv began by saying her husband told her that Sandy had been calling him at Jim Swan's house. She said he'd admitted talking to Sandy and claimed she said some nasty things to him.

"Mrs. Harvey, do you think your husband may have hurt Pen Meyer?"

"No, I don't."

"Do you think he had anything to do with her disappearance?"

"No."

Harv said she never directly asked Carpenter whether or not he was involved in the crime. When they spoke, she said, they'd come to the conclusion that Pen got drunk— implying anything could happen to her in that state. Harv buried her face on the table.

"Why would the Lord put me through this?" she asked.

Skahan placed a compassionate hand on hers. "Would you like me to pray with you?" he asked. She nodded. The two of them held hands and bowed their heads, asking God for the strength to understand and overcome. It was a sincere gesture of faith from Skahan.

"Did Ken have any business being on Pen's road Wednesday morning?"

"He did not."

"Can you think of any reason why he might go there?"

"No." Harv said she told her husband that she could

not be forced to testify against him and she would support him. But Carpenter had told her there was nothing to tell.

"Mrs. Harvey, how did Ken end up in the hospital tonight?"

She said he called her at work from the hospital because he was having thoughts of killing himself. "It's not the first time he's had suicidal thoughts. He's been talking about killing himself since August."

"Has he ever tried to harm himself?"

"Twice. He tried to hang himself and he tried to slit his wrists."

"Why do you think he feels this way now?"

Harv said Carpenter suffered from borderline personality disorder, a psychiatric condition marked by emotional instability, in the same family of conditions as narcissism and antisocial psychopathy. Harv said her husband had gone to a specialist in Massachusetts for the diagnosis. She said Carpenter displayed nine of the eleven traits for the disorder.

Harv then mentioned, with open disgust, that Sandy had been calling her house and Jim Swan's looking for Carpenter. "She's obviously not that afraid of him."

Skahan told Harv that the state police had been monitoring the calls between Carpenter and Sandy. Harv became enraged. She stood up from the table, saying she wanted to leave. Skahan worked quickly to calm her down and get her to sit down again.

Through clenched teeth, Harv asked, "What did he say to her?"

Skahan treaded carefully, but he told her about Carpenter's effort to soothe Sandy's nerves and the theories he'd shared about Pen's whereabouts. He hoped to tell Harv enough to win her trust, but kept some details close to the vest.

"Who made the first phone call after Pen disappeared?" she asked. Skahan said he honestly didn't know.

Harv said she and Carpenter had talked about the possibility of their phones being tapped. The way she spoke, it was as if she thought the police recorded only the calls going to Jim Swan's house, and she told the detective that Sandy had called her home on Saturday. Skahan said he knew Sandy had called her house because he had told her to.

"In fact, we were the ones who instructed her to make all the phone calls to Ken."

Harv's face twisted. She stood up from the table and said she needed to go talk to her husband. She put her hand on the doorknob, then turned to face the detective again.

"Tell me one specific thing that my husband said to her."

Skahan paused and thought about it. "He asked her if she wanted to order a pizza."

Harv clinched her fists. "Pizza?" she huffed about some marital slight known only to she and Carpenter. "I couldn't have pizza for two years!" With that, she stormed out of the break room.

*   *   *

Sergeant Lamson felt they finally had enough to get a search warrant for Carpenter's home in Lempster. A state police evidence team of four troopers, including Fred Lulka and John Encarnacao, waited patiently as Lamson typed up the affidavit and sought out a judge to approve the warrant. Despite the increasing snowfall and the late hour, he felt the evidence team needed to get out there right away. The snow had piled up enough in the past few hours that they had to call in a truck to plow the road to the little cottage on Quimby Farm Road.

Around 9:00 p.m., with the full force of the nor'easter coming down, the troopers radioed back that they had arrived at the Carpenter home. Harv was apparently still at work so the investigators entered through a rear window. There was no sign of Pen Meyer. But moments later they contacted Lamson with the news that they may have found something.

Trooper John Encarnacao stood over a fire pit outside the home of Ken Carpenter and Cynthia Harvey. The pit had been neatly dug out of the ground and was surrounded by a dozen cement cinder blocks. It was obviously something built in warmer weather for a recreational purpose, perhaps summer stargazing or socializing around burning brush.

Encarnacao had been with the New Hampshire State Police for about eight years. Most of that time, he had been working undercover for the Narcotics Division. That long-term operation was now over, and all those drug dealers he'd rubbed elbows with now knew he was a cop. His experience with surveillance equipment and related techniques made him a strong candidate for the Major Crimes Unit. The newly clean-cut and squared-away Encarnacao had been an evidence technician for just three weeks when he found himself on the Carpenter property in the middle of a blizzard.

On the night of February 28, the fire pit's contents were still warm and slightly smoldering. The top was covered with twigs and small branches, blanketed by bits of newspaper. There were no hot embers, but Encarnacao found the pit still hot enough to the touch that he donned a pair of gloves. He started pulling out individual branches and examining them. Once all of the sticks and tinder had been removed, what remained was a bowl of white and gray bits of ash and particulate matter. The top layer of debris was very loose, so he didn't have to dig, just take a scoop of debris and cautiously sift through it.

It wasn't long before he saw the first bit of bone.

It was about an inch long and looked like a chicken bone. He didn't know for certain it was Pen—they couldn't even be certain it was human—but they had to assume it was. Encarnacao continued to work, packaging and documenting each bit of evidence, when all the while snow and ice were blowing sideways into his face. Feeling his way through the mess, he grabbed something else that was hard like a stone. It was another bone.

Encarnacao's eye was drawn to something else in the smoldering pit. A thin wire was poking out of the sand-like ash. As he freed it from the hot dirt, the trooper realized it wasn't just a wire. It was the frame to a pair of eyeglasses. He might not know a chicken bone from a human bone, but he was pretty sure chickens didn't wear glasses.

One thing left innocently near the fire pit, but totally out of place, was a stick standing straight up in the thick snow. Encarnacao pulled it out and gave it the once-over. The stick was five feet long and about as thick as a baseball bat. The bottom end of the stick was charred black and worn to a slight point. It looked like it had been used to stoke the fire, to churn all its contents.

The four technicians gathered together. The snowdrifts were nearly up to their knees and the winds kept biting at the skin of their bare cheeks. The snow was so thick that the beams from their flashlights could illuminate only the white specks falling around them. "We can't work for much longer in these conditions," Lulka said. "This property is a huge crime scene. We need the equipment in the crime van and we need decent lighting."

"We'll have a secure the scene and come back in the morning when the weather breaks."

"What about the debris smoldering in the fire? Will the heat destroy any more evidence?"

"The heat is low. It's not the problem," said Encarnacao.

"It's the snow. It's going to bury the pit if we don't do something."

"It's going to take hours, maybe days, to process that fire pit. We'll have to cover it with a tarp and start first thing in the morning."

The crew put a blue plastic tarp over the ash heap and prayed it would do the trick. They kicked their feet and fought through the snow to get back to their vehicles, leaving behind a single state trooper to make sure nobody came or left the property while they were gone.

The effort to locate Pen Meyer was over. But in many ways, the search for her had only just begun.

FOURTEEN

Notebook

Sergeant Russell Lamson's investigation suddenly had more moving parts than he realized. His suspect, Ken Carpenter, was in Valley Regional Hospital with supposedly suicidal thoughts. From what they gathered from Harv, it was a voluntary admission, so he could voluntarily check himself out at any time. Medical privacy rules being what they were, the hospital wasn't freely going to let a trooper sit in the hallway outside his room in the psych ward. Lamson ordered a detail to stake out the hospital and make sure Carpenter didn't discharge himself and skip town. Though the hospital infrastructure was a frustrating layer between the state police and their suspect, it also worked in the investigator's favor. They knew where Carpenter was if they needed him.

The discovery of bits of bone in the fire pit did not sound the triumphant note that investigators were looking for. In their minds, Pen was dead, but they didn't have enough for an arrest and they didn't have enough to notify the family. As far as the press would be concerned, this was still an open missing person case, but Senior Assistant Attorney General Will Delker would be the spokesman for the investigation. If reporters wanted to speculate why the AG was now front and center, let them.

The state police told Harv that she would need to stay with friends for an extended time, as they expected the processing of her family home and property to take several days. As the investigators gathered on the morning of March 1, 2005, the fire pit felt more like a Herculean obstacle than the answer to a mystery. The pit was at least twenty inches deep with burned debris.

"How do we process that?" Lamson asked his team. They were silent. New Hampshire is a small state that averages about two-dozen homicides a year, most of them very by-the-book shootings. Occasionally, they had been called to examine a body found inside a building after an arson. In those cases, their job was to determine whether the victim was dead before the building was set on fire. But even then, there was a complete body with a skeleton and organs to examine. They were at a loss as to how to recover all the biological matter mixed in with the piles of ash, and then make a positive identification that this was, in fact, Pen Meyer.

The team began brainstorming ideas. Someone asked how archeologists recovered bones and fossils from sand.

"They use a set of screens," Trooper Fred Lulka said. "They have a series of stackable screens, each screen's holes slightly finer than the next. They pour the sand on the screen and sift through. The largest debris gets caught at the top. Then they repeat the process for a smaller screen and then yet another smaller one. Each time it passes through, the screen collects material of a certain size. They can sift all the way down to grains of sand."

"We can do some preliminary sifting, but we can't do all of that on-site, in this weather," Trooper John Encarnacao said. "We need to do that in a controlled environment."

Lamson agreed. He instructed the evidence team to collect all of the ash debris, package it, and bring it to the state Medical Examiner's Office. He'd already sent the few bones they had to the office. Lamson then called the state Division of Historical Resources and talked to an archeologist about obtaining some screens.

When they returned to the home on Quimby Farm Road in Lempster the morning of Monday, March 1, the landscape had a peaceful, clean look to it. The snow from the previous night's nor'easter had settled into the cracks and crevasses made by man, bandaging all sign of activity. Everything was a heavenly white, and it reflected the newly returned sun so brightly the troopers risked snow blindness.

Encarnacao forced his way through the snowpack to get to where he'd left the smoldering fire pit hours before. There was a good layer of snow on top of the tarp, but not so much that he couldn't lift it free.

When he pulled the tarp, the first thing Encarnacao noticed was the smell emanating from the pit. He got a strong whiff of gasoline or some other petroleum product. It was an odor he'd definitely picked up on the night before, but today it was extremely intense. The tarp had captured the fumes evaporating, and when he removed it, they erupted in a thick, invisible cloud. There was also another malodorous note beneath the fuel: the smell of something sickly sweet.

Encarnacao did some sifting on-site. Using the largest of the screens, the trooper poured the dirt on to the screen's surface and gave it tiny shakes to encourage the matter through. Mostly everything passed except for cigar-sized twigs and branches. The large screens helped capture even more pieces of bone. They were various sizes, up to six inches long. Some were flat and some were rounded. Each was cooked to a different color, from charcoal gray to black. Encarnacao bagged these and marked them with his initials.

He had brought with him several white five-gallon buckets to fill. After skimming with the screen, methodically he would take the top layer of the fire pit—still cooling—and place the fragments into a bucket. He would

Edith "Pen" Meyer lived a tranquil life of serenity and style. A familiar face around Sullivan County, Pen was never without her sheepdog sidekick, Fluff. *(Courtesy of Jonathan Purick)*

Pen loved to hike the many wooded trails of Goshen with Fluff. This footbridge around Lake Gunnison was dedicated in her honor.

Pen lived in the New Hampshire hamlet of Goshen. The town was so quiet, the only full-time police officer was the chief.

Pen Meyer loved life on Lake Gunnison—known to the locals as "the Goshen Ocean." Her home and garden were sources of great pride.

Among his fellow Alcoholics Anonymous members, Kenneth Carpenter was known for being suave and charismatic. He often trolled for women during Twelve Step meetings.
(James M. Patterson, Valley News)

Pen and her friends sought serenity during meetings at Millie's Place, a gathering spot for Alcoholics Anonymous. It was here that Ken Carpenter became acquainted with Sandy Merritt and Pen Meyer.

The undeveloped terrain around Ken Carpenter's secluded cabin in the woods of Lempster, New Hampshire, proved challenging for crime scene investigators.
(New Hampshire Department of Justice)

Fighting both time and a blizzard, state police investigators needed a snowplow to cleave a path through the woods to get to Ken Carpenter's home. *(New Hampshire Department of Justice)*

Investigators dug through several inches of ash and debris in this fire pit to recover key pieces of evidence, including personal items belonging to Pen Meyer. *(New Hampshire Department of Justice)*

Months after their search of the snow-covered property, investigators discovered additional evidence in the stump of this hollowed elm tree. *(New Hampshire Department of Justice)*

Pieces of Pen's distinctive jewelry, adorned with Southwestern imagery, were recovered from the hollow stump. *(New Hampshire Department of Justice)*

Investigators were directed by an anonymous tipster to check out this pay phone at the Goshen Country Store. Secured beneath the phone with orange duct tape was an important clue.

Above Left: This roll of orange duct tape—which seemed to match the tape found at the pay phone—was discovered in the back of Carpenter's truck. *(New Hampshire Department of Justice)*

Above Right: While searching his shed, investigators found a .22 rifle wrapped inside a yellow raincoat that had Carpenter's name written on it. *(New Hampshire Department of Justice)*

Carpenter reacts to his attorneys, Mark Sisti (left) and Aime Cook
(right), during his trial for the murder of Pen Meyer.
(James M. Patterson, Valley News)

Above Left: Defense Attorney Mark Sisti had a brash style that suited
him well. He believed the state had many weaknesses in its case.

Above Right: Russ Lamson was detective sergeant of the state police
Troop C. Lamson assured headquarters that the detectives of his
small rural outpost could handle this growing investigation.

Eric Berube was new to the detective bureau at Troop C. While listening to dozens of hours of jailhouse phone calls, Berube deciphered clues that would help resolve the case.

Above Left: Senior Assistant Attorney General Will Delker (left) brought an intellectual cool to the prosecution's case. But Delker needed to connect with the jury on a personal level to win a conviction. *(Jennifer Hauck, Valley News)*

Above Right: Assistant Attorney General Kirsten Wilson took the Pen Meyer case to heart. Wilson had never identified more closely with any homicide victim than she did with Pen.

(©2012 Leeann Pierce, Focusure Studios)

mark each bucket with his initials and an evidence number. They would be able to determine to some extent how deep in the pit each bucket worth of debris came from.

While placing small scoopful after scoopful into a bucket, eyeing bits of white, black, and gray matter, Encarnacao noticed something metal. He didn't wait for a sifting screen to pluck this out. It was another key, possibly for a post-office box. This was on a key chain. Attached to the ring was a flat metal trinket. The trooper gently brushed the grit away for a closer look. The trinket was in the shape of a teddy bear.

The fire pit was not the only area the troopers would need to process. Trooper Fred Lulka and the other investigators took turns scooping ash from the pit and examining the rest of the property.

The property had several outbuildings, including two sheds. They propped open their doors, and armed with a bunch of numbered yellow tent signs, they got to work identifying potential evidence inside.

The smaller of the two sheds could have been mistaken for an outhouse. It was constructed out of old wood and had a dirt floor. It contained shovels and garden hoses and coffee cans filled with nails. Given the situation, the things that immediately stood out were the fuel containers. Five of them were red plastic containers of gasoline. There was a yellow diesel fuel container. There was a can of charcoal lighter fluid. Lulka had his men take liquid samples of each fuel in case they could match them to any accelerants found in the pit.

"Check this out."

Lulka had discovered a black backpack. When he picked it up, he could tell it was full. The trooper unzipped it and started cataloging what was inside.

"Some gloves . . . a flashlight . . . a belt . . ."

"What else?" asked Encarnacao.

"Krazy Glue . . . a lighter . . . a lock . . . some condoms . . ."

"Interesting combination of supplies. What's he packing for?"

Lulka went on. "Some type of tree cutter . . . several knives . . . some tie-down-type cords."

"Could be a kidnapping kit," they speculated. "Let's bag it."

The troopers soon turned their attention on the other shed. It, too, was filled with all the accoutrements of rural life: chain saw, bolt cutters, dead batteries, and jugs of antifreeze. Stuffed in the corner, somewhat out of place, was a yellow rain jacket. It wasn't hanging neatly on a nail. It had been bundled slightly; it was covering something. Encarnacao peeled back the raincoat to see what was beneath. It was a .22 Marlin rifle, propped up with the muzzle pointing down. He took the Marlin and opened the bolt. There was a round in the chamber and more in the magazine. He counted out eleven .22 rounds.

Holding the butt of the rifle, the trooper examined

the raincoat in his other hand. On the inside of the lining, writing in permanent marker, was the word "Ken."

New Hampshire State Police had twenty-five K-9 units, but only three of the dogs were trained in cadaver detection. Lamson asked the Major Crimes Unit to send one to Lempster and assist the evidence team.

The dog's name was Gunther and his handler was Trooper James Martin. The two of them had been assigned to so many cases in every corner of the state that they had a running joke at NHSP—"Have dog, will travel." Gunther was trained "to indicate"—to paw and scratch at something—when he got the scent of human remains. The odor comes from the decaying body.

Martin walked Gunther through the property and its outskirts in twenty-five minute shifts over two days. Martin led the dog on a leash, ordering "Seek, seek," as the German shepherd rooted around the yard. After each shift, the dog would rest his nose for another twenty-five minutes before getting back to it.

The task was a difficult one for this K-9 unit. After the nor'easter, the snow was nearly to the trooper's waist. A pack of snow would be just the kind of thing that could bury the scent of decay. Also, if they were hunting for remains that had all of the biological material burned off it, there would be nothing left to decay and let off a smell. After two days, the only thing Gunther found was some thin ice over a brook that Martin crashed through up to his wet knees.

The team had Ken Carpenter's Nissan pickup truck and Cynthia Harvey's Ford Escort impounded so they could do a thorough examination. From what they heard from neighbors and saw from the gas station video, they presumed Carpenter was driving the Escort the morning of February 23. They hoped to find some trace evidence—blood, fibers, fingerprints—in the car. Trooper Jaye Almstrom had already done a perfunctory check on the Escort the morning of the twenty-fourth, and Almstorm and Detective Eric Berube got inside and looked at it again that same night. The state police brought the vehicles to a secure garage, where they could do some forensic tests.

Lamson was unsure what they'd find in the Escort. He already knew there wasn't anything obvious, like a bloodstain, to discover. He kept going back to that CD of the gas station video. When he was filling up, Carpenter kept looking into the backseat of the car. On the video, the backseat contents are dark and shapeless—perhaps covered with a tarp or blanket. No matter how hard their technicians tried, detectives couldn't get a better view of what was in the backseat of the Escort.

"Do you think it was Pen's body?" Senior Assistant AG Delker asked him.

Lamson's face would curl up, like he wanted to say

something that his body wouldn't let him. For cops, there's "what you think" and "what you know." For homicide prosecutors, there's "what you know" and "what you can prove." The question of what was in the backseat couldn't be answered. "I can't say," was the best he could do.

It did occur to Lamson that if it had been Pen's body and she was covered with a blanket, they might recover trace evidence from the blanket, if they could ever find it. Investigators refused to underestimate what tricks and techniques the *CSI*-loving Carpenter might have employed.

The truck's contents were far more interesting. On the floor was a candy wrapper—one for Life Savers Creme Savers. It was the same brand of candy wrapper the troopers had found in the pockets of Pen's jeans. Lamson remembered that in Almstrom's notes of their first visit with Carpenter, the suspect mentioned that he and Pen both liked the same flavor of candy. It seemed like a very odd tidbit to volunteer.

The back of the truck's bench seat folded forward for extra storage. Behind the passenger's seat was a roll of duct tape—orange duct tape. Stuck to the seat there was also a six-inch strip of orange duct tape. So far these items were only circumstantial; the investigators had to find a way to definitively tie them to the crime.

Also in the truck was a box of Federal brand .22 bullets, the same caliber of the recovered rifle.

As he watched the technicians rummage through the truck, Sergeant Lamson's mind wandered to the fire pit still to be processed. *All that ash* . . . It inspired Lamson to put on a latex glove and look inside the truck's ashtray.

"Look at this."

Lamson pulled out something hard and white that he was pretty sure was a bone.

Back at the site in Lempster, while some members of the investigative team were scooping and sifting debris from the fire pit, the other troopers continued to comb through the Carpenter property for more evidence. The camper that was parked by some of Carpenter's heavy equipment was unlocked. Inside they found the cardboard box that the .22 Marlin was originally packaged in.

Inside the main house, Lulka and Encarnacao started collecting shoes and gloves in case imprints could be recovered. In the living room they also found two Stetson hats hanging on the wall, consistent with the cowboy hat Carpenter was seen wearing at the Goshen Country Store before the key was discovered beneath the pay phone.

The men spent a lot of time going through miscellaneous papers and correspondence in the house, anything that might give them some insight into Carpenter's personal situation at the time of Pen's disappearance.

The house was small; it had just four rooms and one bath. The living room was 24 by 14 feet, wood-paneled with a cathedral ceiling. It led to an open kitchen area of about the same size. In the far back corner was a 10-by-11-foot bedroom, just wide enough to accommodate a double bed. There was an unfinished room off the bathroom that was used as a large storage closet.

Encarnacao rummaged around the storage area. There were a few footlockers and suitcases mixed about, and forgotten clothes hanging on racks providing a musty smell. On the shelf above the coatrack was a cardboard box. He brought it down, lifted the cover, then started to thumb through the papers stored inside.

"Lulka! Get in here."

The other trooper bounced to the rear of the home. Encarnacao, his hands encased in white latex gloves, was holding up a single document folded in thirds. Trooper Lulka moved in for a closer look. At the top, it said: "Agreement to Sell Personal Property."

It was a one-page purchase and sales agreement template. But the template was not filled out. It didn't say in any of the blank lines what was being sold or what the price was. Lulka scanned the document further. Although the agreement detail at the top had been left blank, the date of the transaction had been filled in with pen: February 23, 2005—the day Pen Meyer vanished.

The document also had two signatures written in cursive at the bottom. The seller had signed her name "Edith K. Meyer." The buyer had countersigned as "Ken Carpenter."

Word of the sales agreement got back to Sergeant Russell Lamson in a flash. What was Pen going to sell to

Carpenter? Was it a willing transaction or a forced one? Why would Pen sign a blank sales agreement? Was it even her signature? Lamson thought back to the date on the contract: February 23. Carpenter had told troopers on the twenty-fourth he hadn't seen Pen in about two weeks, but this deal they allegedly worked out was the day before.

Lamson was in his police cruiser transporting some evidence when it struck him. In the phone call, Pen told Sandy that she was leaving her house to Carpenter and the two of them should move in together. *But if that's it, why is the contract blank?*

Lamson pulled into the Goshen Post Office and asked to see the postmaster. They walked over to Box 306. Lamson brought with him the key on the teddy bear chain they'd pulled out of the fire pit. The lead investigator slid the key into the mailbox, Pen Meyer's mailbox. The door popped open without a hitch.

Investigators executed a search warrant at Jim Swan's home for his guest room, which he freely allowed them access to. They seized some of Carpenter's belongings, his clothes, and a pair of his work boots. One of the boots had a gash in the toe, as if it had been nicked with a chain saw.

Back at the Carpenter house, the troopers continued looking for items of evidentiary value. The little cottage had no basement, but there was an unfinished loft above the kitchen. It was only accessible through a crawl-space-sized door by a stepladder.

The inside of the loft was framed by two-by-fours with rolls of pink fiberglass insulation tucked into the eves. There were boxes and milk crates filled with junk that the residents just hadn't gotten around to throwing out. The investigators moved the boxes from one end of the loft to the other but found nothing of value hidden there.

After recovering and bagging all the items of interest on the floor in the living room, the troopers did a more in-depth probe of the room. They went through drawers, looked under furniture, and peeked behind shelves.

Trooper Encarnacao was examining a red leather chair. It was a nice piece of furniture, soft with nail head trimming, though the arms were showing some wear and starting to crack. The seat cushion was detachable, and Encarnacao slid his hand underneath. He pulled out a blue notebook. The writing inside was Carpenter's. They knew from Harv and Dot Monahan that he kept a journal of his activities and his feelings.

"What's in my head? Smaller picture, I don't want to die today, not yet anyway."

The entry was from January 31, three weeks before Pen's disappearance. The pages read like a stream-of-conscience rant. They were a riot of scribbles and double underlines and triple exclamation points. On this page,

Carpenter was manically going back and forth from obsessing over Sandy watching *CSI* with Ronnie to Pen's unsolicited interference in his love life. The entry was randomly punctuated with "That bitch!" popping in the way a drummer would hit a crash cymbal.

"Are they together? (IF THEY ARE! I CAN LET THIS GO!!!)" Carpenter pleaded with the heavens to just let him know so he could move on with his life. "Why do I feel so lonely inside? Tell me what to do."

It was clear from the passage that Carpenter was still obsessed with Sandy and fixated on Pen. The investigator turned the page to read the next passage. Something about the entry was different. It was a journal entry, but it didn't read like one. This time it didn't read like Carpenter was expressing his own feelings. It was more like he was writing as a character, speaking in someone else's voice.

"I never meant for it to go this far," the narrator said. The voice commanded to wait a week, then offer to testify for Ken. This narrator was giving instructions to someone. The narrator promised to leave a letter for the court to explain "how I pushed you," and then confessed to manipulating the listener.

Why would Carpenter assume a different persona to give orders to someone? Encarnacao wondered. *Because this is a script for someone else to read!*

Had it started as a fantasy, one in which Pen approached Sandy on her own and pleaded Carpenter's case? When did it change from mere wish to step-by-step plan to eliminate his rival?

"I never planned on Ken hanging in there," Pen/Carpenter wrote. The narrator concluded that loving Sandy was the man's only crime. She/he insisted Sandy drop the restraining order, take Carpenter home, and "fuck his brains out."

Investigators believed this notebook was a first draft of the script Pen was forced to read. Also, it indicated that even in the early stages of Carpenter's deadly fantasy, the plan was for Pen Meyer to disappear.

The script called for Pen to reveal she had been carrying on a secret affair with a pilot. "I'm going to Florida then, you won't believe this, Mexico and South America." In her absence, Ken Carpenter would house-sit and drive her car until she returned. She even suggested Sandy and Carpenter move into the lakefront home together.

Also in the blue notebook were letters written by the imaginary Pen, one to the Goshen Police and one to Sandy Merritt. She/he informed the cops that she and Carpenter had resolved their differences and he would be house-sitting for an extended period. In the letter to Sandy, the writer made the most direct pleas yet for her to reconcile with Carpenter.

"Go after him the way I had you stay away from him. Think of aloneness as a drink and stick to him like glue." The writer promised to send Sandy a check to help with bills and to drop a line from Florida or Mexico. The letter was signed, "Pen, (the asshole)." In the postscript, the writer ordered Sandy to say nothing to Jonathan Purick and said Fluff would be going home with Carpenter.

Encarnacao kept on reading through the solid blocks of texts. There was almost no white space between the ink-colored screams, but one line break caught his eye. It was a one-word paragraph, a complete thought sitting alone on a ruled line.

"Burn," it said.

The notebook found under the red leather seat cushion was more than a diary for a sick, angry man. It was a blueprint for murder, notes on a killing.

In the margins of the rant, the investigators noticed a doodle. It was nothing more than stick figures and rudimentary shapes. The drawing was of two people. Nearby was a square house and a fire. One of the stick figures was pointing a stick rifle and shooting the other.

FIFTEEN

Puzzle

Since their discovery of the deadly fire pit the night of February 28, the state police had good luck keeping developments in the case under wraps. The Carpenter home was on the end of a Class VI road off another Class VI road, so the comings and goings of investigators were barely noticed by residents of the area. Normally conspicuous vehicles like the state police crime van simply vanished into the woods for hours at a time. While the Meyer disappearance was the talk of the town, few were able to keep tabs on what detectives were focusing on in their investigation, and reporters were unlikely to stumble across the property by accident.

Senior Assistant Attorney General Will Delker did a good job keeping the local media at bay. He had a knack for ignoring the loaded questions and gave quotes that were substantial enough to satisfy the needs of scribes on deadline. Unlike the serious, pointed questioning attorneys do with clients and with each other, Delker knew *giving* an answer to the press was more important than what that answer actually was. Perhaps it was because he was himself married to a reporter that he understood what they were looking for. He knew a dozen different ways to say "no comment" without actually saying "no comment."

It's the little bits of serendipity that often break news stories. For the TV reporter and videographer driving toward Goshen on March 2, 2005, that moment arrived when they spotted a state police flatbed truck driving in the other direction. The truck had a purple hatchback strapped to the back. They turned and chased the truck for a mile or so, shooting video through the windshield of their station's white Ford Explorer. When the pair eventually arrived in Goshen for the daily briefing with SAAG Delker, they asked if the impounded car had anything to do with the weeklong search for Pen Meyer. Not expecting such a specific question, Delker hesitated for a microsecond before saying he couldn't comment on any evidence gathered in the case. It wasn't an official confirmation they were on to something, but the news crew felt like they very well might be.

After a fruitless search for people to interview in Goshen, the TV crew wandered farther down the road into Lempster. They stopped at the local garage and asked the mechanic if he knew anybody in town who drove a purple car—an unusual color for those parts. He said he knew of no one. The reporter struck out at the post office and the volunteer fire department, too.

The reporter and videographer grabbed lunch at Sturgeon's General Store. The décor was rustic and wooden, like a prototypical general store from the prairie. Its shelves were stocked with the usual staples including farming supplies. There was a large handmade lunch counter where the owner and his wife served fresh deli sandwiches. The storekeeper was warm and hospitable to the reporter, a subtle yet positive departure from the other friendly-but-not-terribly-helpful residents he'd quizzed about the purple car.

The sandwiches were delicious and the reporter stayed casual, laying on the charm about the town and the store. He waited until they had finished every morsel on their plates and emptied their soda cans before asking.

"Do you know anyone in town who drives a purple car?"

The storeowner's face hardened slightly. He lowered his voice in a manner that signaled, "I know I shouldn't be telling you this . . ."

At around 2:00 p.m. on March 2, the Explorer carrying that TV crew stopped at the end of Quimby Farm Road. Stepping out of the truck, the videographer casually opened the hatch, pulled out his tripod and camera, and started taking video of the home and property. Lieutenant Russ Conte and Sergeant Russell Lamson walked down the driveway from the crime scene van to talk to the new arrivals.

The reporter, who kept his hands in his pockets and his eyes on nothing in particular, greeted the troopers with nothing but a "Hey." The troopers knew there was little they could do. The crew remained on the road, a public right-of-way, and they couldn't tell them to leave. The videographer had no idea what he was shooting, but he made sure to shoot everything within view.

"I suppose," the reporter asked Conte and Lamson, "we have to talk to Delker about this?"

They nodded. Without ever breaking protocol or going on the record, the TV crew had what they needed. They drove out of town with a big break in the story: The search for Pen Meyer had brought state police to an isolated home twenty minutes away in Lempster, where officials were referring comment to a state homicide prosecutor.

Even without the story evolving in the media, Will Delker had a difficult case on his hands. The senior assistant attorney general had a possible homicide, but little physical evidence. At this phase, his first concern wasn't whether he could get a jury conviction or even whether get could get a grand jury indictment. Delker first had to convince the attorney general of the state of New Hampshire that there was enough evidence to make an arrest.

Delker and Sergeant Lamson visited with the state's

deputy medical examiner, Jennie Duval. She had agreed to take in the dozen or so five-gallon buckets of fire ash to be sifted and screened in search of evidence. Duval had already contacted a colleague in Maine, a forensic anthropologist, to help identify whatever bones were recovered.

"I heard back from our bone expert about the evidence you sent us," she said. Duval had sent digital photos of the twenty or so pieces of bone they first recovered. "She says the bones are human. This one is part of the humerus. This one here is the fifth metatarsal, to be exact. A bone from the foot."

"How do we know whether it's Pen? Can we get some DNA?"

"We can't," said Duval. "DNA is very brittle and the bonds that hold the nuclear ties together break up under intense heat. The DNA string unravels. It's highly unlikely we can get usable DNA from these bones, even the larger ones."

"Have you found any teeth?" Delker asked Lamson.

"No, not yet."

"There's a chance we could recover some mitochondrial DNA from the teeth," the medical examiner offered. "It's passed on through the mother's genes. It's not as definitive as a full DNA screening, but mtDNA could narrow identification down to a single family or set of relatives."

"I'll write up a warrant for Pen's dental records," Delker said. "We can compare any teeth to her x-rays."

"It may not be enough," Duval warned. "Right now,

I don't have enough to make anything close to a positive identification—let alone a cause of death."

"But it's clearly a homicide."

"I can't definitely say that. None of us know how she got into that fire. She could have had a heart attack or broke her neck in a fall. Right now, I couldn't say if she was stabbed or strangled or shot or hit by a car."

Duval said she wouldn't issue a death certificate until there was more physical evidence to study.

Around noontime on Thursday, March 3, 2005, Detective Shawn Skahan got a panicked call on his cell from Harv. She said she'd just spoken to her husband and he wanted to get out of the hospital, but the doctor wouldn't be in until 2:00. Harv said Carpenter had been talking on the phone to his brother, Dale, who told him he wasn't going to come to the hospital to get him. This resulted in a fight in which Carpenter swore at his brother and slammed the phone down on him.

"I told the nurse that he's not welcome back at my house and she suggested I come to the hospital to talk to him." Skahan urged her not to go to the hospital and to instead try to work things out over the telephone. She promised she'd be in touch.

At about 1:50, Harv called Skahan again. She said she'd just gotten off the phone with Carpenter and told him he wasn't welcome at their home in Lempster, and informed him that she'd obtained an "Order of Trespass" to keep him off the property.

"Why are you trying to get out of the hospital?" Harv had asked her husband. "You're safe where you are."

"I want to go to Florida." He also told her that he was not going to jail. He said if it came to that, he would take his own life. "Or I'll force their hand and put them in a position to kill me."

Harv told Carpenter she felt uncomfortable staying in their house. "Our house is not the crime scene," he said bluntly. "The person you knew didn't do this and the person you know didn't do this."

Harv sounded depressed relaying this to the detective. "It's like my husband has changed and nothing matters to him anymore. Not just the bad things, but everything."

Skahan looked at this watch. Time was running out. Carpenter planned to check out of the hospital and flee the state. Circumstantial evidence or not, they were going to have to make a move.

With less-than-encouraging news from the medical examiner, Delker and Lamson still made their case to the attorney general of the state of New Hampshire on Thursday, March 3. They wanted to issue an arrest warrant for Ken Carpenter, who was still hiding out in the psych ward at Valley Regional Hospital.

Attorney General Kelly Ayotte was a veteran homicide

prosecutor and deputy AG when her boss hastily resigned in June 2004 accused of sexually harassing a state worker in—of all places—an after-hours conga line at a conference discussing sexual abuse prevention. He was later exonerated of wrongdoing, but Ayotte had his post. Now, at age thirty-five, she was about to be battle-tested in her role as the state's top cop.

Delker laid out the circumstantial case against Ken Carpenter. Just walking through what they knew exposed the gaping evidentiary holes in their case. At the moment, they couldn't prove Carpenter was responsible for Pen's murder. They couldn't prove how Pen was murdered—or even prove that she was dead.

Ayotte asked if they were able to prove a crime had occurred and whether they could prove it happened in New Hampshire, as the question of jurisdiction was likely to be exploited by a defense attorney. Carpenter had said he visited Massachusetts in the late morning and was seen driving south from T-bird's gas station. Delker argued if the body was found in New Hampshire, then the legal presumption was that the crime had occurred in the state, but it would be an issue they'd likely have to address in court.

As a prosecutor, Ayotte had a 100 percent conviction rate. Part of the credit for that went to the solid work of police investigators, but much of it was owed to her habits of intense preparation and caution. She was known for leaving nothing to chance, especially during murder trials. She simply wasn't willing to gamble with a conviction, even when she was sure the suspect had committed the crime. Led by Ayotte's example, the prosecutors in the AG's homicide unit didn't seek an arrest or an indictment unless they were 150 percent sure they could secure a conviction.

An investigation with this many holes was not something Ayotte would traditionally have jumped at. Time was often on the state's side; the AG's office could wait weeks or months to gather evidence and build the case before making an arrest. There was less likelihood of making a mistake that way, less likelihood of doing something that would give a defendant grounds for an appeal—or let them walk.

"General, will you issue the warrant for Ken Carpenter's arrest?" Lamson asked.

He was more than a little surprised when AG Ayotte nodded and told the investigators to go for it.

Sergeant Lamson ordered his two detectives, Skahan and Berube, to meet him in the lobby of Valley Regional Hospital in Claremont at 6:00 p.m. He had a warrant for Ken Carpenter's arrest. It was important for Lamson to have his guys there. Several agencies had been involved in the case—dozens of officers had provided critical evidence—but this arrest belonged to Troop C. The three of them were going to be there when they cuffed him.

Before they could execute it, they would need to get authorization to "search" the hospital. Lamson and his men met with one of the hospital administrators. The sergeant showed the man a form, a "Written Consent for Search," which would allow the state police to look for Carpenter in the hospital. The administrator signed the form and—not wanting these armed detectives wandering all over the hospital—offered to escort them to Carpenter's room.

When they got there, Lamson got his first look at Ken Carpenter. He was dressed in jeans and a rumpled shirt, probably the same clothes he'd been wearing when he checked himself in four days previous. The hospital had been a good place to hide out while the police were spinning their wheels, but now that they were moving in on him, he had planned to make another move. He was dressed because he was itching to go.

He's not wearing his shoes, Berube noticed. Why was it that half the guys they arrested for major felonies weren't wearing shoes? *Because those are always the guys who aren't expecting us to show up.*

"Ken Carpenter?" Lamson wasn't asking as much as he was accusing. He'd spent a whole week thinking about nothing but Pen Meyer, learning about her personality and her deeply held convictions. This moment was why he worked so hard on cases like this. This was why he had personally brought the arrest warrant to the hospital. He wanted to see the look on Ken Carpenter's face when he arrested him.

Carpenter responded to his name with a "Yeah?" He

pulled his shoulders back and stood up straighter, like he would punch his way out of the room if he needed to.

"This is for Pen Meyer," Lamson said. "You're under arrest for first-degree murder."

Skahan swiftly moved behind Carpenter, cuffed him, and double locked the cuffs.

Lamson read Carpenter his Miranda rights.

"Would you be willing to make a statement?" he asked.

Carpenter said he wanted to speak to an attorney. The three detectives led their suspect out of the hospital and into Trooper Almstrom's awaiting cruiser. Carpenter was taken to the Claremont Police Department to be booked, his arraignment to be held the next day at Newport District Court.

For the seven days that Pen was missing, Jonathan Purick was a mess. He had slept every night on a different friend's couch. He had no idea where Ken Carpenter was, but he had every reason to fear him. Carpenter had it in for him, too.

Jonathan called the police department at least once a day to offer help or get an update on the search. He couldn't go back to Pen's house and wait for her in the kitchen anymore. The investigation had moved beyond him.

The night after Pen vanished, Purick had gotten a phone call from Pen's youngest daughter, Hayley, who was living in Colorado. She was in tears, upset about her mother. She asked Jonathan to share what he knew. They both cried and comforted each other. It was the only time anyone from Pen's family acknowledged him and his connection to Pen in any way.

Jonathan felt like he was going insane. He'd been to rock bottom before, had drunk his way there, but this was completely different. There was nothing to surrender to in this situation, no amount of steps he could take to achieve serenity.

He found himself sitting at his kitchen table writing letters to Pen, tears streaming down his face.

I know you're probably not alive, and I'm crazy to write to you, but I feel like there is an angel above me . . .

The phone rang. It was Jonathan's sponsor. "Have you heard anything new about Pen?"

"No," Jonathan said. "I'm not immediate family. They're not telling me anything about the case."

His sponsor was someone with lots of local connections, someone who heard things long before others did. "Something's happened. Check the news to see what they're saying."

It was Thursday night. Jonathan flipped on the television and waited for the 6:00 newscast. The reporter said that Pen Meyer was still a missing person and there were no significant developments in the case. Jonathan was relieved; his sponsor was wrong.

When he tuned in again at 11:00, he saw the flashing

graphic announcing "Breaking News." Through the ringing in his ears, Purick heard the anchor say that Pen was dead. Carpenter was under arrest. The anchor said nothing else, except that more details would be released in the coming days.

Jonathan cried himself to sleep that night. The weight on his chest caused by a week of fear and conjecture had been lifted, but that was of little relief as all the emotion that weight had dammed inside him finally burst forth. He had traveled so far in his life, overcome so many pitfalls, he truly thought Pen was his karmic reward for staying clean and sober for so long. Now he didn't know what to think.

The next morning, Jonathan walked into the 7:30 a.m. meeting at Stone Church like a zombie. The format for the meeting was speaker/discussion, so they solicited a volunteer to lead the talk. Jonathan raised his hand. He sighed, opened his eyes, and let all of his feelings pour out.

The arrest of Ken Carpenter was a relief to Sandy Merritt. After the discovery of Pen's bones in the fire pit, investigators were worried about Sandy's safety. She had been his motivation to kill.

Although Carpenter had checked himself into the psych unit and the hospital was under surveillance, Lamson and his team thought the best thing to do would be to move Sandy out of her Newport apartment and into a motel where Carpenter wouldn't be able to find her if he left the hospital undetected. She had done well with the recorded phone calls, but they doubted he'd continue calling. Harv had already told them Carpenter suspected the phones could be tapped and they'd confirmed it for her.

Court records suggest just how difficult Sandy's struggles were, as she battled with both sobriety and psychological issues. According to those records, Sandy had been a blackout drinker in the months before she came to AA. She told her therapist that she drank one to two bottles of wine a day. She also displayed signs of psychosis and thought blocking. She told a physician she thought the birds in the trees were chattering about her. She couldn't tell whether her memories of the past were real or just a symptom of her condition. Sandy had made tremendous progress in finding serenity over the past year, but this latest crisis with Carpenter threatened all of it.

On Friday, with Carpenter in custody and about to be arraigned, a police officer drove Sandy from the motel back home. She'd been gone for the better part of a week, and it was oddly quiet when she returned. Her dog, Moisha, was staying in the main house so there was no one to greet her. She wandered around, peeked into the fridge, unsure of what to do next.

Sandy stared at the green telephone sitting on her counter, the one that had been plugged into all sorts of recording equipment the last time she was home. Someone had left a message on her machine while she was out. Sandy picked up the receiver to see where the call had come from. The phone number was unfamiliar, but the caller ID said it was from Valley Regional Hospital. She played the message.

"Hi, it's me." Carpenter, of course. "I'm just seeing if you got that check and everything left for you. I don't understand that, but . . . but . . . uh . . . you suck."

The recording frightened her even though she knew Carpenter was locked up. She had no idea what he was talking about.

Sandy went to collect her mail, which had piled up in her absence. She flipped through the many envelopes, making note of which looked like bills and which looked like junk mail. In the stack she came across a handwritten envelope that had arrived the first part of the week. It had to have been dropped in the mail the previous Friday or Saturday.

She opened the envelope and took out a bank check written out to her in the amount of $400. It was signed by Pen. Also in the letter was a legal document she'd never seen before.

Agreement to Sell Personal Property
PURCHASE AND SALES AGREEMENT made
between <u>Edith K. Meyer and Sandra Merritt</u>

The names in the form had been filled in with a type-writer. On the next line "Edith K. Meyer," followed by a line of 37 periods, was listed as "(seller)." "Sandra Merritt" and 38 consecutive periods were on the next line as "(buyer)."

Line 1 of the contract specified exactly what property was being exchanged.

"Entire" conents [sic] of "Seller's" house Center Rd.
Goshen, N.H. 03752
Also included contents of garage (Same adress [sic])

The list price for this transaction: one dollar. The date of the title transfer was typed in as "Febuary [sic] 23, 2005," the same day that Pen Meyer vanished. Under "other terms" of the contract, this rider was listed:

Must take fluff (dog) (check enclosed)
P.S. I love you guy's [sic].

The contract was signed at the bottom by both Pen and Sandy, but Sandy knew someone had forged her signature. They likely had forged Pen's, too. Now the phone message made sense to her. Shaking, she picked up the phone and dialed the state police.

PART THREE

Collision

Come, let's away to prison:
We two alone will sing like birds I'th'cage.

—WILLIAM SHAKESPEARE, *KING LEAR*

SIXTEEN

Loyalty

After her husband's arrest, Cynthia Harvey consulted with her friends and her spiritual advisors. The past two weeks—between Pen's disappearance and Carpenter's arrest—had been a whirlwind. Alone in her home after the state police had finally left, Harv prayed for guidance. It had been difficult, but hadn't she and her husband been making progress?

When she first visited him at the county jail, Carpenter proclaimed his innocence. He humbled himself in front of her and confessed that he had been abusing his anti-depressant medication. Carpenter also admitted to her that he had "picked up," or used, drugs. He admitted he'd snorted heroin and crystal meth recently. Twenty-three years of sobriety were gone, and now he'd have to go to a meeting and pick up a white chip.

As a detainee in the county jail, Carpenter had telephone privileges. The calls were collect, expensive, and recorded. There were only certain numbers a prisoner could call. Very soon after his arrest, he began placing a call to Harv in a campaign to proclaim his innocence and repair their marriage.

"Hello?"

"Honey?" he asked, unsure if she'd accept the call. "How you doin'?"

"Not good." That was an understatement. Harv was exhausted. On top of that, the state police had left her home a mess, the kerosene tank was low, and now the satellite TV wasn't working. She had been abandoned by her husband in all sorts of small ways, which only added salt to the wound of the big one.

"I was prayin' about this every single minute I'm awake and prayin' about you every single minute," he said. "It's gonna be okay. I'm tellin' ya."

"Okay." She sniffed back a tear.

"God is pullin' for us here, you know." Carpenter then told his wife that in the few days he was behind bars, he'd found religion. He told her he'd been reading the Bible cover to cover. He said he'd attended regular AA meetings in the jail. His tone was sugar-sweet and earnest with his God-fearing wife.

"Now honey," he continued. "Don't talk to anybody, okay?"

"Yeah."

"Please? My life is on the line here, okay?"

"Yes, I know that."

Carpenter's voice began to rise. "I'm fuckin' tellin' you that. Okay?"

Harv's voice trembled. "Okay."

"I am deadly serious here. My lawyer is sure that we can do this. This is not over. But you cannot go openin' up your mouth because you wanna talk to somebody. I don't mean to sound abrupt, but gee whiz, I read in the police statements that Dot says, 'Oh yeah, we've always been afraid of Ken.'"

"I can't speak for Dot."

"Maybe you outta talk to her about havin' a little compassion."

"Don't talk to me about what other people are saying."

"Help me out a little here, huh?"

Harv didn't take kindly to that. "Excuse me?"

"Please, I know we can get through this. And then whatever you decide to do, if we're gonna stay together, fine, we'll stay together." Carpenter's voice dropped low again, to that tone he had so much luck manipulating her with. "I just wanna be with you, baby."

The whole seduction move struck Harv as ridiculous, and she burst out laughing. "Sorry," she said after covering her mouth.

"You're an asshole," he said. "Please don't do that to me."

"I heard you tell Sandy the same things."

"Do you really need to do this right now? Why don't you come down during visiting hours and tell me how much I suck, okay?"

"Stop it," she scolded him.

"I need another chance to make it up to you. It's not fair and I agree with you. But let me deal with this and then I can kiss your ass for the rest of my life in Macy's window, okay?"

The first step in the criminal process for Ken Carpenter was his arraignment in district court on first-degree murder charges. As he was being charged with a felony, a crime that would be adjudicated in the superior court, no plea from the defendant could be entered. The prosecutors would say nothing publicly that wasn't already in the terse arrest warrant: that Kenneth Carpenter purposely caused the death of Edith "Pen" Meyer and incinerated her body. The revelation about the fire pit titillated the press. The prosecution moved that the file be sealed from the public indefinitely while the investigation continued. The judge ordered the suspect held without bail and scheduled a probable cause hearing for the following week. After the hearing, the state would need to get an indictment from a grand jury and then proceed to trial.

Will Delker now had a co-chair for the case, Assistant Attorney General Kirsten Wilson. Wilson had an impressive head of full, ash-blond hair and smoky gray eyes. In her mid-thirties, she would have been a dead ringer for

Ann-Margret, circa *Tommy*, if it weren't for her square, athletic jawline and slightly crooked smile (the investigators noted Wilson had a passing resemblance to another important person in the case: a young Pen Meyer). Wilson's style and sex appeal were in stark contrast to Delker's last-kid-picked persona. They were a formidable team in the courtroom, however. Delker brought the intellectual analysis; Wilson brought the empathy and the passion.

Delker and Wilson were hoping the defense team would waive the probable cause hearing. It was common in felony cases to skip this court appearance. The state would present a brief overview of the evidence in the case to a judge. The burden of proof was not "beyond a reasonable doubt" as it was in a jury trial; the burden was "preponderance of the evidence," a much lower standard to meet. It wasn't worth a defense attorney putting up the fight—unless he suspected the state's evidence was bad and he could get the case thrown out.

The evidence in the Pen Meyer investigation wasn't bad, but it wasn't as rock solid as the prosecutors would like. Publicly the government declared their faith in the evidence. Behind closed doors, in discussions with police investigators, the team was ill at ease with what they had.

"The medical examiner has yet to issue a death certificate in this case," Wilson said. "If she doesn't have enough evidence for a death certificate, do we have enough to get a conviction?"

"Do we have enough for a probable cause hearing?

Absolutely," Delker said to her. "Do we have enough for trial? We hope so."

"Do you *need* to prove how she died?" Sergeant Lamson asked. Having the incinerated bones of your arch-enemy discovered on your property was pretty damning in and of itself. The lead investigator wasn't being flippant when he questioned whether a cause of death was an extraneous detail.

"The law says we don't have to provide a cause of death," Delker replied, "but a jury might feel otherwise."

Lamson told Delker and Wilson that the crime lab was going to analyze the material it did have: the written property agreements, the duct tape, and the bloodstained towel. His detectives were spending every day at the Medical Examiner's Office sifting through the more than sixty gallons of ash and debris scooped out of the fire pit. They were still finding bits of bone, which were to be sent to the forensic anthropologist for further analysis, but the conversation consistently turned to what they hadn't yet found.

"If he shot her with that twenty-two, the only way we could prove it now would be to find a bone with a bullet hole in it. If he fatally stabbed her, there might be blade marks on a bone. Of course, all the bones we've found have been in tiny pieces."

"An adult skeleton, even one as small as Pen's, would still contain over two hundred bones," Wilson said. "That pit should have been overflowing with bones."

"It's possible the fire burned long enough and hot enough to reduce them to ash," Lamson theorized.

"Some of the bones," countered Delker, "but not others."

"It's possible there could be more than one burn site," the detective said. "Or some of the bones were dumped at a different location."

"So we're still waiting for our best evidence to be discovered?"

Lamson nodded.

Carpenter's attorney was not going to give the State a pass on probable cause and waive the hearing. Public defender John Newman wanted to get a good, long peek at the prosecution's hand. A veteran defense lawyer, Newman probably suspected the government was having trouble collecting everything it would need in a conventional case.

The PC hearing was held March 10, 2005, only a week after Carpenter's arrest. Senior Assistant AG Will Delker planned to handle the offer of proof, as Assistant AG Kirsten Wilson was still getting up to speed on the crime. The hearing would consist of testimony from one witness: Detective Sergeant Russell Lamson.

Carpenter arrived at court wearing a thick orange jumpsuit. He'd spent the last week in the Sullivan County House of Corrections in Claremont. Carpenter walked up the steps to the district court with his hands cuffed together in front of him, a sheriff's deputy leading him by the arm. For the public—getting their first look at the suspect in this brutal attack—Carpenter's long hair, shaggy beard, and wide-eyed gaze made him look like a wild man. The press immediately began speculating whether an insanity defense was a possibility.

Inside the small courtroom—the same courtroom in which Carpenter, Sandy, and Pen had all confronted one another three months earlier—the defendant found his seat next to Attorney Newman. The room stood as the judge entered and the hearing was under way.

Delker called Lamson to the stand. With the case file having been sealed at arraignment, the public still didn't know the details of how Pen Meyer disappeared and was allegedly killed by Ken Carpenter. The detective explained how the defendant had a grudge against Pen because she'd interfered with his extramarital affair. He told the story of how Sandy had received an unusual phone call at work.

"She remembered Pen telling her that Ken had a near-fatal accident with a chain saw and that she should drop the stalking order and get back with him. That they loved each other once, and should get back together."

"Was this characteristic?"

"It was contrary to everything she'd done before."

Lamson ticked off virtually everything they had at the moment. They'd recovered fifteen to eighteen bone fragments from the fire pit. They had the property agreements from Carpenter's home and the handwritten deed with forged signatures that had been sent to Sandy. A neighbor had seen a man who resembled Carpenter waiting in a car outside Pen's home before she disappeared. Lamson also added that an anonymous caller who sounded like the defendant had directed them to the pay phone where Pen's safe-deposit key was found taped.

When it was his turn to cross-examine Sergeant Lamson, Newman wasted no time going after the weakness in the case.

"Is there any trace evidence directly linking Mr. Carpenter to Ms. Meyer?"

"Not all of the evidence has been fully processed."

"So the answer is 'no'?"

Lamson capitulated. "No."

"No hair? No fibers? No fingerprints?"

"No."

"Any confession?"

"No."

"Has the ME even issued a death certificate yet?"

"No."

"Is there any direct proof that the remains found in that fire pit are Ms. Meyer's?"

"As I said," Lamson explained, "not all of the evidence has been fully processed."

Newman made an impassioned plea to get the charges dropped and his client released. "There are tremendous gaps in this evidence. There is no proof of probable cause," he told the judge. "There is no confession. There are no witnesses. There is no cause of death. There is no murder weapon. There is no link between the defendant and any trace evidence and Ms. Meyer. There is no evidence that Ms. Meyer has been killed in this case."

Delker objected. "Your honor, under state law, the prosecution is not obligated to determine cause of death. This case epitomizes why there is no such requirement because all the defendant needs to do is obliterate the body."

Despite the strong arguments against it, the judge ruled there was enough probable cause to hold the defendant and refer the case to the grand jury. The case file would be unsealed. Both attorneys got a taste of what the other's strategy at trial was going to be; that was the victory each team walked away with.

Another important tidbit was revealed in court that day. It was clear from the testimony that bone fragments had been recovered in only one location: the fire pit. The state police made no mention of finding human remains anywhere else. That fact may have been lost on many of the observers in the courtroom, but it was not lost on Ken Carpenter.

Harv agreed to visit her husband on Saturday nights during county jail visiting hours. The corrections officers wouldn't let him have a hair tie, so his shaggy mane hung around his face. The face-to-face visits seemed to be good for them. Harv seemed to enjoy the talks, even if she still wasn't quite satisfied with Carpenter's level of transparency.

"I still have questions," she said, "about things going on."

He told her to write the questions down and he would answer them.

Five days after the probable cause hearing on March 10, Harv accepted a collect call from her husband. He was very casual, eager to make small talk, and happy just to gab about his day in the rec yard. Harv was quiet, answering questions with "yeah" and "okay" and not really present for the conversation.

"I got a couple of questions of my own," she finally said.

"Okay. Did you write them down?"

"No. I'm going to ask you directly."

"I can't be on the phone answering questions," he said. Harv said nothing in response. His wife's silence soon got to him, and he buckled. "Go ahead."

"I read in the paper—which was a mistake—that you called Sandy from the hospital."

"I don't remember saying that."

"Did you?"

"I don't remember saying that." Then he snapped his fingers. "Oh, that's when I told her she sucked."

Harv started to get steamed. "You called her from the hospital? Why hasn't she changed her phone number?"

"'Cause she's an asshole, that's why."

"The paper says you called her about the transfer of property. That's why you called her."

"No," he said. "Why? Was that in the paper?"

"Ken, what I'm saying is it didn't say in the paper that you called her and you told her she sucked," Harv shot back. "It said that you called her about the transfer of property."

"I asked why it wasn't in the paper or wasn't on TV."

"You just told me you called her to say she sucked."

"Yeah," Carpenter responded. "I said that, too."

"They also found a document here at the house with your name and Pen's name."

"I know what it is," he said curtly. "Is your question answered?"

For Harv, the questions hadn't been answered at all. Not in the least.

SEVENTEEN

Curiosity

Detective Eric Berube of the New Hampshire State Police completely immersed himself in the Ken Carpenter investigation. Berube was still a greenhorn. NHSP was his first job in law enforcement. He'd been hired in December 2002 and had been made a detective in February 2005. His first call as a detective was a noisy dog complaint. His second call was a neighbor complaint. His third was the Pen Meyer case.

As a uniformed road trooper, Berube caught the attention of Sergeant Lamson by single-handedly solving an unusual case. On the night of July Fourth, 2004, a stray bullet fell from the sky and through the roof of a camper, nearly striking a sleeping child in the head. The camper was parked in the middle of Sullivan County's deepest woods and the 39mm round likely came from an AK-47, meaning it could have been fired in the air anywhere in a five-mile radius. *Gunshots in the woods on the Fourth of July?* the other troopers at the barracks snickered. They laughed at Berube's bad luck catching the call, universally declaring the case unsolvable.

On July fifth, Trooper Berube began knocking on doors, leapfrogging a dozen houses at a time. He fanned northeast from ground zero, asking residents if they'd heard anything that didn't sound exactly like fireworks the previous night. The answers changed from "no" to "maybe" to eventually "I saw three yahoos shooting automatic rifles in the air on top of Aaron's Ledge." A little more legwork and Berube found the three guys who—unaware of what had become of their stray rounds—readily admitted to the trooper they were shooting off AKs on Independence Day. The men were charged with reckless conduct, and Berube had guaranteed himself a spot in the Troop C detective bureau as soon as one opened up.

Even with the few bones they had, Detective Berube thought there was enough evidence to put Carpenter away for a million years, but his mentor, Sergeant Lamson, kept insisting there was never enough evidence to get in a case like this.

Lamson had Berube dig into the "anonymous" phone call that led them to the Goshen Country Store pay phone. The facts were that Carpenter had been seen at the store (and was videotaped) at around 4:00 p.m. The call came into the police station at 4:51 p.m. Other than Detective Skahan's swearing the voice on the phone was

Carpenter's, Berube was charged with finding another way to prove it had been Carpenter who'd made the call.

Berube examined the phone records provided to state police by Verizon. It showed that the mysterious incoming call was placed at a pay phone on Glidden Street in Claremont, New Hampshire, about twenty-two miles away from the pay phone where the safe-deposit key was found. A call placed at that distance, from outside the local exchange, would have been considered "in-state long distance." It couldn't be paid for with a quarter. The phone records showed the call was paid for with a prepaid calling card.

"Could he tape the key to the pay phone in Goshen," Lamson asked Berube, "and still have enough time to drive to Claremont and make the call?"

Using a timer, Berube drove his police cruiser from the Goshen Country Store to the Claremont pay phone. He took Route 10, the most direct path, and kept his speed at only five miles over the limit, in order to emulate most civilian driving habits. The detective made the trip in twenty-four minutes. He tried a different route on the way back and had the same result. There had been about fifty minutes between the Carpenter sighting in Goshen and the call, so they had proved their suspect had the time to do it.

Detective Berube went back to the personal items that were seized from Carpenter when he was arrested. In his wallet was an AT&T prepaid phone card from Walmart. When he ran the number, he found that it matched the number of the card that paid for the anonymous call.

* * *

Berube drove to the Sullivan County House of Corrections to get a swab of DNA from Carpenter. The corrections officers placed the prisoner in an entry room. Berube showed Carpenter his badge and handed him a copy of the subpoena for his DNA.

"When are you guys going to release my truck and my car?"

Berube told him he wasn't authorized to discuss the investigation with him. Carpenter became angry, telling him there was no need to keep his vehicles. The detective recommended he instead read the subpoena, which he did.

"What does my DNA have to do with anything?"

"Again, I'm not authorized to discuss the case with you, sir."

"I'd like to call my attorney."

Berube patiently told him that the law did not require presence or advice of counsel, and failing to comply was punishable by law. Carpenter wanted to know what the punishment was, but the detective said he was not in a position to answer that.

Carpenter agreed to submit, and opened his mouth while Berube ran four oral swabs across his cheeks. As the corrections officer was leading him away, Carpenter stopped and asked, "When this is all over, are you going to apologize to me?"

Berube looked at him queerly. "Do you mean me, personally?"

"That's what I mean."

"No sir," he said.

"Oh," Carpenter mugged. "'Cause that's not your job." Then he called Detective Berube an asshole.

Much of the evidence collected on Quimby Farm Road in Lempster was sent to the state crime lab in Concord for analysis. Other items were delivered to the Major Crimes Unit. A box of notebooks and journals was sent back to Troop C for Detective Berube to photocopy and review (no particular reason was ever given for why this job fell back on Troop C; it's possible no one in Major Crimes wanted to do it themselves).

The process of photocopying each page of Carpenter's recovered writings took three days. Berube read each page, looking for further insight into Carpenter's thinking and motivation. The one thing that he came away with was the sense that Carpenter had spent days and days devising his plan for Pen's sudden, forced change of mind.

"Never will you find someone so caring and loving," Carpenter wrote in his notebook as his Pen persona. "I wanted him to love me like that."

The writings then turned again to something more sinister. Berube attached a yellow adhesive flag to certain passages so Lamson could flip to them. At times, Carpenter seemed to be troubleshooting the shortcomings of his plan. "Big fire outside stove . . . Where did she go? Travel, visit someone sick, just disappeared."

Next in the notebook were more scripts for Pen to read to Sandy. It was as if Carpenter was continuing to audition each of the lines, trying to find the most effective arguments with which Pen could convince Sandy to drop the charges and get back together with him. Mixed in the stream-of-conscienceness rambling were further plans to commit the crime and cover his tracks.

"In and out and simple," it read. "Prior to leaving, tell friends don't worry, I need time away." The plan called for obtaining addresses of Pen's friends and sending cards. Carpenter also sketched out the logistics for opening bank accounts to pay Pen's mortgage, bills, and taxes. He made special note to "keep JP away," a reference to Pen's boyfriend, Jonathan Purick, who would surely push him for answers.

As spring 2005 rolled along, the pressure was on the investigators to find more evidence against Carpenter. The Medical Examiner's Office still would not issue a certificate pronouncing Pen Meyer dead. After the probable cause hearing, the next step for Delker and Wilson was to bring the case to a grand jury, and no one on the team knew if they had enough to get an indictment. The grand jury met just once a month, and the state was willing to wait as many months as it could before the defense pressed the issue. At some point the public defender would bring a motion: *Indict or release.*

Berube got a message from the watch captain at the Sullivan House of Corrections. As a matter of routine, the jail recorded all the outgoing telephone calls of prisoners, and Ken Carpenter was no exception. The captain heard something in one of Carpenter's calls and thought the detectives might want to monitor his communications with family and friends. Berube agreed and filled out the paperwork to get copies of those recordings. They were sent to him on compact discs, which he listened to whenever he had the opportunity.

One thing that became abundantly clear from listening to the calls was Carpenter's insincerity when it came to matters of religion. When he was on the phone with Harv, he told her about how hard he was praying and how frequently he was reading his Bible. He would evangelize about God and His plan for the two of them. He told his wife that his arrest was God's test for them, and that was the reason they should stay together and see this through.

When Berube heard Carpenter speak to other friends or relatives, however, he joked about how he was using Harv's faith as a leash to stay tethered to her. He was certain that by dropping the right buzzwords—just like he had for twenty years in AA—he could control her indefinitely.

One call in particular caught Berube's attention. Carpenter had placed a collect call to his son, Michael. It was the first call he'd made to his son and there was no record of Michael Carpenter visiting the House of Corrections.

Michael Carpenter was a day laborer living in Massachusetts, the child Ken Carpenter had had with his first wife. He was close to Ken's mother, his grandmother, but didn't hear from his father much. Over the winter, Michael had made plans to fly to Hollywood, Florida, in March to visit his grandmother. Out of the blue, he'd gotten a call from his father from the woods of New Hampshire. On the phone he'd told his son about his deteriorating marriage and his girlfriend on the side. They made plans to meet for lunch at the airport before Michael's flight.

The first week of March, just before he was about to leave for Florida, Michael was working out on a treadmill in the local gym, watching the Boston TV news. He watched his father being hauled into a New Hampshire courtroom to be arraigned for murder. He figured the lunch wasn't going to happen.

When his father finally called him in the spring, Michael agreed to accept the $3.59 charge for the first minute and 59 cents for each one thereafter. Carpenter's mood was joyous at hearing his son's voice.

"I'm sorry for the way things are right now," Carpenter said. "I'm still gonna write to you once in a while here, okay?"

"Okay." Most of Michael's answers were monosyllabic.

"Let me just jump to this, okay? Now, everything I say up here is recorded."

"Um-hm," said his son.

"Now, where did the blankets and stuff originate?"

"I want to say a couple days after I got back from Florida, Uncle Dale dropped off a bunch of paintings that were wrapped up in them."

"They were already wrapped up?"

"Yeah, stuff was in the blankets."

Detective Berube, listening to this call days later, wondered why Carpenter was interested in some blankets.

"Okay, now don't say what it is," Carpenter cautioned his son, "but there was something about the size of a computer there."

"Ah, okay."

"Okay. Now they didn't ask about it, right?"

"No."

"Okay. Now this is, careful with this, all right?"

"Okay," Michael said.

"There is no disc in that thing, is there."

"I don't know . . ."

"No," he said firmly. "There *is* no disc in that thing right now, is there."

"No, there's not," the son responded obediently.

They then talked about Michael's trip to see his grandmother and Carpenter turned that conversation into another thinly coded message.

"Pa taught me a long, long time ago, whenever I'm asked by the police, you can't lie."

"Yup."

"There's always 'yes sir,' there's 'no sir,' and there's 'I don't recall.'"

"Um-hm."

"Okay? And Pa was big on 'I don't recall' because he told me to respect them and answer their questions," Carpenter prodded. "But 'I don't recall' is a really good answer."

* * *

Berube called Michael Carpenter and found the young man to be very thoughtful. He said he was glad a police officer had reached out to him, because he'd had a conversation with his father that had concerned him. Berube offered to come right over.

Michael greeted the detective warmly at his two-bedroom condo in Dracut, Massachusetts. They sat at his table, and Berube could sense the son's anguish about the situation. He told the detective that his father had seemed really concerned about some blankets that were at his Uncle Dale's house. Michael also said his father kept referencing something, but he didn't want him to mention it on the recorded call.

"What was it?"

Michael led the detective into the other room and showed him what the mystery was about. It wasn't a computer per se. It was a Brother word processor. The machine had a detachable keyboard and a box-shaped CPU that accepted typing paper in a toaster slot in the top.

"When my dad started asking about this word processor, I started checking out the files saved on the disc," Michael said. "But I thought something here might be considered evidence, so I thought better of it."

Michael pushed a button and a 3.5-inch floppy disc popped from the machine. Berube asked if he'd added or deleted anything to the files and Michael said he hadn't. The detective asked if he could take the word processor with him. The son agreed readily, as if he were expunging something dirty from his home.

Detective Berube drove to the home of Ken Carpenter's brother, Dale. He was greeted stoically, but not reluctantly, by Dale and his wife, Betty Ann. Dale Carpenter had nothing but sympathy for the family of Pen Meyer. Berube thought his deportment was very much like his nephew's: They couldn't deny Ken Carpenter was family, but some moral callings are thicker than blood.

Dale said, at Harv's insistence, that he'd retrieved Ken's personal items from the Lempster home and given them to Michael. The possessions were a hodgepodge of belongings that were uninteresting to both Harv and investigators, such as the antiquated word processor. There were boxes of clothes and shoes and a couple of art prints that had been wrapped in blankets for transport.

"Do you still have these blankets?" Berube asked.

Dale Carpenter nodded and asked Betty Ann to fetch them.

While they were alone, Dale told Berube that the previous year had been difficult for his brother. Carpenter was always behind in his bills and the mortgage. He complained about the state of his relationships and about being depressed, but no matter what encouragement he got from Dale, Carpenter refused to do anything to better his lot.

The brother said he'd received some letters from Ken in prison. The first message was extremely angry.

Carpenter blamed Dale for not coming to get him at the hospital. Discouraged, Dale Carpenter threw the letter away. But the subsequent letters were kinder, more reflective, and he kept those.

"He doesn't say anything incriminating in them," Dale said as he passed the folded papers to Berube, "but you might find them interesting."

The detective scanned the first letter—a single page. After hours and hours of listening to his speech patterns, he could hear Carpenter's voice in the sentences. Berube could also spot Carpenter's manipulation playbook throughout the message, trying to get his brother to consider what a terrible place he was in and that he might actually be innocent.

In the other letters, Carpenter continued to apologize to his brother and urged him to look in on his son and their mother. He joked about being in prison. "Boy is my butt sore (only kidding)," he wrote, then described his cell like it was a swank real estate listing.

"Here you go," said Betty Ann, handing Berube the blankets. "You know, I had a restraining order against Ken at one time."

"Yes, I know," said the detective. A flash of surprise crossed Betty Ann's face. The restraining order paperwork had been the first thing the NH State Police received when they did a records check on Carpenter when Pen went missing. "Do you want to tell me about your relationship with Ken?"

Betty Ann took a seat and began.

*   *   *

Dale and Betty Ann had Ken Carpenter to thank for their marriage. After he dropped out of college, Ken asked his then-girlfriend if she knew anyone who might be interested in his older brother, Dale. She introduced him to a pretty girl named Betty Ann and they set her up with Dale. Their relationship blossomed quickly, just as Ken Carpenter's relationship with his girlfriend fizzled. Dale and Betty Ann were a steady couple and they wed in 1974, but she always thought Ken Carpenter was fixated on her and jealous of her relationship with his brother.

When Carpenter decided to get sober in the early 1980s, his plan was to check himself into rehab. The center was Lowell General Hospital, in the next city over from Chelmsford. It was a chilly winter day and his request was that only Betty Ann take him to be admitted. His sister-in-law agreed, but as soon as they were in the car, Carpenter's personality changed. He became more agitated the closer they got to Lowell. He started yelling at Betty Ann, swearing at her, and calling her names. *He's just like Dr. Jekyll and Mr. Hyde*, she thought.

When they got to the parking lot of Lowell General, Carpenter's cold feet kicked in. He didn't want to get out of the car. Betty Ann got out of the driver's side and walked around to the other door. She was dressed in jeans and a puffy winter jacket. When she opened the passenger's side door, Carpenter reached out and grabbed her by the crotch. As he held on to her crotch with one hand, he tried to pull her down with the other.

"Stop it!" she screamed, then pleaded for help. Betty Ann put her hands on Carpenter's arms, trying to force him to let go of her pubic bone. Carpenter bent forward and bit her on the arm. She screamed again. The bite was so strong it punctured the skin beneath her down coat. Betty Ann raised both hands and brought them down on Carpenter's head again and again until he let her go.

After Carpenter was subdued by security, Betty Ann begged the hospital staff to take him away. They said that since he'd changed his mind about going to rehab, they couldn't involuntarily admit him.

"You have to take him back," they told her.

"I will not." Instead, she opted for the Lowell Police to arrest him.

Now sober, Ken Carpenter took over the role as assistant manager at his parents' drive-in in Chelmsford. That lasted until the mid-1980s, when his parents sold the land to condo developers in a quick payday. Carpenter started his own business, a road-striping operation aptly named Zebra Paving. Landlords and vendors found him unremarkable. He paid all his bills on time, never caused any problems. When the business fell on hard times, he dutifully closed up shop and started plowing snow for a living.

Dale and Betty Ann were living with their children at

the home of the family patriarch, Alfred Carpenter. Betty Ann worked at the University of Lowell. The relationship between Betty and Ken was strained, but civil. Things continued that way until around 1992, when the elder Carpenter became gravely ill and had to be hospitalized.

One evening, when the rest of the family was at Lowell General visiting Fred Carpenter, and Betty Ann was home with the children, the phone rang in the kitchen. It was Ken Carpenter.

"What's up?" The words were angry and rude.

Betty Ann didn't know what might have put him in that mood. "I'm sorry. What do you mean?"

"What do I mean?" he exploded into the receiver. "Just who do you think you are anyway? You got some nerve . . ."

Carpenter's rant continued, but Betty Ann calmly hung up the phone. She then dialed her mother and started telling her about what had just happened.

Ten minutes into the conversation the front door slammed open. Betty Ann swung around to see Ken Carpenter storming up to her.

"Get out of this house right now!" He got up in her face and continued to scream at her. At six feet, he towered over the woman. His yellowish eyes reminded Betty Ann of the attack in the hospital parking lot a decade earlier.

He's completely nuts, she thought.

"Get out, Ken!"

"I'm going to kill you!"

"Ken! Get out!"

Betty Ann retreated behind the kitchen table and kept herself 180° from the intruder. As Carpenter started to move to his right, so did Betty Ann. He stopped and came back to his left. His prey mirrored each of his moves. He tried to overtake her with speed and he ran to the other side of the table, but she had already sprinted to the spot he had just vacated. As he chased her around the table, the children scattered into corners and were all blubbering.

"I'm going to get you," he promised, "and you're not going to know when it's going to happen!"

In the meantime, Betty Ann's mother could hear the entire fracas on the phone. She was screaming into the receiver for Carpenter to leave her daughter alone. On one lap around the table, Betty Ann picked up the phone and told her mother to call the cops just before she hung up the handset.

"This is not the time to do this," Betty Ann said, attempting to distract the coiled beast. "Your father is in the hospital. You should be there with him."

"Get out of this house!" he roared and again flushed her from her spot on the other side of the table. "I am going to get you! Do you understand? *Do you understand?*"

On the next lap around, Betty Ann was able to grab the telephone. She dialed the direct line to her father-in-law's hospital room. Dale answered and she begged him to come straight home.

"Dale's on his way," she said, clutching the back of a

kitchen chair. "You don't want to be here when he gets home."

Carpenter looked at her from the opposing side of the table. He slunk away from the table and slammed the door behind him.

After the incident, Carpenter stalked his sister-in-law. He would rev his engine when he passed the house. He would circle the block where she worked and give her the finger. He left a threatening message for her on her answering machine.

After listening to the message, Dale encouraged Betty Ann to get a restraining order. It compelled Carpenter to keep twenty-five yards away from his sister-in-law and her children. It was in effect for one year. During that time, Carpenter never explicitly violated it, but the intimidation continued. He would drive the streets she used to bring her kids to school and he would point at her as she went by, mouthing the words "I'm gonna get you."

Detective Berube thanked Dale and Betty Ann for their cooperation. It would have been easy for them to stall, to obfuscate. He left their home realizing that—even in the middle of extraordinary circumstances—decent people will always be decent.

EIGHTEEN

Discovery

Harv remained troubled by the whole notion that a murder had occurred on her property. She invited the Monahans and her minister to the home so they could pray over the fire pit. Harv wanted to believe her husband when he said he had nothing to do with the killing. He had given her an alibi—one that he had not yet shared with his attorney—that exonerated him. He told her that he simply had to prove it and he was sure he'd be let out of jail.

"Once I get outta here, I can actually get somethin' done," he told her, meaning he could solve the case.

"That's not your job," Harv scolded.

"I know, but it'd be nice that I could solve it."

"You're not Thomas Magnum," she said, "or Jim Rockford, you know."

The gruesome details of the murder danced in Harv's head when she was alone or things were quiet. They would appear when she was working at the nursing home or watching *CSI*. They cropped up at nursing school, especially when the coursework veered into human anatomy.

"There are two hundred and six bones in the human body," the instructor said. Harv looked up from her notebook and watched the instructor pass around plastic bones. She stared at the medical skeleton suspended at the front of the classroom. Something wasn't right.

Two hundred and six bones, she thought *There's no way there were two hundred and six bones in that fire pit. Even if it had been burning for eight or nine hours. They found fewer than two dozen fragments.*

Harv kept staring at the skeleton. The nursing students had been told it had come from a man in India. A man, yes, but a small man. *Was that man the same size as Pen?*

A tear slid down her cheek as her classmates passed each other ribs and femurs. The instructor started telling stories about serial killers and different bones the police would find at crime scenes. *Does he know?* she wondered. *Is he going to bring up Ken?*

"But if the bones are incinerated enough, the DNA can't be tested."

Harv scribbled this in her notes. "What about carbon dating?" she asked. They could perform that test to see how old the bones were, but not use it as an identification tool, her instructor explained.

Harv wondered what this information meant for her husband, Ken.

On Saturday, June 25, 2005, Harv brought up the issue of the bones while visiting her husband in jail. She knew it was a big deal. The grand jury had already met that month behind closed doors and no indictment against Carpenter had been announced. The law said the state had to indict within ninety days and that deadline had passed. There was still no death certificate. The defense was now seeking a bail hearing, reasoning that if the government could not produce a case against Ken, he should at least be able to get out on bail. Harv thought the drought of bone evidence had to work in his favor.

"This could be the thing that gets you out," she told him.

Harv continued to pester him about the bones. He tried to ignore the questions, but they kept coming up. He asked his wife to be patient for another couple of weeks, just until his bail hearing could happen.

"When I get home, I'll walk you all over our property and tell you all about it."

He talked to her about cleaning things up, but Harv still wasn't satisfied. Carpenter was getting annoyed. He drew a little map of their yard, one which she could not take with her, and asked her to do something for him.

* * *

Harv didn't like doing Carpenter's bidding while he was in jail. There was no question that she had run hot and cold with him—and the police—in the three months since he was arrested. Her faith had been tested, but not like this.

When she got home, Harv considered following the path on the map—she'd stared at it for so long that she'd memorized it. She didn't want to go where it would lead her, but her curiosity eventually got the best of her.

It was early evening and there was still light in the sky, but the long shadows of the trees would darken her land until morning. Harv walked out her front door and followed the path that she'd visualized a dozen times. She walked across the yellowed grass to the edge of the tree line. There was an old elm that had been cut down with a chain saw and was nothing but a smoothed-off stump. The stump was rotten inside; the tree had been dying before it was cut. Harv looked down into the tree that nature had hollowed out and found nothing.

The stump was cradled within inches of another tree, a foe whose roots it had entwined and whose branches it had challenged for sunlight and water. Resting in this spot beside the old stump, Harv saw an uneven mound of black dirt. She drew closer. The dirt on the ground was not bark or sawdust or even dirt at all. Its color had come from flame. It was burned debris.

Along with the twigs and wind-felled branches, there were additional shapes she could make out in the pile. There were several rounded semicircles. Harv picked one up. It had a hard metallic feel between her fingers, but its shine had faded away. It was about the size of a coffee mug's handle. It was a piece of jewelry. She reached for another. This one was wider. It had turned gray and had flecks of rust. She held it up in the fading light. It had once been a bangle.

She reached for another piece. This one felt different in her hand. It was thin and had been broken. It was discolored but contained no rust.

All at once it struck her what it was. The plastic bones in class she refused to touch did not look like this. Those were full and straight and ivory white. This was chipped like an Indian arrowhead. Once she knew what it was, Harv knew what the dozens and dozens of other blue-gray bits were scattered around the stump. It was as if the solution to one of those visual puzzles had revealed itself, and she couldn't un-see it anymore.

Harv collapsed on to the ground by the remains of the elm tree and wept. She had found Pen Meyer.

Cynthia Harvey sobbed in her backyard for ten minutes before walking away from the stump. She went to the phone and called her pastor. *What should I do?* Harv asked him. They prayed together. The pastor told her that God wanted her to do the right thing, so Harv hung up and called the state police barracks in Keene. She asked for Detective Shawn Skahan, one of Troop C's three detectives. Skahan was, like Harv, a religious person and he had prayed with her before, earning her trust. She learned that Skahan was out of town. Harv told the sergeant on duty that she'd found additional evidence in the case and he said he'd send a car over to get it.

The state police sergeant had been curt with her, bordering on rude. Harv hated being talked down to, especially by a police officer. She called her pastor back.

"I'm not doing it," she said. Harv wanted to say they'd treated her like shit, but thought better of it. Again, the pastor calmed her nerves and urged her to see this through.

By 8:30 p.m., a uniformed trooper pulled up Quimby Farm Road and found Harv waiting at the end of her driveway. She stood with a flashlight and led the trooper to the spot north of the house. While they walked, Harv explained how she had pulled some jewelry out of the stump. It wasn't until they were standing over it that she blurted out, "There are also some bone fragments that I found."

The trooper turned around and went back to radio his sergeant. The commanding officer told the trooper to stay put until the detectives could get there.

Detective Sergeant Russell Lamson called Eric Berube at home and told him to meet him at the Carpenter place immediately. They both took just enough time to slip out of their casual weekend clothes to make themselves look professional before going.

Lamson and Berube arrived before 10:00 p.m. and got a debriefing from the trooper who'd been guarding the driveway. Lamson asked Berube to go in the house and get Harv to sign a consent form for the search of her property.

The rookie detective marched up the stairs and found Harv pacing the floor inside. She was highly agitated, and Berube thought he was pressing his luck even being inside the home.

"You don't have to answer my questions," Berube said. "You're not under arrest, and you're not the subject of my investigation." He unfolded the Consent to Search form and passed it to her. As they filled it out, Harv told him that Carpenter had led her to the location of the ashes. She signed the form with an unsteady hand.

Berube huddled up with Lamson. They agreed that in her current state of shock, Harv could revoke consent at any moment. They knew she'd nearly pulled the plug after the other sergeant rubbed her the wrong way. They couldn't wait for a team from Major Crimes to come from Concord. They had to photograph the scene and collect the evidence themselves. And they had to do it fast.

The trooper led Lamson and Berube by flashlight out to the elm stump. Lamson carried with him evidence bags that were in his cruiser. He kneeled down and aimed his light into the ash pile. The bits of jewelry were obvious.

They were all still intact. He visually scanned around the debris and saw many bits of bone. Lamson spotted some flat pieces he knew to be skull bone. He could identify the sutures that fused the cranium together. He knew this was Pen's resting place.

"Start taking pictures," Lamson told Berube before pointing at the house. "Then go talk to her and keep her talking."

There is a moment of tantric relief that follows a discovery like this. The investigators had been looking for Pen since late February, when this tree stump had been buried underneath a foot of snow. Lamson and his team had invested so much energy, so much of themselves, into finding her. The fire pit yielded just a fraction of what they were looking for. It had told them that Pen was dead, but it didn't reveal where she truly was.

Russell Lamson had seen death before. He'd seen all kinds of death. Young and old. Peaceful and violent. Accidental and homicidal. Lamson had had people die in his arms. This was something completely different for him. As he leaned over the stump, illuminated only by two flashlights, he started to collect the bracelets and other jewelry with gloved hands. Then with care that bordered on reverence, Lamson gathered the tiny remains of Pen Meyer. *We're bringing Pen home to her family*, he thought.

Falling back on his training with the Major Crimes Unit, Lamson continued to place the bits of bone in bags, seal them, and write his initials. His gloved finger scratched over a piece of wire. He reached in and gingerly shook it free from the ash. It was part of the frame from a pair of eyeglasses.

After he'd finished taking photographs of the stump, Berube returned to the house to talk to Harv. They sat at the kitchen table. Harv's eyes were red and swollen from crying. Berube took off the suit jacket he had hastily thrown on an hour earlier and placed it on the back of the kitchen chair. He believed a dress suit could sometimes be intimidating to the rural residents of Sullivan County, so talking to them in shirtsleeves helped people open up to him.

"I can't tell you everything, but I can tell you some things," she said.

Through more tears, Harv told Berube that Carpenter had told her he had dragged a burn barrel out of the fire and that it had made drag marks. He brought it to a point about eighty feet from the house and dumped it out. Carpenter told his wife that he remembered seeing what he thought was a bone shaped like a horseshoe in the barrel.

She told Berube that she and her husband had talked about it some more during her jail visit. Carpenter had scoffed at rumors in the press that he had cut up the body because he couldn't stand the sight of blood. Harv told Berube this much was true. Carpenter had washed out of a nursing program because he couldn't stand even the idea of needles. Her husband would flee the bathroom even if there were used tampons in the wastebasket.

Harv then said that the more they spoke about the

burn barrel, the more uncomfortable the visit became. She wasn't going to look at the stump when she came home, but she couldn't help herself. Berube asked if she'd taken anything or added anything to the ash pile. She said she hadn't.

"I'm concerned about my safety now."

"Why is that?" the detective asked.

Harv looked down. "I can't say. It has nothing to do with Ken."

"Mrs. Harvey, if you have a real safety concern, the police should know about it so we can address it properly." She declined to say anything more.

Berube asked about the location of this barrel. Harv said it had been crushed by a skidder, but was still on the property.

"He didn't do this, you know," Harv stated. "I can't tell you why I feel that way."

Berube changed the subject to a different part of his investigation. "Did you happen to give Ken's brother, Dale, any blankets when he came to take Ken's things?"

Harv crossed her arms and looked away. "I don't remember giving any blankets to Dale." Berube had noted that throughout their conversation, Harv had displayed signs of honesty and cooperation. Now her behavior had shifted toward signs of deception.

"You're not making eye contact with me," Berube pointed out.

Harv spun in her chair and stared him in the face. "I'm thinking!" she complained.

"I do have blankets in my possession," the detective said. "I got them from Dale, who said he got them from you."

"There were two blankets," Harv said. "One was white with a dinosaur print. One was blue with flowers. I don't know where they came from but they weren't mine. Maybe they came from the sheds."

Berube got up to leave, taking the suit jacket off the chair and sliding his arms through the sleeves.

"Is there anything else we need to know about?"

Harv sneaked a quick glance at the ceiling and then said, "No."

At 10:28 the next morning, Sunday, June 26, Ken Carpenter called home sounding chipper.

"Hi, babe," he started, sounding like he didn't have a care in the world. His wife, however, was very quiet, very different from how she'd been during her visit the day before.

"What's up?" Her lingering silence disturbed him. "Honey?"

"The police were here last night."

"Why? Honey?"

She held her breath, then the words tumbled out. "They took the stuff from the stump."

"How could they? How could they?" His voice was rising. He kept asking her, "What did you do? What did you do?"

"I called the police."

Carpenter screamed, "Why?"

"I had to."

"Oh, Harv!" He wailed like his soul had been ripped out. "Harv! Harv! No! No, you couldn't've. Tell me this is not happening!"

"You told me about it. You had no right to tell me! Why did you put me in this—"

"Why? Oh, honey! Don't tell me you did this! Please, please, please to my God. Why did you do this?"

"Because it's what God wanted me to do!" she yelled. "I had to!"

"No! No! No! That was Satan on your shoulder," he spat back. "That was Satan fightin' you because I'm getting that much closer to God and it's pissin' him off that he can't get at me!"

"No it wasn't."

"I don't . . . you just . . . I don't believe this." For once the master manipulator was stupefied with nothing to say. "Why didn't you just let it go?! Why didn't you just let it go?! I don't believe this."

Harv stiffened her backbone. "Because God was ready for me to find it."

Carpenter's head was spinning. He told Harv she'd fallen for a trick of the Devil, just like Eve in the Garden of Eden. Then, referencing the following week's bail hearing, he asked, "Why didn't you just let it go until I get home?"

"Why did you even tell me?" Harv asked.

"Because *you* kept pressuring me to do that!"

"Ken, look in the mirror. Don't turn this around on me."

"I can't believe you fuckin' did that! I . . . I . . . I . . . I . . . I can't! I really can't! It's like a death sentence. I can't believe this!"

Harv whimpered this wasn't her fault.

Carpenter put his denial aside to take care of other business on the recorded line. "I'm glad I never admitted that I did anything because I didn't do it! I might've *known* where stuff was . . . but I didn't do it!"

"I told them that. I told them that you told me where to look."

"I'm pretty fucked right now!" he said. "I might as well just shoot myself now. They'll never believe me. They'll never fuckin' believe me!"

"They'll believe me," Harv assured him. "Because I didn't have to call them."

"My life is over. They'll never believe me."

"God will see that justice is done. That's what I've been praying for. This isn't just about you." Then she conspiratorially admonished her husband. "You held back the truth."

"I couldn't," he exclaimed, "because he was going to kill me. I couldn't because he'd come back and kill you."

"Well, that might happen," Harv said. If investigators were puzzled hearing Carpenter describe the existence of a possible accomplice or co-conspirator to this murder, Harv did not seem to be. She seemed to speak knowingly

NOTES ON A KILLING

of Carpenter's story. Whatever he told her, she seemed to believe it.

"That was my ace in the hole, okay?" he said. "That was my ace in the hole."

"I knew the police were going to come back and I didn't want them to find anything on their own. I wanted them to know that this was from you."

"I told you what I told you and you've already given it to them."

"I haven't given them the rest of it," Harv said. "God knows the truth. You have to stand before Him and account for your actions."

Sergeant Russell Lamson called Pen Meyer's children and her sister and asked if they could all meet to discuss some developments in the case. They gathered at the home of a family friend on Thursday, June 30. Justin Campbell was there with his wife, Brandi. Kira Campbell brought her husband, Aaron Dotter. Hayley, the youngest daughter, had returned from the West Coast and was there with her aunt, Jessie Meyer-Eisendrath.

Lamson laid out thirty photographs on the kitchen table. Each one had been numbered. He explained that the pictures were of items recovered during the investigation and he wanted to know if any of them could identify them as belongings of Pen.

The group sat in the living room while one by one they filed into the kitchen to look over the items.

The photo array was mostly of the individual pieces of jewelry recovered from the stump. Each had been set aside, photographed on a white background. Some had been placed alongside rulers for scale or next to markers that indicated they were evidence. The pieces shined no more. They were all battleship gray from the fire. It was as if Pen's spirit had been the thing that powered them, and now that she was gone, the jewelry withered away.

It was a solemn event, as solemn as any identification done in a morgue. Most of them simply pointed to the pieces with which they were familiar. There were several pieces that all of them recognized. There were a couple of bracelets. There was a large bangle cuff with a buffalo on it they all identified. There was a key with a teddy bear key chain.

When it was Kira Campbell's turn, she didn't just point to the photos like so many suspects in a lineup. She examined them all with wistful longing for her mother. They had never had a chance to make up from their quarrel. Now these pictures were her mother's story, and she was among the few who could read it aloud.

"This one," she said, pointing to photo number four, a single earring, "she bought it when we were visiting the Southwest after I graduated from high school, so maybe 1997. She used to wear a lot of smaller jewelry, but her style changed after that trip."

Lamson made a note. Kira pointed to more pieces. "Those came from out West. And that Hopi necklace, too," she said. "Number ten. This bracelet was made by a local artist she absolutely loved, Ron Craven. She loved his stuff. Number nineteen—Ron did that one, too. And twenty-one, she bought that at the League of New Hampshire Craftsmen."

Kira picked up photograph number twelve and looked closely at it. "This necklace," she said, "the one with the silver beads. The inside had been strung with cotton. She couldn't wear it in the shower. It was always an issue."

Lamson nodded his head and watched her channel her mother's spirit.

"I bought her another necklace like this from the same store, but before I gave it to her, I restrung the beads myself with wire. That way she could wear it whenever. She was so pleased that I restrung this one for her, too."

Kira put the photo down and wiped away a brave tear. Of the twenty-seven jewelry pieces displayed, Kira had recognized twenty-three of them. With Pen's body completely obliterated, this was the closest the family would ever get to positively identifying her.

The last three photos in the set weren't of jewelry. They were of the three blankets Dale Carpenter had given to Detective Berube. Kira and Hayley Campbell said maybe, maybe the white one belonged to their mother, but nobody really recognized the bedding.

On July 1, 2005, Sergeant Lamson met with Deputy Medical Examiner Jennie Duval at her office in Concord.

They were sifting through the remains Lamson had recovered from the stump the previous weekend. The amount of bone fragments was impressive, but not conclusive.

"There's a lot more here we have to work with, including a skull, but I don't think we've come close to finding all the remains of the victim." Duval pulled aside some of the bone fragments and held them under the examination light. "I think these might be teeth."

Duval called a local dentist who had training in forensic odontology. There wasn't much call in tiny New Hampshire for a forensic dentist, but the state had used Dr. Ralph Phalen in those rare cases when it was necessary. Phalen came directly to the lab when he understood the nature of the call. Duval provided him with copies of Pen's dental x-rays they had in the case file.

"Are these all the teeth you have recovered?"

"Yes." There were twenty-six teeth and teeth fragments. There were also two man-made crowns.

Phalen took his time, but he was definitive. "These teeth are consistent with Pen Meyer's x-rays," he claimed. "Or should I say, there are no *inconsistencies* which would exclude them from belonging to her."

Duval considered the findings of her colleague and the other new evidence unearthed by the investigators. She sat at her desk and—finally—wrote out a death certificate for Edith Pen Meyer. The cause of death was listed as "homicidal violence."

* * *

Russell Lamson spent the weekend looking at the photos that Detective Berube had taken the night of June 25. In addition to the close-ups of the stump, there were several wide-angle shots of the property. Everything was harshly lit by the flash from the camera and was otherwise black as pitch. He was looking for something specific.

Harv had said something to Berube that was still running around Lamson's brain. She said Carpenter had transported the charred bones from the fire pit to the stump using a metal barrel. She said a skidder had crushed the barrel and that it was still on the property.

In one photo, Lamson thought he could make out a brown rusted barrel, folded in half on itself, stuck among a couple of felled trees on the property. The bottom of the barrel appeared to be blackened, as if it had sat in a fire for some time.

Lamson called up Senior Assistant AG Will Delker. "I'm not making any excuses," he said. "That barrel was on the property in February, but it was under two feet of snow. If there's a chance that he burned Pen's body in that barrel, we should seize it."

Delker agreed. The forensics team could literally scrape the bottom of the barrel in search of biological matter. Delker told Lamson to write up another warrant seeking to search the Lempster property for the barrel. Each warrant had to list all of the known probable facts in the case, and although Lamson could just add the latest information to the tail end of the previous warrant, the document he would be bringing to the judge in this twisting-turning case was more than sixteen pages.

Lamson supervised a team that returned to Harv's home on Sunday, July 3. The sergeant spotted the rusted barrel right away. It was crimped like a crushed Dixie cup. It was a thirty-gallon drum, much smaller than the typical fifty-five-gallon drum used commercially. Inside the barrel he could see sticks and other burned debris.

There was enough room for Lamson to get an arm inside and feel around. He pulled out the wood and rooted around blindly. It was hard to distinguish solely by touch what objects were tinder and which were bone fragments. Then Lamson's fingers discovered something that was neither.

"No shit."

He pulled his arm out of the barrel and held his fingers up to the summer sun. It was only about a half an inch long and looked like a small cigarette butt. On its bottom was stamped REM, short for "Remington." It was a spent shell casing from a .22 bullet, the same caliber as the rifle taken from the shed.

NINETEEN

Phil

Ken Carpenter's pastor came for a jailhouse visit the first week in July. When he arrived, the reverend asked the corrections officers if he could have a "through the glass" meeting with Carpenter.

"Why do you want to meet through the glass?" the commander asked. "You two usually meet face-to-face in the visitor's room."

The pastor said that Carpenter was mad at him because he had talked Harv into calling the police. The staff observed the meeting between the two men at a safe distance. They couldn't hear what was being said, but Carpenter seemed angry and animated.

* * *

Harv felt that by calling the state police about her findings at the stump, she had somehow betrayed her husband. The problem, as she saw it, was that they didn't know the whole story. If the police just knew everything that she knew, then they'd see that Carpenter was innocent.

Harv called Detective Berube and asked him to come back to her home. She wanted to explain more of what she knew. Berube, again in shirtsleeves with his suit coat hanging on the back of the kitchen chair, listened intently.

"A couple of weeks ago I asked Ken to tell me the truth," she began. "His lawyer said not to tell me anything but he told me anyways." Berube began taking notes. "This is what happened the day Pen Meyer died . . ."

Ken Carpenter told his wife that on February 23, 2005, he got up early to go snowshoeing like he usually did. While he was making his way through the open field at the Newport High School, a black SUV pulled alongside him. Carpenter approached the vehicle and the driver rolled down the window. The man in the SUV introduced himself as "Phil." He said he was a friend of Pen Meyer's.

"I understand you're trying to get back together with your old girlfriend," said Phil. Carpenter said this was true. "I can make that happen," the stranger said.

Phil was a white man with a full head of hair, slightly taller than Carpenter. He thought the stranger might have been from New York. Phil told Carpenter all he had to do was bring Pen to his home in Lempster at 3:00 that afternoon and that he would take care of the rest.

Carpenter drove his wife's Escort over to Pen's house. While pulling in front of the home, he met Pen out walking her dog in the fresh snow. He said he struck up a friendly conversation with her. Pen voluntarily got into the car with him. Fluff initially jumped in the Ford, but Pen brought the dog back inside before she left with Carpenter.

The two of them spent the day together. Pen accompanied Carpenter as he drove to Greenfield, Massachusetts, to the Carpenter family farm. They then went to the cemetery where his father was buried, but they couldn't get in because it had yet to be plowed. They stopped for gas. The two of them had pleasant conversation the entire day and talked of a great many things they'd never discussed with each other before. They talked about his emotional problems and the medications he was on.

Carpenter drove back to his home on Quimby Farm Road with Pen riding shotgun. They pulled in at 3:00, and not long after, Phil arrived in his black SUV. Pen greeted Phil as if they knew each other. Carpenter felt as though Phil might be an ex-boyfriend of hers.

"I need to step out for a few minutes," Carpenter told them. "I'm staying at Jim Swan's house and I have to go back to walk his coonhounds." He told Harv he left Pen and Phil in the driveway, and he drove back to Newport to take care of the dogs.

Carpenter returned a short time later. Phil was standing alone burning something by the fire pit.

"Where is Pen?" he asked. Phil refused to answer. "I mean it! Where is Pen?"

"Your problem is solved," he said and began to walk away.

"Wait," Carpenter shouted. "You have to give me an answer."

Phil spun on his heels and faced him. The man leaned over and exposed a handgun in a shoulder holster tucked beneath his winter coat. "I'm sure I can find a barrel big enough for you, too. And for your wife."

Phil told him to keep the fire going and not to let it burn out. The stranger then got back in his black SUV and drove off into the winter dusk.

Harv was uneasy explaining this tale to Berube, but she clearly believed every word of it. She said that since Carpenter's arrest she'd lived in fear that "Phil" would return to do her harm if her husband were to reveal the story. She said that Carpenter's mother and brother had received threatening phone calls. Harv thought the calls might have been from the media, but Carpenter told her they were from Phil.

"Ken thought it was strange that Phil wanted them to meet at his house, but when Pen greeted Phil as a friend—she wasn't frightened—he just assumed everything would be all right." She said Carpenter had admitted to dumping out the barrel to protect his family and that he wanted to get out of jail so he could solve the crime.

After his arrest, Carpenter told Harv to lock the doors and put up NO TRESPASSING signs. He told her never to mention Phil on the phone or in writing. Carpenter himself did use the name "Phil" in two separate letters to her. This so unnerved Harv that she destroyed both letters.

Carpenter also told Harv that the police's story about finding a house key with the remains had to be untrue because Pen told him that she always left her doors unlocked. He told her he had placed a handgun for her on layaway at Walmart and urged her to pick it up. When Harv went to the store, however, no one could find a record of Carpenter purchasing a weapon.

"He told me," Harv said, "that if Phil were to attack him or attack me, that it would prove that he was innocent."

Berube put down his pen and looked sympathetically at the woman before him. "I know that Ken has lied to you since your marriage began." She agreed he had. "Why do you believe him now?"

"Ken has led me to the Lord. My faith has increased as of late." Harv said God spoke to her and told her to remain loyal to her husband, to see him through this. "I don't see any part of his personality that would have caused him to be violent. He's lied to me a lot, but he doesn't lie well. I've always known when he was lying to me—except when he lied about his affairs with other women."

"Is there anything about this entire ordeal that you do not understand?" he asked.

Harv thought a moment and then said it didn't make sense that the property transfer documents they found existed.

"Why would he create a trail back to himself?"

She also didn't understand why Carpenter and Pen would have spent the entire day together if they weren't having an affair or something. He'd always denied he had any romantic interest in Pen, and as he had previously confessed to his extramarital affairs, there wasn't any reason to lie about one more. Harv said she was pretty sure they weren't having an affair, but didn't know why they'd spend all of February 23 driving around together.

On his way out the door, Berube said he was interested in finding Phil and would likely discuss the situation with the public defender. Harv seemed greatly relieved and touched that the police took the Phil story seriously.

The detectives at Troop C actually got a laugh out of the "Phil" story. It was so ridiculous and beyond credibility that it was hard to believe that Ken Carpenter had come up with it. This was the man, after all, who had reverse-engineered his favorite TV police procedurals into virtually erasing a human body. He had sketched out draft after draft of a murder plot in his blue notebook until he got something he thought he could pull off. The story of

Phil sounded less like an alibi and more like an out-of-body projection of his own criminal activities.

They knew the story was good for one thing: stringing along Harv. He still had that power over her, and they were likely to hear references to Phil on recorded phone calls and the like.

The entire tale of Phil was so ham-fisted, it was hard for any of them to imagine it was about to upend the entire criminal case.

The defense lost its hearing on July 13, 2005, to get Ken Carpenter released on bail. Attorney John Newman argued that holding Carpenter for more than 150 days without an indictment posed "serious constitutional issues." What had seemed like such a promising gambit only a month ago went down in flames.

Senior Assistant AG Will Delker countered the public defender's claims that the case against Carpenter was in crisis by recalling Sergeant Lamson to the stand. Just like at the probable cause hearing in March, Lamson walked the court through the evidence they had collected. This time, the investigator was able to present new information about teeth and the bullet casing. And unlike the previous court appearance, this time, the prosecution had a death certificate for their victim in hand.

On August 3, 2005, the very next time the grand jury convened, it indicted Carpenter on one count of first-degree murder. A trial date was scheduled for late 2006.

* * *

Harv continued to attend AA meetings at Millie's Place and the local churches, and to see the same people who'd loved Pen and opposed Carpenter. The program still provided much-needed support for her, even if it did create moments of uncomfortable silence.

During the summer, a new member picked up a white chip and joined the meetings at Millie's. "My name is Phil," he said, "and I'm an alcoholic."

Harv was terrified. The man did not seem threatening in any way and had nothing but typical interactions with her, but she couldn't be sure this wasn't the man who had killed Pen and framed her husband. Carpenter had been so vague with her about what "Phil" looked like, she was seeing him everywhere.

"Have you thought any more about a physical description?" she asked Carpenter on the phone. "Ken, I see this guy at every fucking meeting! It's driving me crazy!"

"I don't think it's him," he said with some measure of confidence. "Why would it be? Why would he even hang around here? I thought he was from New York."

"You said she knew him."

"Yeah, she did. But it doesn't mean that he's not from New York." Carpenter burped into the phone and then excused himself. "They'll never believe me now. They don't have to. They'll just put me away for the crime. They don't need Phil. They'll figure that this is solved and I can stay in jail for thirty years until Phil decides, 'Oh, I'll give them that I did this other crime.'"

"But all your lies make you seem guilty as hell."

"The only lie I have to actually apologize to you for is telling you that I 'picked up,'" he said. "Because I didn't."

Harv was once again stunned. Carpenter had told her when he was arrested that he had fallen off the wagon. "What do you mean you didn't?"

"I never did. I never picked up a drink and I never picked up a drug."

"Why did you tell me you did?"

With shame in his voice, Carpenter said, "I needed to have your sympathy because I'm stuck here."

"You son of a bitch!" Harv thought she had endured the indignity of the wronged wife with some grace. Carpenter's extramarital offenses against her were not works of fantasy. He committed those sins and needed to face them no matter how painful to the two of them. As they were both in Alcoholics Anonymous, there was another covenant they had with each other about sobriety. If he broke that covenant, it was another one of life's difficulties that they had to overcome together. For Carpenter to simply lie that a horrible transgression happened, to hurt her *needlessly*, was an indignity she never thought she'd bear. People are human, so sometimes the truth hurts. There is nothing you can do about reality. So why should a lie hurt so much worse than a hard truth? Because we all have control of our fictions. Until now, Harv had been an indirect victim of Carpenter's actions, the collateral damage of an affair and of a homicide investigation. Now the transgression was squarely against her.

The next day, Harv's phone rang at 12:56 p.m.

The recorded voice began, "You have a collect call from—"

"Honey, please pick up the phone again, please, please . . ."

"An inmate at Sullivan Department of Corrections."

Right from the get-go, the call was tense. Harv remained standoffish while Carpenter circled, tried his best to get his arms around the woman on the outside that he so desperately needed on his side.

"Does it make any difference if I relapsed?"

"Yeah, it does," she said. "I want to know what the truth is."

"Whether I picked up heroin or Jack Daniels or another girl, isn't a drug a drug a drug?"

"You told me that you snorted heroin and crystal meth."

"Okay."

"True or not?"

"True."

Harv was flabbergasted. "Why did you tell me yesterday it was a lie?"

"Because it didn't make any difference."

"Ken, why did you fuck with my head yesterday and tell me you hadn't?"

"All I wanted for you to do was not worry about the shit that I'm going through . . ."

Harv would have none of it. "Oh, no no no no no no. Don't even go there. You are still fucking with my head!"

"Will you just call your shrink," he asked, "so we can just get you to calm down a little?"

Harv threw the phone down on the ground. She gathered herself and picked up the receiver. "This is all a plot to get my money!" she blurted out.

"Honey, I don't want your fuckin' money!"

"Just to let you know, you're not in my will. You know that?"

"I don't care. That's why I signed the divorce papers."

She'd forgotten about that. She'd sent him divorce papers weeks ago, but never filed them. At one point it had looked like her husband was never going to be a free man and that ending the marriage was a sensible thing to do. But then she began to believe that God had a different path for them, in no small part because that was what Ken had told her to believe.

Harv broke down sobbing for the umpteenth time. "If I'm dead before the divorce, then you'd get the money. Well, you can't, because you're not in the will."

"Honey, all I want is for you to be okay."

"I hate you," she said. "It's not going to work this time."

"Honey, take a deep breath."

"You know what, Ken? I wouldn't have been this upset if you hadn't lied to me yesterday about the drugs. You can't talk yourself out of it. You can't talk your way out of it this time."

She was slipping farther way. "Honey, please."

"You just lied about lying. You lied about lying about lying about lying. That's how deep you are, Ken."

"No, I—"

"How could you lie about telling me the truth when you should tell the truth about lying? And you lie about lying and you lie about everything."

Carpenter couldn't suppress her. He was like an octopus flopping one tentacle after another over her, but still the grip was unsure. She kept wriggling away.

"I trusted God because God told me to stay with you," Harv confessed. "Now I don't know what to think." She understood then that Carpenter hadn't turned himself over to God like he said he had, that the whole thing had been a ruse.

Carpenter turned the subject to the man at Millie's Place named Phil, hoping to stoke the fear that had kept her close. He suggested his lawyer or a private investigator should look into this guy to see if he was the man who killed Pen.

"Remember I said the guy was a little bit bigger than me? A little taller than me and weighed a little bit more than I did?"

"What else?"

"I thought the guy was stupid. He wasn't smart enough to think about what he did so I knew he had to be workin' for somebody."

"I'm talking about a *physical* description."

"I don't know if he had sunglasses . . . He had glasses. And he was bald in front. I said he had a hat on."

"No," Harv interrupted. "You said you didn't remember whether he had a hat on. You said he had a full head of hair and that maybe he had a hat on."

"Okay."

"What did his face look like?"

"Oh, he had this scruffy beard."

"You told me he was clean shaven."

"Well, he was clean shaven. *You* told me he had a scruffy beard." Harv just laughed at him.

"You've told me everything the opposite of what you told me before."

Carpenter went through it again. Phil was six-two, about 220 pounds. He had eyeglasses like aviator's glasses. He had a full head of hair, but it could have been a hat. Maybe it was a hairpiece. "I was sitting in my truck. He was sitting in his SUV. I wasn't in his face."

"You told me you were standing outside the car."

"No, I . . ." Carpenter began to stammer. "Well, I . . . honey . . . I don't . . . no . . . wait a minute. Um . . ."

"If this is your fucking alibi, you'd better get your story straight."

Carpenter tripped his way through the rest of his wife's interrogation. He begged her not to cause trouble for the guy named Phil at Millie's and hoped it wasn't the same person.

Harv wondered if the whole thing wasn't just a setup.

Why did he tell me about the stump? If Phil learned there was other evidence and returned to the scene to murder her, didn't it prove Carpenter's claim? What if the murder of Pen was a whole conspiracy between him and Sandy to get Pen's land—and now Carpenter was just covering for his lover? New theories crept into Harv's imagination as quickly as her faith in Ken was leaving it.

"Do you realize," she said, "that you have devastated every single life you have come in contact with? I'm starting to think you're the fucking Antichrist and these are the End Times. Seriously."

TWENTY

Pivot

Few people had more insight into the marriage of Ken Carpenter and Cynthia Harvey than Detective Eric Berube. He had spent more than eighty hours listening to the recorded jailhouse phone conversations of the couple.

A week after his incarceration, Carpenter asked Harv to tell people not to talk badly about him, whether "it's true or not." In one conversation, Harv asked Carpenter if he was going to go down to the jail infirmary and try to make a break. Carpenter quickly admonished her and reminded her that the call was being recorded. Later, Carpenter told his wife that the guard found a plastic bag that he had hidden in his cell; he said he was going to use it to kill himself if things got too bad. Not long after the NHSP seized the burn barrel, Carpenter and Harv had a conversation about living on an island outside the United States, and it sounded more like a plot than a wish.

As the summer wore on, Berube noted that it seemed Harv was going through the motions with Carpenter. She still didn't understand all the actions he'd taken and continued looking for ulterior motivations, something evidenced by her continuing to accept his calls.

Carpenter had also admitted to Harv that he'd placed the anonymous phone call because he was scared the police were getting too close.

"But that doesn't explain the safe-deposit box key," she said. Making the call meant that he had placed the key under the pay phone with the orange duct tape, too.

"It doesn't explain why you went to Pen's house in the first place. If you really look at it, you'll see your deep-down desire was to get back with Sandy and you would do anything to get back with her. So when this person offered you an opportunity to do that and said he would smooth things over with Pen, you jumped at it."

"Okay, but let's ask a legitimate question," he offered. "How could that possibly happen? What kind of magic wand does Pen have?" Carpenter was staking a position that his own motive for the crime didn't make sense.

"It doesn't matter what was real. And it really had nothing to do with Pen." Listening along, Berube thought Harv was doing a decent job of cross-examining the defendant, even if her motivation was to find some sort of personal peace.

"Of course, killing Pen would have absolutely no guarantee that you'd get back with Sandy. If anything, logically, it would make it worse. But in your sick mind, in your addictive mind, what were you thinking?"

Detective Berube made good on his promise to track down "Phil." It wasn't because the state police thought for a moment that Phil existed. They knew the defense would grill them on the stand if they didn't follow up on the lead, trying to show that investigators made a "rush to judgment" about who killed Pen regardless of facts.

Based on this call between Harv and Carpenter, Berube went to Millie's Place and asked the directors if he could talk to the member named Phil. The detective was very transparent about why he wanted to see him, hoping they could get beyond the anonymous part of Alcoholics Anonymous. The directors acted as go-betweens and arranged a meeting between Berube and Phil.

The discussion didn't last long. This Phil was very soft spoken, very willing to answer questions from the detective. Berube made a note that he found him easy to talk to.

"Do you happen to own a black SUV?"

"No," he replied. "I lost my license thirty years ago for drunk driving. I've never had it renewed."

Phil from Millie's was eliminated as a suspect and thanked for his cooperation.

*   *   *

On the afternoon of Wednesday September 13, 2005, Cynthia Harvey walked into the dispatch center of the Troop C barracks and dropped off five pages of documents, all handwritten on lined paper. There was also a small tree branch. She asked that Detective Shawn Skahan receive these.

When Skahan got in the next day, he examined the papers. He was familiar with Carpenter's handwriting—having been one of the detectives who'd viewed his many homicidal diatribes in his notebook. This handwriting, however, was not Ken Carpenter's. At least from what the papers said, the notes had been written by Pen Meyer.

Skahan called Harv to ask her from where these pages had come. She told him they'd been hidden in the attic of her home in Lempster. Although the state police had done a cursory search of the cabin's attic back in February, they obviously missed these papers stuffed behind the fiberglass insulation. Harv said she'd learned about the existence of this evidence during her jailhouse visit on June 25. "I didn't have the courage to check the attic until yesterday."

Harv said Carpenter told her of the letters to prove that Pen had spent the day with him of her own free will. He told her no one would believe him that they were together under innocent circumstances, and had offered up the letters as evidence of just that.

Harv told him that her husband said he and Pen had driven to Greenfield, Massachusetts, and parked in the driveway of his family's home. There, Carpenter claimed he dictated a letter to Pen about his problems, and she freely acted as his recording secretary.

Lamson was eager to share the documents with the Attorney General's Office. Will Delker and Kirsten Wilson pored over the letters with the lead investigator.

The writer declared it to be February twenty-third and an incredible day at that. She said she had spent this time talking truths with Ken Carpenter and her overwhelming wish was for him to heal. "I have freely spent a day together traveling in harmony. God bless you, Ken." The letter was signed, "Pen Meyer."

The handwriting was clearly not Carpenter's. Lamson had copies of Pen's signature from the safe-deposit box card and other documents. He was no expert, but it certainly looked the same.

"We'll contact the FBI about getting a handwriting analysis."

The existence of this letter troubled the team. It did read as if it had been written at the end of the day, not first thing in the morning. Like the phone call to Sandy, it had most certainly been coerced at gunpoint. But why would Carpenter want to get Pen on record saying they spent the day "freely" together? Had his future alibi been that well planned?

Pages two, three, and four were also in Pen's handwriting, but the words were Carpenter's. The narrator declared he had been diagnosed with a borderline personality disorder, and a near-death chain saw accident had helped him appreciate the gift of life. The narrator asked Sandy directly for her forgiveness, attributing his unhealthy ways to the powerlessness of his disorder and long-standing abandonment issues. "Sick as it may seem, the harder you ran away, the more I ran to you."

Underneath this message, on the last line of the page, was one more insert. This one was written in a completely different handwriting. Those who'd seen it before knew it to be Ken Carpenter's. It said:

I need you—I want you—I love you

Right below this insert, a piece of the page had been torn away. This part of the message was also terribly unusual. Carpenter was forcing Pen to help him give Sandy more space?

"He spent some time making her write these letters," Lamson said. "How much? I don't know. But we do know the window of opportunity was only between seven a.m.— when the neighbor saw her on her walk—and nine a.m.— when the painters arrived."

"We know he stopped for gas in Claremont," added Delker. "Is it possible he really took Pen to Greenfield, spent the day with her—under duress or not—and killed her there or someplace else?"

"No!" Wilson insisted. She felt by now she knew Pen and what she would do. "Pen would *not* have left her house with him. Gun or not." Wilson was emphatic.

Wilson couldn't help feeling the terror that Pen Meyer must have felt writing these letters. As much as she had come to know Carpenter and Harv, the prosecutor felt the most affinity for Pen. She was a woman who'd raised her kids on her own terms, was an outspoken advocate for causes she believed in, and had a sense of style all her own. These were traits that the far younger Wilson thought she had in common with the victim. Pen had a talent on the loom and a deep appreciation for art. As an undergraduate, Wilson had studied studio art. There was—as several people had pointed out—a passing physical resemblance between Pen and Wilson. Both had high, defined cheekbones, gray eyes, and a love for the outdoors. The prosecutor had come to admire Pen Meyer tremendously, and felt a posthumous tug for the woman that, had they met in life, she was sure would have blossomed into a deep friendship.

Later that same day, Carpenter called Harv collect from jail. They spent much of the call engaged in small talk, mostly about Harv's sinus infection. After ten minutes or so, she told him she'd retrieved the hidden letters he'd told her about and then turned the letters over to the state police.

"Why?" he asked.

"Because I had to give the letters to them. What am I supposed to do with them?"

"Throw 'em away." It seemed like such an obvious thing to *him*.

"Yeah, okay," she seemed to concede.

"Honey, I . . . I . . . I don't believe it. I really . . ."

"What do you expect, Ken?"

"Why didn't you give him the notebooks?"

"Well, I burned those like you asked me to."

Carpenter let out an exasperated sigh. "You know you're bein' recorded. Don't say things like that."

"It's evidence, Ken."

"If I tell you where the rest of the stuff is?" Carpenter stopped himself. "Never mind," he said.

About a week later, Harv told her husband to stop calling her. She said she needed some time to process all the things he'd told her, and sort through her own feelings of betrayal. She removed her home phone from the list of approved numbers Carpenter could call from jail, and even sent a message to Detective Skahan letting him know that she and her husband were no longer in contact.

Carpenter was largely cut off from the outside now. He could still write letters to Harv, even if they'd go unanswered. At his probable cause hearing in March, he knew that the state police had not found all the evidence he'd hidden. He had hopes his wife would do right by him and dispose of it. Now, six months later, she'd ratted t and given the government more ammunition to

ainst him at trial.

spite this betrayal, Carpenter still knew he needed

. Whatever the reason, love or addiction or other

gns, he was not willing to let her go. He needed a way

bring Harv back into the fold. Carpenter needed to

que her interest and get Harv believing once again that

e was an innocent man.

Carpenter wrote a letter to Dot Monahan's husband, Nicholas. He asked him not to share the information with anyone other than Harv. He wrote that his defense attorney had learned a New York man had been arrested at a casino in Massachusetts during a murder-for-hire sting. During questioning, this suspect told cops he had killed and incinerated a woman from Northern New England.

"His name is <u>PHIL WATERS</u> from New York!!!!!" Carpenter wrote, the capital letters, underscoring, and five exclamation marks all included. Carpenter told Nicholas Monahan that this new information would likely exonerate him—at the very least get him a new bail hearing so he could be released while all the state and federal authorities sorted the case out.

The Monahans turned the letter over to the state police almost immediately. They were familiar with the Phil story, as they'd remained constant confidants for Harv, and didn't think much of the ramblings. They saw the whole tale as a ploy to contact Harv and get her believing that Phil existed, was in custody, and would take the fall for Pen's murder.

Although Carpenter had finally assigned a last name
his imaginary friend—Phil Waters—the part of the lette
the Monahans most felt needed urgent attention wa
found in the next paragraph. They felt it was a plea for help
in an escape plot. Carpenter asked Nicholas to get his Star
Yamaha motorcycle gassed up and leave him a rain suit
and a full face helmet for the middle of next week.

The first week in October 2005, Dot Monahan's phone
rang. When she answered, she heard a recording asking
her to accept a collect call from the jail in Sullivan County.
She accepted the call, but told Carpenter she was expecting company and couldn't talk long.

"Um, I got your letter yesterday," she said. "So anything new you want to share or no?"

"No. That's all set, though, right?"

Dot was puzzled. "What's all set?"

"As far as 'Star'?"

"If I get your meaning," she said carefully, "I don't
think that's a good idea."

Carpenter pressed Dot on what Harv's reaction was to
the new developments, but she didn't have an answer. He
expressed shock that even after a two-week break, she
didn't want to talk to him.

Later that month, Harv finally allowed Carpenter to call
her from jail. Before long he brought up the idea that Phil
Waters was in custody in Massachusetts.

"I thought that maybe it would be in the paper," said

Harv. "I mean, when they arrest somebody at a casino, wouldn't that be in the paper?"

"He wasn't robbing the casino. He was having an argument with somebody."

"Which one?"

"Um, I don't know. Mohegan Sun?"

"No. Mohegan Sun is in Connecticut."

"What's the other down there? Foxwoods?"

Both Mohegan Sun and Foxwoods were in Connecticut. There were no casinos, on an American Indian reservation or otherwise, in Massachusetts.

"How do you know this?" she probed.

"I got it from John."

Detective Eric Berube was called upon to look for "Phil" again, this time armed with the casino arrest story.

Berube checked with the state police in Massachusetts and Connecticut and security at both Foxwoods and Mohegan Sun asking about an arrest of a Phil Waters. He called the FBI, the CIA, the Postal Inspector, Homeland Security, the Secret Service, and every federal agency he could think of to see if any of them had a case that sounded remotely like Carpenter's story. No one had any investigations on file regarding a Phil Waters.

Berube did a criminal records search for "Phil Waters." He did find a man with a past criminal history named Phil Waters living in Massachusetts. Berube asked the Mass State Police to accompany him to Mr. Waters's house. When the authorities arrived, they were greeted at the door by a six-foot-seven black man. He had a shaved head and was built like a professional basketball player. This Phil Waters had gotten into some scrapes as a teen, but was now living a life as law-abiding as the next guy. Berube officially ruled him out as a suspect.

The detectives of Troop C sat spinning in their chairs, wondering exactly how they could make hay out of their suspect's tall tale.

"Why invent a phony alibi if you're innocent?" Sergeant Lamson asked rhetorically.

"Because you're not innocent," Berube answered. "We already know that."

"He makes up the lie because he has a guilty conscience," Skahan offered. "And in New Hampshire, evidence of a guilty conscience can be admitted as evidence against the defendant."

Lamson drummed his fingers on his desk. *How do we prove the Phil story is a product of a guilty conscience?* "When Harv asked, who did he say told him about Phil's arrest?"

Berube picked up the typed transcript. "'I got it from John,'" he read. "His attorney."

The idea was straightforward, but would be complicated to execute. It wasn't enough simply to argue, "The facts

of the case show the Phil Waters story could not be true."
Alibis and alternative theories of crimes are what criminal
defense is all about. One cannot simply say that an alternative theory—even if disproved at trial—is a de facto lie
meant to ease a guilt-ridden defendant's mind.

In both the letter to Nicholas Monahan and the phone
call to Harv, Carpenter had given them something
they could use. How could jail inmate Ken Carpenter
have learned the elaborate details of Phil Waters being
arrested in an Indian casino in another state? Over and
over again, he claimed he'd heard it from his attorney,
John Newman. If Newman didn't provide the story to
his client, they could prove beyond a reasonable doubt
that the whole thing was a lie born of Carpenter's twisted
imagination.

This legal tactic was fraught with potential difficulties.
There was not one, but two sets of privileges the state
would have to bushwhack through. They felt pretty good
about getting around the spousal privilege. Both husband
and wife knew their phone calls were being recorded by
the county jail; they really could not argue any expecta-
tion of privacy.

The attorney-client privilege was a much harder one
to punch through. It was one of the most revered tenants
of the American legal system, but the privilege was not
absolute. Will Delker and Kirsten Wilson drafted a narrowly defined motion to subpoena John Newman's testimony regarding the Phil Waters story.

* * *

The passing months did not heal the heart of Pen's boy-friend, Jonathan Purick. He found himself feeling more alone than he had ever felt before. He envisioned himself on an island with the waters rising all around him. On one side was the tide of anger; the other was the tide of despair. If he dipped a toe in the water, he'd quickly find himself up to his chest in its currents. He clawed his way back on to the island and stranded himself there.

"I could see it coming," he'd tell friends. In hindsight, the fatal trajectories of Pen and Carpenter were easy to track. There were reactions and interactions he replayed in his head. The night Carpenter showed up in her drive-way, Jonathan should have known. A good pickpocket will have someone else bump into his victim, gauge the reaction before attempting to swipe the wallet. Jonathan was sure that was Carpenter's bump.

In the days immediately after Pen's death, Jonathan called the phone company to change his number. He asked for hers. The employee said he'd have to wait three months after it was disconnected to apply for it. Jonathan circled the date on his calendar and called back three months later and got it.

He got a new vanity license plate for his truck. Some thought PENSCOB was some sort of variation on "Penob-scot," the county and river in Maine named after the Native American tribe. Few recognized it as his love note: *Pen's cob*.

Before the murder, Jonathan had been planning on moving to Goshen to be with Pen. A small home on the opposite end of Center Road went on the market and Jonathan scooped it up. He would have loved to have purchased Pen's waterfront home on Center Road, but the asking price was not something he could afford. He was sure that Pen's family wouldn't sell him the property anyway.

As a mourner, he still felt like an outsider. Pen's famously private family didn't share condolences with him. He felt like they saw him as an interloper and expected him to go away, to abdicate his right to publicly grieve the woman he loved. Jonathan respected Pen's children, respected the family's right to grieve in whatever manner they chose, but he didn't understand them. He didn't know why they insisted on keeping the details of Pen's life secret from the press, discouraging even the police and prosecutors from praising the legacy of the most remarkable woman he'd ever known. He couldn't fathom why they would say that Pen's life in Alcoholics Anonymous was more of a social commitment for her, that she didn't really seem to have a drinking problem and was actually drawn to AA because of her desire to help people. Were they that deep in denial? Were they that out of touch with the woman Pen had become? Jonathan didn't know.

On January 20, 2006, almost a year after the death of Pen Meyer, Detective Skahan received a letter in the mail from Harv. She wrote to say there were two black toolboxes at the end of her driveway. Inside were some keys wrapped in duct tape that she wanted the police to pick up.

Skahan drove to Quimby Farm Road once again, asked Harv to sign a search form, and took the keys from the toolbox. He unwrapped the tape and examined the key. It said GERRISH on it, the name of a local Honda dealership. Also wrapped with it was an AA medallion. Skahan noticed there were fibers of pink cellulose insulation stuck to the adhesive side of the tape.

"How did you discover this?"

"Ken told me where to find it." She made it sound as if it were a recent conversation, but she was vague. They'd later hear a recording of a conversation that took place in early December.

"Were the keys in this toolbox all along?"

"Do I have to answer that?" Harv posed.

"No."

She refused to answer any more questions. Skahan left with the evidence.

What Harv had left out was that inside the toolboxes had been more notebooks written by Carpenter, and that she'd burned them in the woodstove at her husband's direction. He still had control over her.

Attorney John Newman was not pleased that the State planned to depose him and call him as a witness against his own client. The Office of NH Public Defender prepared to fight any subpoena vigorously. The AG's motion was narrowly drawn, focusing only on three questions regarding Phil, and wasn't an all-out fishing expedition. While unorthodox, legal observers thought the motion had a better than 50 percent chance of being upheld.

Newman had been prepping for more than a year for the Carpenter trial. In June 2006, he was forced to withdraw from the case. He certainly could not represent Carpenter and testify for the prosecution. Not only was he out, but the whole Public Defender's Office was out.

This left defendant Ken Carpenter without a lawyer, and Judge David Sullivan was faced with the tough task of getting him one. In the decades before *Miranda* and the national public defenders movement, the indigent defendant would receive representation from lawyers chosen at random by judges. No one wanted to be defended by a tax attorney when they were facing a capital crime, but it happened fairly frequently. Carpenter was going to get a pig in a poke for the biggest trial Sullivan County had seen in many years.

At a pretrial hearing, Judge Sullivan turned to the members of the Bar assembled in his courtroom awaiting their own hearings. He asked an unusual question to those assembled: Were there any qualified attorneys who would be willing to represent Kenneth Carpenter and get paid the public defender rate for their work?

One man stood up immediately and waved his hand at the judge. He was short and stocky, dressed in an ill-fitting suit. His thin, curly hair was long and tied in a ponytail that hung limply down his back. The ponytail did nothing to disguise the fact that he was nearly bald on top.

"I'll take the case, your honor."

The defendant didn't know who this man was, but everyone else in the courtroom did. By sheer luck and good timing, Kenneth Carpenter had just retained the state's preeminent criminal defense attorney.

PART FOUR

Ruin

Those who are kind benefit themselves, but the cruel bring ruin on themselves.

—PROVERBS 11:17

TWENTY-ONE

Forensics

The disciplines of modern police forensic work are so varied that no one technician can be proficient in them all. In larger labs, one person might do nothing but analyze impressions of tire tracks. In New Hampshire's small lab, however, the staff is routinely cross-trained in multiple disciplines.

Criminalist Marc Dupre was one of the supervisors at the lab and a jack of many trades. Dupre was considered an expert in firearms, tool marks, fingerprints, serial number restoration, and glass analysis (determining evidence from shatter patterns or chemically matching broken shards from a crime scene to a suspect's clothing).

Dupre was given the Marlin 60SB rifle that was recovered from the shed on Carpenter's property. The first thing he noticed was that the bore of the .22 had a sooty residue on the inside. The rifle had been fired since its last cleaning, but he couldn't tell when that might have been.

Dupre shot the rifle in a test fire tank and the weapon worked just fine. Then he examined the spent cartridges to study what marks were left by the rifle's firing pin. The Marlin made a rectangular indentation on the rim of the cartridge case. He placed one of those .22s under a comparison microscope with the .22 casing that Lamson had pulled from the burn barrel on Carpenter's property.

The markings were similar, but Dupre couldn't find very many individual characteristics from the firing pin. There wasn't anything on the .22 from the barrel that indicated it was fired by a different weapon, but there wasn't enough to say it had definitively come from Carpenter's.

New Hampshire State Police Criminalist Stephen Ostrowski was asked to look for fingerprints on documents recovered by investigators, including the property transfer documents. One such document had been found in a box in Carpenter's closet; the other had been sent to Sandy Merritt in the mail.

Ostrowski dipped the pieces of paper in a solution called an anhydrate. The solution would react with the amino acids in human sweat left by fingerprints. After this process, all the technician would need to do was apply heat (in the form of a simple house iron) and the fingerprint patterns on the document would turn purple.

There were two sets of fingerprint cards taken of Ken Carpenter—one set after his stalking arrest and a full set of impressions that included palm prints after being charged with murder. Ostrowski would have no trouble doing a comparison. There were no known sets of fingerprints from Pen Meyer, however. She had never been arrested, joined the military, or taken part in any profession where getting printed was a requirement. Technicians could not use any of the common objects in her home because there was no way to know who had left those impressions. Even if the same print turned up a million times in her home, her car, her safe-deposit box, it wouldn't stand up to legal scrutiny.

Ostrowski took a look at the document found in Carpenter's home, the contract that was blank except for the signatures. There were two prints on the front. Both of them were about two-thirds of the way down the page on the right-hand side. He pegged one of them as being Ken Carpenter's right thumb. The other was also a right thumb left by someone for whom they had no sets of prints. Given the location of the fingerprints, it was consistent with someone holding a piece of paper and passing it to someone else.

There was another round mark at the bottom of the paper. It had been made by a drop of fluid. The team had no way of testing it, but they had a theory based on its size and the splash pattern that it was likely a teardrop.

Ostrowski looked at the contract sent to Sandy through the mail and the envelope it came in. There were no usable prints on those documents. The fingerprints and shoe impressions found inside Pen's house were either unsuitable or excluded Carpenter.

He also determined the bloodstain found in Pen's bathroom had likely come from a shaving nick.

Criminalist Ostrowski also examined the sections of orange duct tape collected to see if they could be matched to one another. There were three specimens to work with: The piece used to tape the plastic bag with the safe-deposit key to the pay phone, the piece on Carpenter's truck seat, and the roll found in Carpenter's truck.

Ostrowski cut a fresh piece off the roll for comparison. The three pieces all looked like they came from the same brand of tape. The color on both sides was the same. The thickness was the same. They all had a pattern of forty-four fibers.

The technician used a stereo microscope to examine the torn end from the section he removed from the roll. Judging by the ridges and valleys along the random tear, two of the ends matched up. The piece found at the pay phone had, in fact, been the last piece ripped off that roll.

Ostrowski then looked at the other ragged end of that piece of tape. Under the microscope, the other side was a perfect fit for the piece that had been found on the seat of Carpenter's Nissan. In other words, all three pieces had once been part of the same long roll of tape.

*   *   *

Senior Criminalist Timothy Alan Jackson had been an examiner for sixteen years. Much of his time had been spent dealing with latent fingerprints and footwear. He also had a more obscure competency: the area of fabric impressions. Jackson was proficient in studying markings and residue left behind by gloves and other items.

The orange duct tape and Ziploc bag found at the pay phone did not have any fingerprints on them, but the forensic team thought there might be a glove impression there. Jackson put the evidence in a chamber and heated up some superglue. The fumes from the glue stuck to the moisture and contaminates left behind by the glove. Next, he added a stain to make the print fluoresce under colored light. He also used the oldest technique in crime scene processing: brushing the surface with black powder.

On the bag, there was a squared impression right where the Ziploc logo was imprinted. It looked like the mark was left when the bag was zipped closed. Jackson also found squared fabric impressions at either end of the duct tape, likely left by someone holding the length of tape with two hands. The impressions were made by the same glove.

The troopers that scoured the Carpenter residence in Lempster and Jim Swan's guest room in Newport collected seventeen pairs of gloves. Some were winter gloves or work gloves. There were some that were still attached at the cuff with a manufacturer's tag. Some were singles without a match.

Jackson created overlays of all the gloves. He put some powder on the fingertips and rolled them on some clear acetate. Jackson then laid the acetate over a scale photograph of the fiber impressions collected. After comparing markings from all the gloves, all the pairs were eliminated except one. It was a pair of Gates brand gloves with a green camouflage pattern. They had little nubs on the fingertips that matched the square indentations perfectly.

The small tree branch that Harv gave to state police when she turned over the memos written by Pen turned out to have no evidentiary value whatsoever. Investigators were at a loss as to why she brought the branch in, other than the fact that it had been in the attic with the papers.

Sergeant Lamson contacted the sales department at the car dealership where Pen's CR-V had been sold after her death. The investigator tracked down the new owner and asked if he could inspect the vehicle.

Lamson brought with him the key that Harv allegedly discovered wrapped in duct tape in a toolbox. He wanted to try it in the ignition. The new owner brought Lamson into his garage and opened the Honda's door.

"Wait a minute," the guy said. "Was somebody killed in my car?"

Lamson felt for the guy. "I can't tell you that." No one really knew *where* Pen had been killed.

The key slid into the ignition lock and started the engine. It was Pen's.

The job of analyzing the soil samples from the fire pit went to Criminalist Linda Bouchard. One of her specialties was ignitable liquids. She was given cans that were three-quarters of the way filled with dirt from under the pit. To find out if there were any molecules of ignitable liquid trapped in the debris, Bouchard heated the can up in an oven. She then added an activated charcoal strip to capture the released molecules.

She used ethyl ether as a solvent on the charcoal strip, then placed the sample in a mass spectrometer. Bouchard discovered that in the soil had been a mixture of gasoline and a liquid containing a naphthenic-paraffinic product. This other fluid could have been lamp fuel or insecticide. It also could have been the lighter fluid recovered from Carpenter's shed.

Bouchard was later given the Brother word processor to examine. The device contained a ribbon encased in a plastic cartridge. Unlike typewriter ribbons of the past, this ribbon was not made with cloth that could be used over and over. This ribbon was a thin strip of clear plastic tape with ink on the outer edge. When a key was struck, it left a clean mark on the tape almost like a punch-out. It was a single-use ribbon; the word processor so perfectly applied the letter, there wasn't any ink left on the ribbon to type again.

Bouchard began to unspool the ribbon from the cartridge. It spooled from right to left, and when she freed the ribbon, she could see letters pressed out. It was hard to read as everything was reappearing backward. Bouchard began to lay the strips out, bottom to top, right to left, on a clean piece of acetate. The document began to take shape.

.s'yugevolI.S.P(desolcnekcehc)(god)ffulfekattsuM

Bouchard rolled out several more strips of ribbon on to the acetate, the static electricity in the air causing the ribbon to curl up around her latex gloves. She pasted down several more lines of backward letters before noticing a string of 37 periods, a name, then a string of 38 periods.

When she had filled her whole sheet of acetate, she flipped it over to read it the correct way.

"Entire"conentsof"Seller's"houseCenterRd.Goshen,N.H. 03752
    Alsoincludedcontentsofgarage(Sameadress) Febuary23,2005
    Musttakefluff(dog)(checkenclosed)P.S.Iloveyouguy's.

The ribbon contained word for word—misspellings included—the contents of the seller's agreement purportedly signed by Pen and Sandy. The document had been typed up on the word processor found among Carpenter's personal belongings.

John Sardone was a forensic document examiner for the FBI. He had spent more than twenty-five years studying handwriting and forgeries for both the Bureau and the New York City Police Department. He was asked by the New Hampshire State Police to look at the signatures on the documents in the Carpenter case.

Sardone was given writing exemplars from Carpenter and Sandy, and several legal documents known to have been signed by Pen. He magnified the writing on the seized documents looking for tremors and hesitations, different pen pressure and drag strokes.

Both the envelope mailed to Sandy and the $400 check were written out and signed by Pen. Sardone found she had a very particular way of signing "Edith," the first name that she used when writing out her signature. The *E* dragged into the *d*, followed by a little tick mark. She used *V*-like movements to make the *i*, *t*, and *h*. It was a pattern repeated over and over in her penmanship.

Sardone concluded that while Pen had addressed the envelope and signed the $400 check, she hadn't signed the property contract contained within. Sardone said her signature on that document—the one that had been filled in by the word processor—was a fake. It looked like someone had traced her name from another paper; indentation marks showed each letter was individually made. Sandy

Merritt's signature as the buyer on that same document was also a forgery.

The blue notebook was given to Sardone, and he determined that its author was Carpenter. This included the letter inside that was signed, "Pen, (the asshole)."

The FBI technician scrutinized the five pages of notes that Harv had found in the attic and turned over to state police. Sardone verified that all of them were written by Pen, with the exception of the "I need you, I want you, I love you" near the bottom of page four. The very bottom of page four had been torn away, but Sardone examined page five (which was otherwise blank). He discovered indentations of what had been written and ripped off from the page above. It read:

Always, Ken (me)

Sardone's professional opinion was a qualified one. He thought it very likely that Ken Carpenter had written those inserts, but it wasn't entirely conclusive.

The New Hampshire State Police Crime Lab had—literally—buckets and buckets of evidence to sift through in the Pen Meyer case. The most important area of the evidence analysis was being farmed out. Marcella Sorg, Ph.D., the forensic anthropologist from the University of Maine, was trying to reconstruct the skeleton with the bone bits recovered from the fire pit and the tree stump.

The task was not a hobby-grade endeavor. There were almost no bones left intact (some of the smaller bones in the hand and the foot were damaged by fire but not by crushing). While they burned on the Lempster property, they had been simultaneously pounded with the end of a stick that was used to stir the entire witch's brew. What was left were hundreds of Chiclet-sized fragments indistinguishable from one another—indistinguishable to someone other than Marcy Sorg.

Sorg had a scientist's eye and a saint's patience. She'd practiced for thirty years as a researcher, lecturer, and consultant to law enforcement. Sorg was one of only sixty or so board-certified forensic anthropologists in the United States and the only one in New England. She'd been consulting with the state of Maine since 1977 and with New Hampshire since 1981. There was nothing semantic about calling Sorg a "forensic expert." She was the real deal.

Sorg was brought into the Pen Meyer case very early on. When Trooper John Encarnacao pulled out the first chunks of bone from the fire pit that snowy night, everyone knew they had to get a photo to Dr. Sorg immediately. NH Deputy Medical Examiner Jennie Duval e-mailed Sorg a picture of what they had. The question in the e-mail was, "Is this human?"

The remains at that point were scant. No one was ruling out that they could have been dealing with a bone from a cow or some other animal. Sorg zoomed in as much as she could on her computer and started looking at the pieces that were there. Some were completely cylindrical; others were bending and tapering before their brittle brakes. Of the dozen or so pieces, Sorg focused on one of the larger ones. It was the knee end of the thighbone. It was a distinctively human piece of anatomy. Based on that, Sorg was able to tell the state police that their debris did contain human remains.

The condition of all the bones was troubling to Sorg. They weren't simply broken down into smaller bits. The great majority were also burned to varying degrees and all colors. Some of the remains were gray like old charcoal. Others were blackened, like tar. Bones were ashy white on one side, but brown and crispy on the other.

Sorg attributed the unusual discoloration to a few things. One was that the fire had burned unevenly. She estimated that temperatures in the fire pit had ranged between 600° and 1,800°, a wide spectrum. It was likely that during the burning process, the fire went out and had to be restarted.

It was clear to Sorg that the bones had been stirred while they burned. At high temperatures the bones would shatter like glass when stirred. This would also account for why some pieces were scorched on one surface but not the other.

Sorg had small sections from the bones in the right forearm—the radius and the ulna. These two bones lie side by side in the arm, and crisscross in an X with a twist of the wrist. While examining these bones, Sorg noticed that the surfaces were burned unevenly. What was interesting about these remains were the surfaces that were burned the most were not those on the outside facing the skin. They were the inner surfaces, the parts of the parallel bones that faced one another in the relative protection of muscle and sinew. In their natural anatomic state, the forearm bones' outer edges would have burned first. To Sorg, it was a sign the bones had been separated and cooked akimbo in the pit.

Sorg also identified a black, shiny sheen on some of the fragments. It created a distinct texture on the bone surface. The term used was "patina." This occurred on bones when an accelerant such as gasoline or lighter fluid was used on the remains. Sorg didn't need to discover patina to guess the suspect had used an accelerant. All the bones reeked of petroleum.

Dr. Sorg would sort the bones the same way when additional remains were sent to her from Lempster. First she would examine each individual fragment to determine whether or not it was a human bone. Some pieces were as small as grains of rice; others were six inches long.

Not everything that was thought to be bone turned out to be so. Sorg couldn't quite place from where in the body the bone recovered from the ashtray in Carpenter's truck had come. Sorg scrutinized it under the microscope for a long time before realizing it wasn't bone at all. It was a small piece of bread that had dried up and looked to the lead investigator like human remains.

Sorg separated the fragments into different sections, trying to group them anatomically. Cranial bones in this pile; bones from the torso there. Then she'd start the process of piecing them together.

Dr. Sorg was not put off by those who would compare her work to someone putting together a jigsaw puzzle. It *was* very much like a puzzle. The average puzzle builder started with the corner pieces and those with a straight edge, and other indications such as colors and patterns that meant two pieces would lock together. Sorg would find those sections of bone with natural edges and butt them together, seeking ridges and patterns that said the pieces belonged to one another. Sorg would spend a year doing this with hundreds of disparate splinters. Her goal was singular: to prove that these remains were Pen Meyer, and that she had been murdered. Sorg was able to tell Sergeant Russell Lamson this much about the remains: They appeared to be those of a short, middle-aged woman.

"Will you be able to explain to a jury how you came to that conclusion?"

Sorg said the bones of a female are often smaller than those of a male. "There is no evidence of muscularity, which often happens with men. The muscle attachments didn't leave any mark. This was a petite person."

"And an adult?"

"Yes. The teeth and bones are all adult-sized and fully developed. Take the upper arm, for instance. In a teenager, that part of the arm is made up of three separate bones from the elbow to the shoulder. As an adult, those three bones fuse together into one bone, the humerus. That's what we have in this set of remains."

There were other signs of aging detected. From what Sorg had of the skull, she saw that the cranial sutures had started to fuse. They recovered third molars, or wisdom teeth, which develop during adolescence, so their victim was not a young adult. There was some mild arthritis (normal for someone older than forty) but none of the natural bone deterioration seen in adults over the age of sixty. Sorg identified the age of the victim as somewhere in that twenty-year window. Pen had been fifty-five.

An important discovery was that it appeared this was only one set of remains. Among the hundreds of fragments, there were no duplicates. The bones Sorg was examining represented all areas of the body. The bones were slightly smaller than the average adult's, but they were all the same proportion.

A closer inspection of some of the bones revealed tiny cracks in the surface, which were typically caused by fire. There were additional warpings and grooves caused by the extreme heat detected. These half-moon markings—called thumbnail fractures—have been identified by archeologists on the bones of ancient Romans burned in funeral pyres. This meant flesh was on the bone when it burned.

When investigators delivered the new set of bones from the stump, Sorg decided she needed some way of tracking which fragments had come from which location. She marked each bone from the fire pit (presumably because there were far fewer of those to mark) with a tiny red dot.

It gave her the freedom to mix and jumble the bits without losing track of their sites of origin.

While working with fragments recovered from the stump, Sorg came across a rounded piece she recognized as a one-inch section of neck bone. Like a good puzzle builder, she remembered having looked over a similar piece earlier. Both bits were from the first cervical vertebra. One piece had been recovered from the ash pile at the stump; the other had been pulled from the fire pit. As both splinters had come from the same vertebra, Sorg was able to link for prosecutors that bones burned in that fire pit had indeed been moved to that dump site.

In total, Sorg estimated they had found about one-third of the skeleton. There were fewer bones from the hands and torso recovered compared to what they had. There was no indication of "scavenger modification," which often happens when remains are left unprotected from wildlife for long periods of time. Sorg said the missing material could have been cremated in the fire pit or there was yet another dump site that hadn't been discovered.

Sorg's hope was that the skull could be reconstructed. It was their best chance at finding something that revealed the way Pen Meyer died.

The people prosecuting this case had been given a stack of scientific findings, but even the most obvious and elementary of findings are open for interpretation in a court of law. All of this evidence combined did not definitively answer the question that would be asked of the jury: Did Ken Carpenter murder Pen Meyer?

Mark Sisti, Carpenter's new attorney, was a master in the art of court argument. He had his sights set not just on the State's findings, but on the technicians who had made them.

TWENTY-TWO

Arguments

In a state with little sensational crime Mark Sisti was renowned in a profession in which few people have such an opportunity. Even to residents who'd never stepped foot in a courtroom, Sisti had the reputation as the state's premier criminal defense attorney. Along with his former partner, Paul Twomey, Sisti had defended Pamela Smart in an infamous 1991 case. Smart was accused of seducing one of her high school students to murder her husband. The trial was among the first to be broadcast live on television. Fascination with the Pam Smart case spawned three books, two movies, and one profitable law firm: Sisti and Twomey.

Although they lost the Smart case, Sisti and Twomey became the go-to defense team for those who could afford them. The bills for the firm were paid on drunk driving charges and drug possessions, but the pair were best known for their aggressive defenses in homicide cases. Paul Twomey left the criminal firm he helped found in the early 2000s. Burned out on murder cases, he began a new career championing election law. Sisti stayed on to carry the torch.

Mark Sisti grew up in Buffalo, New York, in a blue-collar family. His dad was employed as an ironworker, honest labor that paid for his son's education. The younger Sisti became a welder and mechanic, but found ironwork too dangerous so he went back to school. He was drawn to the law and saw criminal defense as a patriotic pursuit. Only in America are the accused considered innocent until proven guilty. Only in America are the accused provided an attorney to give a competent defense. Only in America are the accused spared the injustice of forcibly incriminating themselves. To Sisti, these rights were not those of "criminals"; they were the rights of Americans.

If billings at the Sisti Law Firm were healthy, one would never know it by an examination of its principal partner. Mark Sisti did not drive a fancy luxury car. He didn't wear expensive Italian suits. His sport coats were wrinkled at the elbows and shoulders, and the tails were creased from sitting down on them. His receding dirty blond hair grew long in the back and was often styled in a ponytail. He was stocky and animated, reminding some of a used-car salesman. If clothes made the man, then Sisti would not be where he was. Those who underestimated Mark Sisti were often burned by their assumptions. Too often, those burned included his opposing counsel.

The trial of Ken Carpenter had been scheduled for November 2006, but was repeatedly delayed. After losing the argument about deserving a speedy indictment, Carpenter formally waived his right to a speedy trial. The thought was it would provide the defense enough time to scrutinize the complicated evidence still being collected. The first postponement came after public defender John Newman withdrew; the other continuances were requested by Attorney Sisti. Delker and Wilson objected to the delays, saying Pen's family wanted the case to go to trial and be finished.

A murder trial can be won or lost months before a jury is seated. It all depends on the scope of evidence allowed into court. Sisti had a couple of fights brewing in him over this case. The greatest of all was the State's effort to depose John Newman. It went against everything he believed about the American system of justice.

Assistant Attorney General Kirsten Wilson appeared in court on February 16, 2007, to convince the judge to grant their request to depose the public defender about the "Phil" story.

"The issue with the privilege with John Newman and the defendant is twofold," she argued. "He waived any privilege that did exist. He says that this story is confidential, but he's chosen to go forward." Wilson pointed to both the letters and the recorded phone calls.

"Second is the crime fraud exception to the privilege." Wilson pointed to five other cases as precedent. She said it amounted to witness tampering. "It's a big deal to the defendant that [Harv] is having this communication [with the state police] and he needs to keep her on his side. He reaches out to Dot and Nicholas Monahan to say, 'It's not just me saying that Phil did it. My attorney also is saying it and here's all this information that he's providing that supports the Phil story. So you've got to get Harv to believe me and stay with me.'"

Attorney Jacalyn Colburn spoke on behalf of the New Hamshire Public Defenders. Her position was that Carpenter had not explicitly waived his attorney-client privilege. "There are some serious policy concerns here, including, obviously, the potential chilling effect between criminal defendants and their attorneys and their ability to be forthcoming with their attorneys, which is certainly the cornerstone of representation."

When it was his turn to speak, Sisti did not disappoint. He put his hand on Ken Carpenter's shoulder as he rose from his chair. "If you were held to task for everything your client either said about you, if we were being used to contradict our client's story, we'd be in deposition every day. It's not only a slippery slope—forget about the slope—it's jumping off a cliff."

Sisti told the judge that the defense wasn't going to argue there was any truth to the Phil story, so it was pointless to go down this rabbit hole. "All we're doing is arguing some kind of weird academic law school problem because the bottom line is it's irrelevant."

Judge Philip Mangones said he'd take the whole mess under advisement.

Sisti had other jailhouse-related problems to quash besides Carpenter's phone calls. Corrections officials had been concerned that Carpenter might be planning an escape. Of course, his letters and calls to the Monahans about his motorcycle and full-face helmet were not exactly subtle. There was also the call to Harv in which she had asked him if he going to the infirmary to make a break. The prosecution had other bad acts that it wanted to tell the jury about and that Sisti wanted blocked.

In April 2005, after being in jail for about a month, corrections officers caught Carpenter testing the fence in the recreation area for weaknesses. A few months later, Carpenter was spotted asking another inmate for help. He had made a sign and showed it to the other man. Carpenter then made a motion with his fingers, like shooting a gun. Then he tore the sign up and flushed it down the toilet. Later that same day, they caught Carpenter smearing something over the lens of a security camera. When questioned by corrections officials, Carpenter said he had been playing a joke.

In January 2007, Senior Assistant Attorney General

Will Delker got a phone call from the U.S. Attorney's Office. The federal prosecutor said that Carpenter had approached another inmate during a courthouse transfer and asked for his help in escaping. The other prisoner was a white supremacist facing a federal racketeering charge. Carpenter assumed he was in the Aryan Brotherhood, a powerful prison gang.

"A guy in a wheelchair killed the girl," Carpenter told him. "I helped dispose of her body."

Carpenter thought the skinhead could be trusted. The skinhead obviously didn't feel the same amount of trust toward Carpenter, as he promptly reported the solicitation to his own attorney.

Delker notified the jail and officers tossed Carpenter's cell. They discovered a map he had drawn up of the jail and the rec yard. There were also brochures for property in the Lesser Antilles islands. Carpenter had once had a phone conversation with Harv talking about what life would be like living outside the United States.

Officials also uncovered a page of drawings of a man's face sketched over and over again. Each time the face, which had Carpenter's shape, was rendered in a new combination of features: glasses/no glasses, full beard/goatee/Fu Manchu mustache/clean shaven, toupee/shaved bald. The disguise matrix also included notes about black eye patches or having an arm in a sling. There was a diagram about how to add a pillow to the waist and pad the shoulders under a baggy shirt to appear fat.

* * *

One of the most important pieces of evidence at trial would be the testimony of Sandy Merritt describing the phone call from Pen on the morning of February 23, 2005. Sisti filed motions to block the use of this testimony as hearsay.

The State had its own problem with Sandy as a witness. Much like Harv, Sandy had been hot and cold in her relationship with investigators. Both Delker and Wilson were prepping to do her direct examination, as her demeanor toward men would vacillate. But Sandy was pushing back against appearing in open court. She had been depressed, and started drinking again. She told the prosecutors that she had a mental illness and a social phobia and didn't want to testify. The team drew up a motion to allow Sandy to videotape her testimony, but Sisti objected. He wanted to preserve the right of his client to face his accuser.

Sisti desperately wanted the chance to cross-examine Sandy. He'd already subpoenaed her personal medical records and planned to use her alcoholism and mental state to impeach her on the stand. They showed that in the two years since the murder of Pen Meyer, Sandy had admitted to counselors that she was overwhelmed by compulsive behaviors. She had walked into the ER at Valley Regional Hospital after drinking heavily, but had denied any health problems. She left against medical advice. When asked whether she would be relapsing, the medical record said, "She noted she would be looking forward to some O'Doul's beer later that evening."

Other care providers wrote in her records that Sandy had difficulty focusing and couldn't recall things that had happened to her as recently as within the same week. Sisti was going to argue that Sandy had trouble distinguishing between fantasy and reality. Delker began researching cases on whether a witness's alcoholism or mental delusions had a bearing on their character or truthfulness at trial.

Just when the Phil story couldn't get any more bizarre, six weeks before the trial the Monahans turned over another letter from Carpenter in which he doubled down. He said, thinking back to that day, the SUV that Phil drove might have had Maine license plates. And the guy's name was not Phil Waters, but Phil Jordan.

Detective Berube asked Sergeant Lamson if he wanted him to try to chase down a "Phil Jordan" now. Lamson told him it was a snipe hunt and not worth their time.

Judge Mangones sided with the prosecution on its request to depose public defender John Newman. He said the State could ask the former defense attorney two questions limited to the Phil story. The ruling infuriated Sisti, who filed an appeal to the State Supreme Court. In order to allow for the appeal to be heard, Mangones further delayed the Carpenter trial. Instead of May, jury selection wasn't going to begin until August 30, 2007.

The Sullivan County Courthouse was a gem of a building, but at over one hundred years, it showed its age. The court had poor lighting, no air conditioning, and none of the modern conveniences lawyers have come to expect of these facilities. At times it seemed quaint, like an episode of *Matlock*. But mostly it was loud and uncomfortable. It was probably the worst place to hold a murder trial in all of New Hampshire.

The Courthouse was ninety minutes away from Will Delker's home, two hours for Kirsten Wilson. The State had arranged for them and the third member of their team, victim advocate Jennifer Hunt, to stay in an uncomfortable motel in Newport during hearings and the trial. The crew probably could have powered through it, had it not been for a run-in with a skunk. The three smartly pooled their per diems and rented an off-season waterfront house overlooking Lake Sunapee. Wilson left casseroles for her husband the weeks she was gone; Delker's wife often brought dinners to the lake house for the prosecution to share.

Judge Mangones announced his rulings on the outstanding motions. He'd allow Sandy's testimony about the phone call from Pen, but she'd have to do it in open court. Her medical record could not be used by the defense to impeach her credibility. The judge also said the state could present evidence about Ken's schemes to escape the jail.

The New Hampshire Supreme Court failed to issue a ruling in the appeal over defense attorney John Newman's testimony. The justices wanted to know exactly what two questions were going to be asked. If the prosecution were to submit these questions, Sisti could renew his appeal.

"This will likely delay us further, at least until the Supreme Court can issue an opinion," Judge Mangones warned. Delker stood sweating in the hundred-year-old courtroom.

"Your Honor, it's been two and a half years since Pen Meyer was killed. The victim's family very much wants these proceedings to begin. The state will withdraw its motion to depose Attorney Newman."

"Fine. We'll begin jury selection on Thursday as planned," the judge said. Then, as an afterthought, he said, "Counselors, I've been told the jury room has a mold infestation. So for this trial the jurors will be using the grand jury room instead."

Delker filed an emergency motion forty-eight hours before jury selection was to begin. He asked the judge to admit a letter written by Carpenter to another prisoner. Authorities said on that Monday, Carpenter and the other inmate, listed only as W.T., were both being transported to the courthouse when he solicited W.T.'s help in contacting Sandy Merritt. Carpenter asked the inmate to get his wife to find Sandy and convince her not to testify. He suggested buying Sandy a plane ticket or "getting her lost" in the woods. In return, Carpenter had written he would give W.T. a 1985 bucket truck he had in Lempster.

As soon as the jail caught wind of the letter, State Police Detective Eric Berube was dispatched to talk to W.T. and his cellmate, S.C. Berube was told that Carpenter also wanted something to be done about Jonathan Purick. They said he wanted Pen's boyfriend dead.

On Thursday, August 30, 2007, potential jurors were turned away from the Sullivan County Courthouse, unaware the trial had been delayed yet another day because of further legal issues. When brought up in open court, the new allegations were shocking. But Mark Sisti had the most surprising statement of all.

"Your Honor, I have represented both W.T. and S.C. I would want to cross-examine them and that would be a pure conflict of interest."

Delker countered that the letter itself could be admitted and testimony from the inmates would be unnecessary. Sisti disagreed, saying he would withdraw from the case if the letter or testimony from these men was introduced. Judge Mangones said he needed to take some time to rule and spent three hours in recess trying to decide this latest legal obstacle.

During the recess, Delker and Wilson had lunch next door at the Salt Hill Pub, an Irish bar in what had until recently been an abandoned building.

"Are we ready for this?" Wilson asked. "God knows I don't want to face Sisti, but if he pulls out, it'll delay this trial by another year."

Delker said he had spoken with Jennifer Hunt, the AG's victim advocate. "Pen's family is really disturbed about the possibility of a continuance. They need to get this piece done."

The slap-dash meal was interrupted by Delker's cell phone. After a series of rapid, "Yep, yep's," he snapped the cover shut and went for his legal pad. "The judge has made a decision." They dashed back to the courthouse.

Looking troubled as he retook the bench, Judge Mangones said, "The Court will sustain Mr. Sisti's concern about continuing on as counsel in the event that W.T. or S.C. were called as witnesses."

Another delay would be heartbreaking to the family. Delker rose and said, "The State will go forward without the evidence or the witnesses."

The prosecution bolted from the old courthouse and made a beeline for their lakefront rental. It was less than twenty-four hours before opening arguments and the shape of their case continued to shift.

TWENTY-THREE

Opening

Kirsten Wilson had rituals when it came to dressing for court: dark suits for opening and closing arguments and medical examiner testimony, with the occasional colorful outfit in between. Before this trial she'd splurged on two summer suits, in apricot and turquoise. She never wore the same clothes twice during any trial, which was part superstitious habit, part practical reality. Every day after court, Wilson would get in her car, ditch her jacket in the back, put her hair in a ponytail, and blast music all the way back to the rental house. Those jackets ended up in the dry-cleaning pile in the back of her closet, another part of life she didn't have the time to attend to during trial.

Wilson stood up from the prosecution's table and walked confidently toward the front of the courtroom.

She cut a striking contrast to the professorially attired Will Delker, all the way down to her impeccably polished and impossibly high heels. But if Kirsten Wilson's shoes weren't comfortable, you'd never know it, because if she was anything in court, she was steady as hell on her feet.

"Thank you, Your Honor." Wilson's voice was dark and measured, matching the gaze she laid upon the jury. It was September 19, 2007. After three agonizing weeks of voir dire, nine men and six women had been empanelled.

"Ken Carpenter hated Pen Meyer because he blamed her for his breakup with his girlfriend. His hatred boiled over in February of 2005 and he murdered Pen Meyer and burned her body in a fire pit at his home. On a cold, snowy evening in February of that year, the state police obtained a search warrant, a warrant to go out to his property. A strong snow was falling, and the police went out to that remote location."

Wilson went on as if Ken Carpenter weren't even in the room, as if he weren't sitting a few feet from her, his yellow-red eyes burning into the back of her head.

"A fire pit just to the left of the home was still smoldering, and it was ringed with soot-covered cinder blocks. The state police started digging and sifting in that pit. And slowly, under the snow and ash, they found human bones. Slowly, under the snow and ash, they found human teeth. Slowly, under the snow and ash, they found Pen Meyer."

Wilson paused to make sure she could look at each juror's face as they digested the scene she was describing.

"While Pen was alive, friends and family could tell when Pen was approaching because they could hear the jingling of her silver bracelets that Pen never removed from her body, distinct bracelets and necklaces that Pen collected after travels and that she collected from fellow artists that she respected.

"After Pen's murder . . . her children looked at photographs of burnt, soot-covered jewelry that was found on the defendant's property, and they named the pieces that they knew: a silver bracelet with a buffalo that Pen got in the Southwest; bangles that Pen had worn at her son's wedding; a pendant that she wore to the farmer's market, where she sold some of her weavings. All these pieces and others were identified by Pen's children, as a police detective somberly showed them photo after photo after photo."

Wilson told the jury that all this evidence had been found on Carpenter's property, and described the process of police digging through the fire pit for days and filling buckets full of ash for analysis. She explained how troopers sifted through those buckets, pulling fragments of bone and teeth from the ash and dirt. She also told them of the other item police found in the ash, something her children also identified with ease.

"They found a burnt key ring that had a small teddy bear on it. The small key that was attached to that ring would slip in and open the lock on Pen's post-office box." Wilson then described how the other key found in the pit opened the lock to Pen's empty home on Center Road in Goshen.

"But the burnt remains of Pen's life weren't all that the police found at the defendant's house. Hidden in the loft, tucked behind the insulation, were Pen's car keys and a gold AA medallion. And hidden at the bottom of a box in a closet was a legal form that would give all of Pen's property to the defendant, a man she feared and disliked. All of these things were found inside and around the home of the defendant, a man who hated Pen because she tried to help one of her friends."

If Wilson was feeling anger toward the man accused of killing the woman she felt she'd come to know very well, the jury was unlikely aware of it. Instead they were fixated on the glamorous prosecutor's intense retelling of the facts of the case, her gray eyes making contact with theirs in turn as she unpacked the State's version of events.

Wilson described Pen's life as a gardener, outdoors-woman, weaver, and animal lover. She talked about Pen's three grown children, her dog, Fluff, and her dedication to Alcoholics Anonymous and to the people she met there, the people she felt compelled to help, and would support however and whenever they needed it.

"Sandy Merritt was one such person. Sandy also met the defendant at AA."

Wilson explained how Sandy had begun the affair with Carpenter based on his deception that his marriage to Cynthia Harvey was over. She told the story of how the affair ended, and how the members of AA helped Sandy obtain the restraining order, breaking their anonymity to do so.

"And standing next to Sandy, supporting her at that court process, was her friend, Pen Meyer."

Wilson then told the jury how Carpenter had repeatedly violated the order, and then lied at the final stalking hearing about his attempts to contact Sandy. She explained how Carpenter's growing obsession with controlling the situation fed into his hatred and focus on Pen, and how he told others that Pen Meyer was the single obstacle preventing him from being with Sandy. She told the story of how Carpenter had confronted Pen at her home, and how she'd been concerned enough to call the police. Then she talked about the day that Pen disappeared. The entire time, Carpenter buried any flash of emotion from his face.

"Pen was seen walking her dog by neighbors on the morning of February twenty-third, 2005. There was fresh fallen snow on the ground. And as Pen approached the corner of Brickyard Road, one neighbor was cleaning off his car to go to work. When he sarcastically stated, 'Nice weather we're having,' Pen responded by explaining that she loved it. Pen was smiling as she walked in the new snow toward the house that she loved with her dog beside her. And that was the last time anyone would see Pen Meyer alive."

Wilson paused to let that sink in before launching into a lengthy summary of the investigation that followed Pen's disappearance and eventually led to Carpenter's arrest. She detailed the increasingly bizarre evidence that seemed to turn up each time the case had reached what investigators thought was the most bizarre point it could possibly reach. She described Carpenter's calls to Harv from jail, and his attempts to coerce her into concealing evidence after directing her to yet another burn site, where she found more of Pen's remains and her jewelry.

She detailed the contents of the documents that pointed to Carpenter's intent to seize control of Pen's home and property after her disappearance. She described the notebooks full of plans, scripts, and the word processor used to type up the property transfer documents. Wilson then told the jury about Carpenter's fingering a man named Phil for the murder.

"The defendant murdered Pen Meyer. He had hated Pen for months, and he could not contain his rage. Pen had tried to help and support Sandy when she tried to get away from the defendant, and that act of support cost Pen her life. The defendant had planned to kill Pen, and after she had written the letters on the memo pads, the check to Sandy, and signed away all her belongings, he murdered her. He then burned her remains to cover up his gruesome act and began telling varying accounts of what had happened in order to account for the mounting evidence against him."

Wilson paused to breathe and placed her hands on the rail in front of the jury. She lowered her voice and again swept her eyes left to right, scanning all their faces.

"Ladies and gentleman, at the conclusion of this case,

it will be clear to you beyond any reasonable doubt that the defendant planned and carried out the brutal murder of Pen Meyer. And the only just verdict you can return is one of guilt.

"Thank you."

With that, Kirsten Wilson turned on one gleaming heel and stared for a moment at the man she'd just declared guilty of murder. Carpenter looked right back at her as she strode to the prosecution's table and took her seat behind it.

The judge turned and looked at the opposing table. There were three people seated there: Ken Carpenter, Mark Sisti, and his co-counsel, Attorney Aime Cook. "Does the defense wish to open?"

Sisti stood up, giving the courtroom a full view of his ill-fitting suit.

"I do, Your Honor. Thank you. Thank you."

Sisti launched right into his opening as he walked toward the jury. It was their first look at his signature walk-and-talk style in court.

"Good morning. This is an opportunity where we get to speak right after the prosecution. It's the only time, really." Sisti was also known for asserting that his side was the perpetual underdog. "This sort of thing will get to happen in a case because, as the judge said, these folks have the burden of proof, and it's not a burden of probabilities." Each time Sisti referred to the prosecution, he'd point to their table without looking at it.

"It's not a burden of guessing. It's not a burden where you sit around and say, well, that might have happened, that could have happened, or that's a very interesting theory. It's a burden of proof beyond a reasonable doubt. And it's a burden of proof, ladies and gentlemen, that is steeped in time-honored history in this state and in the United States, and there's a reason for it."

Sisti reminded the jury of their individual questioning during the jury selection process.

"We get to question you to determine whether or not you will have the backbone to hang in there for three, four, five weeks and be persuaded by *evidence* and not *rhetoric*. We get to question you to determine whether or not you will be sitting and expecting a soap opera or science. We get to question you, ladies and gentlemen, not to determine whether or not you will be persuaded by finger-pointing and innuendo, but to determine whether or not you will place your finger on reality, rather than accusations.

"If you've come to a conclusion before you've done your homework, you can fit that square peg into the round hole. You can do it with a sledgehammer. You can do it by cheating the edges of the square peg and driving it in there. I'm going to ask you right now to hold on to your promise and your oath that you took. In this country, people go to trial in courtrooms like this because they trust their peers. They *trust their peers.* You are the folks that stand between the government and *liberty. That* is why you're here."

Sisti began to pace in front of the jury, talking faster as he ambled to and fro.

"Ladies and gentleman, the prosecution went on for over thirty minutes in their opening. They went on and explained to you in some Oprah Winfrey, soap opera way what they were going to do over the next three or four weeks. I'd like to review with you this morning how the State will *fail* to meet its burden of proof by the time they put on their three to four weeks of innuendo and emotional testimony. I'll do it by naming names. I'll do it by telling you that we are going to question people with real names that have *real* scientific backgrounds."

Sisti had given the jury a peek at his hand; now he drove his strategy home.

"You know, one of the problems in this case is because *they don't have a cause of death.* They don't know *when* a death would have occurred, they don't know *where* a death would have occurred, and they don't know *how* a death would have occurred. And ladies and gentlemen, this is a *murder* case."

Sisti was fired up now, breathing heavily in between his emphatic assertions and punctuating them with his index finger on the rail in front of the jury.

"Folks, with regard to the burden of proof, the prosecution cannot even prove beyond a *reasonable doubt* that the remains found on Carpenter's property, the bones, the teeth, the reconstructed skull, are artifacts of Pen Meyer."

Wilson and Delker tried not to move or give any tell that would signal they worried about this. Sisti had, after all, just circled the gaping hole in their case. It was no surprise to the prosecution that a defense attorney of Sisti's skill would hammer at that. In this poker game, the prosecutors kept a stone face. Instead, they scanned the jury box for any notice the twelve people and three alternates were eating it up. The jurors were leaning in, intent on hearing more from Sisti. It wasn't a good sign.

"Now," Sisti continued. "DNA from any of the remains, there's *none*. DNA from Carpenter's house, there's *none*. DNA matching Carpenter to Pen Meyer's house, there's *none*. DNA from Pen Meyer in Carpenter's vehicle? *None*. Cause of death, means of death? Is it a homicide? Was it accidental? Could it have been death caused by natural causes? Starting to get the picture?"

Sisti shook his head in mock disbelief over the State's case as he reiterated the same details that Wilson had listed in her opening statement from the defense point of view.

"You will hear they went through Pen Meyer's home. You will hear that there wasn't one sign—*not one*—of a struggle or a fight or a problem in that house. You will hear *no one* come in to testify that Kenneth Carpenter was even there confronting Pen Meyer, threatening Pen Meyer, abducting Pen Meyer, coercing Pen Meyer."

"Now, is that a problem? That *is* a problem. All the hand wringing and rumors and gossip and all the garbage that goes back and forth between people after an event doesn't make it true beyond a reasonable doubt. And I'm going to ask you now to be true to your oath."

Sisti stopped pacing and stood squarely in front of the jury, appraising them as if assessing their capacity to keep a secret.

"If at the end of a first-degree murder case, after three or four weeks in an American courtroom, if the prosecutor doesn't know where somebody died, how many people may have been with the individual when she died . . . I'm going to ask you at the end of this case to be true to your oath. I'm going to ask you to sweep away the emotion. I'm going to ask you to hold fast to what the judge instructs you to do."

"I'm going to ask *you* to give Ken Carpenter a trial in a courtroom, as officers of the court. I'm going to ask *you* to give Ken Carpenter the due process he deserves on this side of that bar. That bar keeps the *public* out. That bar keeps people that have already made their minds up out. They're out. They're spectators. *We're* the players. And *you're* going to be the judges."

Mark Sisti had built his career on instilling doubt in the minds of juries from day one, even if it meant acknowledging he wasn't necessarily defending saints. As Kirsten Wilson and Will Delker watched him open his case, they knew this was the turn his argument would now take.

"At the end of a case, you can say, there's something wrong here. You know, maybe Ken *was* involved somehow. Something just isn't right. Why were those remains over at his house? Why was he saying the things he was saying?"

Sisti threw his hands up in the air.

"You know what? *So what*. Don't get caught up in that at all. Get caught up in what your job is supposed to be, to objectively look at the evidence, to take the witnesses as they come, on the stand, to make sure that your rights aren't cheapened. Because if you come back at the end of this case with a verdict on *less* than proof beyond a reasonable doubt, oh, sure you're hurting Ken, but you're ruining your own lives."

Sisti began walking back to the defense table and then turned around to make one last point. He gestured at the prosecution's table, where Wilson and Delker sat motionless.

"And at the end of this case, it won't be about sympathy, and it won't be about emotion, I can guarantee you. If they want to come in and make the allegation they made, *make them prove it*."

TWENTY-FOUR

Drill

After openings were concluded, the first witness Will Delker called to the stand was Jonathan Purick. Pen's boyfriend had been through the emotional wringer since her death. He walked to the witness stand with a clear weight on his shoulders, passing Pen's relatives and their supporters on the right-hand side of the room. The reporters were also assembled on the right-hand side, the prosecution side, of the room. They were there for the photo angle. The back of Carpenter's head was not an appealing shot, and their position didn't allow for accidental photos of the jury (which were prohibited by court rule).

The benches on the other side of the courtroom were

almost empty. The only person sitting there to support Kenneth Carpenter was his cousin, Allen Long.

Delker walked Jonathan through an introduction of Alcoholics Anonymous and Al-Anon for the jury before getting to his relationship with Pen. "Can you describe how your relationship developed over time from that first meeting?"

"We just seemed to have similar interests in how we viewed the world," he said. "What I really was impressed with was the fact that she was a great humanitarian. Her integrity—"

"Your Honor, can I just object?" The judge motioned to the attorneys to approach the bench. It was the first objection of the trial and Mark Sisti was steaming.

"It's totally objectionable!" Sisti hissed in hushed tones at the sidebar. "This opinion is being offered for I don't know what reason, with regard to character and integrity and everything else!"

Delker countered, "It's important to any number of foundation questions."

The judge limited what the prosecution could tell the jury about Pen's personality. "In other words," Judge Mangones said, "the alleged homicide of this person shouldn't be any different than the alleged homicide of someone else."

The strength of Pen Meyer's character, while not a germane legal peg to hang a case on, was key to understanding the coldness of this crime. Delker and Wilson would have to push ahead down other roads.

* * *

Day two of testimony began with Sandy Merritt. It was a game time decision, but they thought it would be okay for Delker to do the direct examination instead of Wilson. Prosecutors the day before had used Jonathan to introduce a transcript of the restraining order hearing. Now they were using Sandy to introduce the obsessive letters Carpenter wrote and the check and property agreement she received in the mail. Also, they needed her to tell the jury about the phone call.

"I . . . I was . . . it was very, very different. I just couldn't hear at work and she hardly ever called me at work, but she knew not to call between those times, because we're feeding dogs."

After being questioned on the stand for ninety minutes, Delker turned the witness over to Sisti. The defense asked for a five-minute recess, after which they said they had no questions for Sandy Merritt. Delker and Wilson exchanged glances as Sandy exited the courtroom. They guessed Sisti decided if he couldn't impeach her on the stand, he would win no points with the jury trying.

Fred Evans testified about his own run-ins with Ken Carpenter and how he tried to help Sandy Merritt stay safe while attending meetings at Millie's Place. On direct examination from Delker, he told the jury about the

NOTES ON A KILLING

afternoon Carpenter barged into his house and confronted him about Sandy's restraining order.

On cross, Sisti quizzed Fred about the AA meeting on
December 15, where Carpenter received his 23-year chip.
He asked if the defendant displayed any threatening
behavior toward him or Sandy Merritt or Pen Meyer.

"No."

"No anger, hatred, nothing like that, with regard to
this present situation?"

"My feeling was, I was not comfortable, but I wanted
to try to be friends if we could," Fred said.

"And with those people you're not comfortable with,"
Sisti began with a dramatic flourish for the jury, "do you
generally give them a couple of good old hugs and wish
them a happy birthday and let them hug you back?"

Fred said that on the anniversary of someone's sobriety,
yes, he definitely would.

The next witness for the prosecution was Richard Dow,
the disabled vet who had been staying at Fred Evans's
home. He backed up Fred's testimony about Carpenter's
rage when he learned of the restraining order.

Dow was also at the AA meeting the night of February
24, the night the two state troopers were waiting outside
for Carpenter. Dow sat next to Carpenter and was surprised by his comments to the group.

"He was talking about how fragile a human life could

be and he'd had an accident with a chain saw cutting wood. It struck me as odd because that wasn't what we were talking about."

"Did you smell anything on the defendant?" Delker asked.

"He had a smell of wood smoke on him and a smell that I didn't quite recognize to be wood."

"Can you describe that smell in any more detail?"

"It smelled like a dentist drill, when he's drilling your teeth. The stink that comes from that." There was a faint gasp from the gallery at the wretched descriptions. Dow said after the meeting he specifically walked over to Carpenter to get another whiff. "It just didn't smell right."

"Did you have a physical reaction?"

"I got a little nauseous."

"I don't have any other questions," Delker told the judge. "The defense can go ahead."

Mark Sisti hurried from the defense table to the podium in the middle of the old room. "This was an overpowering, stomach turning, retching smell, that you claim to have observed, right?"

"To me, sir, yes."

"To you," he said, unconvinced. "Because, you know, nobody else has reported that, do you know that?"

Dow said, "I can't speak for them, sir."

"I'm not speaking for them, either," said Sisti, now dancing around the ring. "But are you aware that you were at this meeting with lots of other people?"

"Yes."

"And how many people commented to you at that there was this overpowering . . ."

Delker was on his feet. "Objection. Hearsay."

"I'll allow it," ruled Mangones. "Go ahead."

"I mean, do you have any superhuman sense with regard to smell?"

Dow muttered that he did not. Triumphantly, Sisti gave the jury a nod.

Delker called up the friend whom Pen was on the phone with the night Ken Carpenter pulled into her driveway. Again on cross-examination, Sisti got the witness to concede ground.

"She didn't tell you that she was afraid of the man, correct?"

"No."

"No. In fact, she told you that she didn't fear this person at all, correct?"

"No. Not at all."

"She said to you that she did not think the man would hurt her, correct?"

He nodded. "That's correct."

"May we approach?" Delker gathered the whole team of attorneys at the bench. Jim Swan was slated to take the stand next, but he was indisposed. "Unfortunately, our next witness is gutting a deer right now, actually."

Judge Mangones's eyes popped out of his head. "He's gutting a deer?"

The gathering of men and women in business suits couldn't contain their laughter. Such was life in Sullivan County. The judge sent the jury home a little early and they agreed to pick it up in the morning.

The next day began with testimony from Pen's relatives. Wilson handled the direct examination of Pen's daughter, Kira Campbell. Sisti had been a stickler about making sure evidence in trial was properly introduced. This slightly interrupted the flow for Delker and Wilson. The family was there to testify about Pen's habits and her omnipresent jewelry. They'd have to recall the relatives to the stand to identify the jewelry after the troopers could testify about how it was recovered.

"Her routine was very close to home, very simple," said Kira. "She went for walks, she worked in gardens, she did her weaving, she talked with friends. There wasn't a lot of drama."

Wilson asked about Pen's distinctive jewelry. Kira told the court about how she restrung her favorite necklace.

"Do you recall the time frame to your mom's murder as to when you restrung the beads?"

"It was within a year."

Sisti stood up. With a sympathetic figure like the victim's daughter on the stand, he was careful about appearances. "Your Honor, can we just approach?"

"You may."

At the sidebar, Sisti asked as sweet as pie, "If we could

rephrase our questions from now on to strike the word 'murder,' that would be great. How about 'disappearance'?"

Judge Mangones raised an eyebrow. "Well, is there an issue as to—"

"Everything's an issue. Yes." Sisti wasn't simply arguing that Ken Carpenter didn't kill Pen Meyer. He was going to argue that there was no proof that Pen Meyer was the victim of a crime.

"I suppose the word 'murder' is somewhat prejudicial," the judge conceded. Wilson agreed to rephrase their questions. Over the next month of the homicide trial, the words "murder" or "murderer" were used in open court testimony only nine times, and usually in quotes about the fictitious Phil Waters. The only person who ever used "murderer" and "Ken Carpenter" in the same sentence was Jim Swan.

Kirsten Wilson called Lucy Seabrooke to the stand. She knew there would be problems with her testimony, but they needed her to place Carpenter and his car in front of Pen's house the morning she vanished. She told state police she'd seen a gray wagon.

"I slowed down to look because I asked my daughter, I'm like, well, should we stop and see if he needs help? Then she's like, 'no.'" Seabrooke explained. "She was five."

Sisti wasted no time on cross getting at her. "At the time state police spoke with you, you were intoxicated, correct?'

"I had a six-pack," she said, shifting in her chair. "I don't know. You might think three beers is intoxicated."

Sisti attacked her description of the car's driver. Did he have a hat? Did he have a coat? What kind of shirt was he wearing?

"Flannel," Seabrooke popped out.

Sisti spun on his heels. It wasn't something in her previous statements. "Did you ever describe that to anybody before two seconds ago?"

"I never thought about it. Nobody asked me."

"Anything about the car you can tell us?"

"I just remember I saw a station wagon," she said. "A Subaru."

Seabrooke had previously said it was a Volkswagen. "Subaru. Volkswagen," Sisti droned on. "Anything else?"

"Well, whatever comes like that. There's a million kinds like that."

"Right. A million cars like that?"

Seabrooke was completely flustered. "Well, I mean different brands."

"But this was a gray, small station wagon, correct?"

"Car, I said. Yes."

Sisti pounced again. "Car?"

"Station wagon," she blurted out, hoping to stop the onslaught. "Looked like a station wagon."

Sisti put his hands on his hips. "What was it then?"

"It was a station wagon. Small." When she was finished, even Lucy Seabrooke wasn't sure what she had seen.

* * *

Jim Swan, cleaned up after deer gutting, finally took his place for the prosecution. He was husky, and had a Mediterranean swarthiness to his features. Wilson sensed right away that he had endeared himself to the jury. He came across as a pleasant, colorful character. Who wouldn't love a man who loved his three dogs and had a license plate that read COONHND? The jurors had been all smiles while he spoke.

"Did the defendant ever mention Pen Meyer to you?"

"He went off on a rant about 'that fucking Pen.' And at that point I stopped him, because, I basically said, 'Look, it's not a Pen problem here. It's Ken.'"

At that moment the entire courtroom began to rumble with metal clangs. Someone was trying to fix a pipe a floor below. Wilson fought back the urge to say something sarcastic about the hundred-year-old building.

Swan described the night of February 23, 2005, when he got home from second shift and found Carpenter still awake, watching TV. Swan said he'd just passed a car accident on the corner and asked Carpenter to walk with him to check it out. When the pair returned, Swan said he noticed his roommate had a sickly sweet, smoky smell to him.

Swan said the light on his answering machine was blinking. The message was from the state police asking for Carpenter. Swan's brother had recently been in a car wreck, and assuming the late call was a similar emergency, he handed the phone to Carpenter.

"Kenny shied back and said, 'No one knows I'm here.'" Swan said that after speaking to Harv on the phone, Carpenter told him that Pen Meyer was missing, he had been implicated, and he was going to spend the night at Harv's house.

"I said, 'Geez, Kenny, you're doing great. You're Kenny the liar, Kenny the cheater, Kenny the drunk, and now you're Kenny the ax murderer.' To which he went 'ha-ha.'"

Wilson paused for effect. She prodded him to go on.

"He was going to leave and he was going by the back door of the house, and I said, 'Oh, by the way, Kenny, I got to go do laundry later on. I'm not going to find any bloody clothes or anything in the washing machine, am I?' To which he said, 'No. I burned them.'"

The jurors weren't smiling anymore.

The next day of testimony, Indian summer visited Newport. The courtroom was stifling, despite the giant windows having been opened wide. Wilson had lost so much weight during the trial that her skirt was held up in back with a binder clip, which meant that even during breaks, she couldn't remove her jacket.

The logger that Carpenter had hired to clear brush from the home made a brief appearance on the stand. He told the court he met with Carpenter at his home on February 23 in preparation for the work to be done the following morning. He noticed Carpenter was burning brush at the fire pit near his house. He thought it was strange that the man would lug wood up to the pit when most people would have burned it right where it had fallen.

The prosecutors then brought to the stand Troopers John Encarnacao and Fred Lulka, the two who had collected most of the evidence in the case. Their appearances would be mostly utilitarian. They were there to introduce the evidence and testify about how it was recovered.

Encarnacao was first. He came to court with dozens of boxes and plastic bags. The trooper told the jury the story of how they'd rolled in to the Lempster home of Ken Carpenter during a February blizzard and discovered the fire pit burning. He also went through the many items he'd collected from the home, the sheds, and the pickup truck. The prosecutor and witness settled into a rhythm of sorts during this testimony. Delker would prompt the trooper by asking him about a bagged exhibit, such as the AA medallion found in Pen's bathroom or the roll of orange duct tape seized from the Nissan. Each time, Encarnacao would briefly explain where and how the item was obtained. Reading the evidence number on the bag, he would confirm the item was the same one he had originally discovered. Then at the request of the prosecutor, Encarnacao would open the bag, remove the evidence, and show it to the jury. The process took all morning and continued after lunch, with Wilson repeating the tedious script with Lulka.

The heat of the day was draining to all, and slowed metabolisms from deli sandwiches and potato chips were quickly sapping the jury. After the midafternoon recess, Wilson requested a sidebar with the judge.

"I just wanted to note for the Court's attention—and it's something to monitor over the course of the trial—juror number five, I have seen sleeping a number of times."

With the jury out of the room, the group of lawyers all glanced at the empty box. Juror five was a young man in the front row, but the whole panel had looked out of it when they last filed out. Wilson said a reporter first brought it to her attention.

"Do you want me to deal with it now or deal with it later?" Judge Mangones asked.

"In all fairness," said a sympathetic Sisti, "*I'm* not even concentrating on it right now. But why don't you make some kind of general announcement, if people are feeling groggy for some reason, need to get up, just indicate it. We don't want anybody nodding off."

Mangones agreed to take more frequent breaks and said he would keep an eye on the situation.

Testimony from Trooper Fred Lulka spilled into the next morning. When he got off the stand, Delker called Trooper Jaye Almstrom. The beefy law enforcement official walked jurors through his visit to Carpenter's home the day after Pen's disappearance.

"Now, let's make sure the jury understands," Sisti said on cross-examination. "Mr. Carpenter had absolutely no obligation whatsoever to allow you on his property at all, correct?"

"That is correct."

"In fact, he could have just said, get lost."

"That's correct."

Sisti grilled him about the burn barrel he noticed propped up behind the parked pickup truck. "The bottom line is you did not describe the amount of so-called 'trash' in the barrel in your report, correct?"

"That's correct."

"And you saw a barrel that was not hot to the touch."

"That's correct."

"You saw a barrel that did not appear to have been dragged from one point to another."

"That's correct."

"And you saw a barrel that did not smell of anything sickly."

"That's correct."

Convinced he'd sewn enough reasonable doubt with the jury, Sisti let Trooper Almstrom go.

Criminalist Tim Jackson told Wilson and the jurors how he was able to link Carpenter's camouflaged gloves to the fabric impressions on the orange duct tape. The previous expert testimony had been deadly dry to sit through, so Wilson tried to keep things moving without missing any key points.

The cross-examination was handled by Sisti's co-counsel, Aime Cook. Cook was an androgynous-looking woman who sported a man's haircut and smart business suits. Sisti had built his own career on being underestimated, and he had an affinity for finding others with the same talent.

After dancing around the different types and classifications of gloves and polymer surfaces by every clothing manufacturer around, Cook said, "So the bottom line here is you can't say to any degree of scientific certainty that those gloves made those impressions, correct?"

"Right," agreed Jackson. "I am saying they could have because they have the same pattern design."

"But the 'could have' does not include any specific unique points that pair made that, correct?"

"That is correct, yes."

Cook thanked the witness and sat down.

The eighth day of full testimony was October 1, 2007. The trial had been in session for more than a calendar month, and they were still plodding through the mounting evidence.

Ken Carpenter walked into court each day and sat passively between Sisti and Cook. The proceedings seemed to be happening around him, despite him. The man who had loomed so large in the lives of Sandy Merritt and Pen Meyer, whose violence had set this tragedy all in motion, had been reduced to a spectator to its conclusion.

Detective Shawn Skahan testified for much of the morning. His highlights included all the recorded telephone calls between Sandy and Carpenter as well as being the recipient of the "anonymous" call that directed the team to the Goshen Country Store's pay phone.

"Can you tell the jury how many attempts there were to contact Mr. Carpenter?" Sisti quizzed Skahan.

"I don't know how many off the top of my head. I believe it was in the twenties."

"In fact," Sisti said, waving a finger in the air, "it almost came to thirty, wasn't it?"

"Well," Skahan said dryly, "that would be in the twenties."

The room came alive again with the whir of power tools hacking into metal. There was suddenly more work being done to the pipes below the chamber. The judge halted the proceedings so a bailiff could find the work crew and get them to knock it off.

Sisti switched gears. He asked Skahan if there was any evidence as to how the plastic bag with the key had been placed under the pay phone. The trooper admitted that since no one had witnessed a person taping the bag there, they couldn't say for sure how or when it had been put there.

The lead investigator, Detective Sergeant Russell Lamson, appeared in his best dark suit for his testimony. He not only had to explain how they'd honed in on Carpenter, but also had to introduce the evidence he'd personally collected at the elm tree stump on the night of June 25, 2005.

"I carefully placed that bone evidence in a separate bag from the other items I collected to . . ." Lamson stopped, his voice choked. He was acutely aware that Pen's family was in the courtroom. He couldn't help becoming emotional describing the moment he found the remains of this special woman. He sniffed back the tears and went on. "Understanding what I believed those remains were as well as how fragile they seemed to be, I placed them in a separate bag and transported them directly to the Medical Examiner's Office."

The cross-examination of Sergeant Lamson was endless. Sisti tossed his own crime scene photos back in his face and pounded him on what he thought were deficiencies with the state police investigation.

"Four days [in February and March 2005] the New Hampshire State Police were at this particular location [in Lempster] processing this particular location, right?"

"That's correct."

"And in fact you just stated to this jury some material was found from a so-called burn pit, right?"

"That's correct."

"Now was it your understanding that there was a barrel sitting out in the area depicted by those photographs I just showed you?"

"I can see a barrel in the photograph, yes," Lamson replied coolly.

"And are you telling this jury that you had police personnel there for over four days and nobody went through and searched or sifted through this barrel, this so-called burn barrel?"

"I do not remember anybody saying they searched through a barrel during that four-day period."

Sisti was on a roll. His voice rose, his unbuttoned jacket flapping with the gesticulations of his arms. "And in fact the first time that anything was retrieved from that area would have been four months after folks were there."

"That's correct."

"And this is an area that would have been unmonitored for four months after you left, right? It was not secured in any way, shape, or form."

Again, Lamson admitted, "That's correct."

Sisti argued there was no way to know when those particular bones were burned, nor when they were dumped at the stump. He said no one could be sure that those remains were deposited on the Lempster property after Carpenter had gone to jail.

"Let me ask you, okay—because you're beating around the bush here. Did you recover anything from that particular debris pile that directly links itself through an identifiable characteristic to Mr. Carpenter?"

"Other than the fact that he told his wife he put it there," Lamson said, "no."

TWENTY-FIVE

Defect

Walking into the courtroom each morning, Kirsten Wilson couldn't help observing how, from behind, Ken Carpenter and Mark Sisti looked exactly alike. Each had long hair in a ponytail resting on the shoulders of his suit coat. Carpenter had cleaned up his appearance over the past two years, but refused to give up his long hair. He had shaved his cheeks of the scraggly beard, keeping only a mustache. He came to court in decent-looking dark suits with pressed shirts and ties. Wilson was determined to see his wardrobe changed for good into the dark green uniforms of the New Hampshire State Prison for Men.

As they moved into more of the forensic testimony, the prosecution was sure they were going to hear a recurring theme from the defense. They were going to sell the idea that this body might not be Pen Meyer. Sisti would do it by underscoring the many conditional and less-than-conclusive findings that a finely obliterated corpse would afford them.

Will Delker had prepared Dr. Ralph Phelan, DDS, for a rough cross from Mark Sisti. While the defense had stipulated to the competency of all of the State's technical witnesses, Sisti had objected to Phelan being certified by the Court as an expert. He was a practicing dentist with experience in forensics, but he wasn't certified in forensics by any board or peer organization. His first fight was about keeping him off the stand.

While introducing Phelan to the court, Delker asked Phelan to explain his credentials. He said that while in the Air Force he had trained to be his base's chief morgue officer of dentistry for two years. He would be called upon to identify remains of crashed pilots, but he never had any victims to study. In private practice, he had been called upon to identify dental remains for New Hampshire law enforcement more than a hundred times, about a third of the victims having been burned. Phelan explained that he never became board certified in forensics because the study also required expertise in the area of bite marks. The State had a tiny amount of cases that involved bite marks, so working on enough to become certified seemed impractical.

After sitting through the prosecution's presentation of each tooth and crown recovered, Sisti was ready to tear into the dentist. He zeroed in on Phelan's analysis that the teeth were "not inconsistent" with Pen Meyer's x-rays.

"You cannot positively identify these teeth, even with the crowns, as being that of Edith Meyer."

"Just consistent with," the dentist tried to clarify.

"Now you're not telling this jury that identifications with regard to dental remains *cannot* be positive, right? There *can* be positives, right?"

"Yes, there can be."

"In this case, they are *not*. Right?"

"They are *consistent with*," he repeated.

"They are not positive, correct?"

"They are *consistent with*, not positive."

"Not positive!" Sisti declared, slamming a hand down on the podium. "I have nothing further."

Cynthia Harvey ended day nine and continued testifying on day ten of the trial. Upon taking the stand, Harv announced that she had finally filed for divorce from Ken Carpenter two weeks earlier.

Sisti and Cook brought a motion to bar Harvey's testimony regarding jailhouse communications on the basis of the marital privilege. "Our Supreme Court said that marital privilege is not a blanket immunity; rather it is a privilege protecting marital confidences," ruled Judge Mangones. He said communications between husband and wife with respect to purely business matters are not such confidences, overruling the defense objection.

Wilson had to be very careful with Harv on the stand. As with Sandy Merritt, she and Delker never knew if they were getting the cooperative wife or the reluctant one. Wilson's strategy was to show the jury Harv, warts and all. Better it come from her than from Sisti.

"After the state police had left your home, what did you do?"

"I started right on that Saturday and I started cleaning and throwing things away."

"Did you find anything pertaining to Sandy Merritt during that time?"

Harv wasn't able to bury her sneer. "I found pictures of her in his dresser. I found a list of what he thought were her good points and bad points."

Wilson then got around to the notebooks she found in the toolbox. Harv testified that she had never read them.

"I found things that led me to believe that Ken had not been completely faithful in our marriage. And I didn't want to read anything else. I didn't want to know anything else."

"What did you do with the notebooks?" Wilson asked.

"I got rid of them," Harv said. "I burned them in the woodstove."

"Why did you burn them in the woodstove?"

Harv looked at the judge, then back to the prosecutor. "Because Ken asked me to."

On cross, Sisti grilled Harv about the security of her property. She admitted she didn't begin locking her door until weeks after Carpenter's arrest—after she began to fear that "Phil" might come for her. He got her to concede that she wouldn't know if someone had come to her home after the state police left and deposited the bones at the stump or placed the letters in the attic.

"In fact," Sisti said, "people could have come and gone from your home without your knowledge even on the twenty-fourth of February 2005, right?"

Harv said it was possible.

When Criminalist Steve Ostrowski presented his testimony, the clocks on the wall ground to a halt. The jury, already fatigued by expert testimony of all shades, began to glaze over as Ostrowski went on a twenty-minute monologue describing the ridges and bifurcations of Ken Carpenter's fingerprint card. Delker tried to move it along, urging the witness to eliminate some of the more extraneous detail. Eventually he made the point that Carpenter's prints had been found on the property agreement. There were no known prints of Pen Meyer's, but a second set of unidentified prints was also on the document.

Under Sisti's cross, Ostrowski allowed that Carpenter's fingerprints were not on other key pieces of evidence, such as the duct tape, the keys, or the envelope. Nor were any of Carpenter's prints ever discovered inside Pen's Center Road home.

"You were at the Meyer home and one of the jobs you had was to check for human blood, right?" Sisti asked. "You came up with nothing, correct?"

"That's correct."

*　*　*

Dale Carpenter, Ken's brother, testified for the prosecution. He told the court that his brother wouldn't level with him about the problems in his marriage to Harv. Dale knew of the affair, and was upset that Carpenter wouldn't seek a divorce.

Dale testified that his brother told him of a different time he drove to Pen Meyer's house to confront her about meddling in his affair. "I believe he was in his Jeep and it was snowing out and she wasn't home. So he turned around and left." As he pulled away, he saw Pen and her dog walking down the road, returning from another of their daily hikes.

"Did he tell you whether he contemplated doing anything?" asked Delker.

"He was emotionally upset and he said he could have just pulled over and hit her." Dale looked down at his hands. "I asked him, 'Why didn't you?' and he says, 'I can't do that. I could not bring myself to do it.'"

The older brother testified about the call he received from Carpenter while he was hiding out in the behavioral unit of Valley Regional Hospital. He asked Dale to come pick him up because he wanted to find the person responsible for Pen's disappearance.

"Did he tell you who was responsible?"

"A guy named Phil," he said. "Phil was responsible for this and he had to find Phil because the police weren't looking for Phil."

*　*　*

Michael Carpenter, Ken's son, was next on the stand. His testimony was brief. The court listened to the recording of his father's phone call urging him to lie about the word processor, then he told the jury he called the state police after conferring with his uncle.

"Have you spoken to your father since that call?" Wilson asked.

"No, I have not."

Dr. Terry Melton was the president and CEO of a company called Mitotyping Technologies. They were the out-of-state firm hired to test the bone fragments for any mitochondrial DNA. Kirsten Wilson let the witness explain the difficulties obtaining a usable DNA sample from remains as thoroughly damaged as these.

"What were the results of your tests?"

"We tested two bones from this case and we got no results from either bone."

When it was Sisti's turn, he asked Melton if she was the actual person who did the testing. She said she was not.

"So I'm here questioning somebody that actually didn't test the material that was sent to you from the State of New Hampshire, correct?"

Melton bristled at the implication. She said she supervised her technicians and they didn't testify in court.

"So you're not the person really from this particular

lab that is the most qualified to be testifying before this jury on the very subject that you were declared an expert on?"

"I disagree with that." Melton said her examiner was highly qualified and had worked on all the remains from the World Trade Center before working for her.

"And this is the person we don't get to question here today, right?"

"I'm here," Melton said.

"Yes you are." Sisti was still unimpressed. "And this person that did all this wonderful work in the past at the World Trade Center and is better qualified than you to select particular questioned fragments of bone is not here to be questioned today."

"No," the doctor said. "She is at another meeting."

Detective Eric Berube testified about the jailhouse recordings he listened to and the letters Carpenter had mailed to family and friends. He described how they led him down other investigative paths, such as looking for "Phil" or recovering the word processor.

In the middle of showing copies of the letters on a screen, the power to the digital projector went out. A passing thunderstorm had disrupted electricity to the old courthouse just long enough to cause the State's laptop to reboot. Watching from the table, Wilson swore this ancient building would be the death of her.

"I'm going to ask you," said Sisti, "did you hear after

listening to eighty hours of tape that Ken Carpenter ever touched Pen Meyer?"

Berube answered, "No."

"Did you hear over the eighty hours of tape that you listened to that Mr. Carpenter killed Pen Meyer?"

"No."

"Nowhere in those letters does it indicate that Ken Carpenter says 'I killed Pen Meyer.' Or 'I kidnapped Pen Meyer.' "

"No."

Sisti asked Berube whether the blankets he received from Dale Carpenter linked either Pen or Carpenter to the crime. They did not, but on redirect, Will Delker came back to the point.

"You testified the defendant showed a particular interest in those blankets," he said. "Why was that significant to you?"

"Because," Berube said, "if the blankets didn't have anything to do with anything, then why would somebody be concerned as to whether or not the police had them?"

Criminalist Mark Dupre testified about his examination of the .22 Marlin rifle seized from Carpenter's shed. If the jurors were hoping to hear that the firearm matched the spent Remington casing retrieved from the burn barrel, they would have been disappointed. He, too, offered only a qualified opinion. The firing pin left similar impressions, but the Marlin could not be definitively linked to that shell.

Sisti also made some hay with the brand of ammo. He noted that while the empty casing was a Remington, all of the ammo found in the weapon and in Carpenter's truck was Federal brand cartridges. Plus, no one could account for how the casing wound up in the barrel in the first place.

"It could have just been left outside?" Sisti pondered.

Dupre agreed it could have.

"I mean, it could have been outside for years, right?"

"That is possible. Yes."

FBI handwriting expert John Sardone began testifying the morning of Tuesday, October 9, 2007. It was the morning after the long Columbus Day weekend. Sardone arrived over the holiday and met with Kirsten Wilson to go over his testimony. The New Yorker was wound up, and expressed disappointment there wasn't anyplace to go on the night of a federal holiday in sleepy Sullivan County.

In court, Sardone presented strongly. He testified that Pen had written the four-page letter discovered in the attic, as well as the envelope and $400 check to Sandy Merritt. He declared her signature on the property agreement to be a forgery. Sardone said the handwriting in the notebooks, as well as the "I need you, I want you, I love you," was Carpenter's.

Sisti's partner, Aime Cook, handled the cross-examination. "You can determine from a handwriting if somebody's hand's shaking, can't you?"

Sardone agreed.

"And if somebody had a gun to their head, they'd have a tremor or handshaking or hesitation?"

"I would think so, yes."

"And you didn't notice any hesitancy in the questioned sample?"

"Not that I could determine. No."

Much of the prosecution's case was now riding on Dr. Marcella Sorg and Dr. Jennie Duval. Intellectually, jurors would never contemplate the meaning of forged signatures and inconvenient fingerprints if they couldn't believe the elementary point: Pen Meyer was murdered. If they couldn't win on that front, nothing else mattered.

Marcy Sorg was not an intimidating presence in the courtroom. She didn't have the physical stature of the burly state troopers who had testified before her. But she carried with her an entirely different kind of gravitas when she testified. She didn't have to say it, but everyone knew she was the smartest person in the room.

Sorg had brought with her photographs from her lab of the hundreds of charred bone fragments she'd had to work with. She explained that after more than a year of work, she was able to partially reconstruct the skeleton. The victim had been a petite, middle-aged woman.

Most important, Sorg had been able to take the cranial bones and reconstruct the skull. Behind the left ear, low toward the neck, Sorg discovered what she referred to as a "defect." She testified that it was a gunshot wound to the head.

"How could you tell this was a gunshot wound?" Wilson asked.

"It's a round hole and it is very clearly sort of punched out. A smoothed edge, round hole. You don't see that kind of roundness in fire damage. You can see this outer bevel that's on the bottom edge."

Using a laser pointer, Sorg circled the area on the digital projections where the bullet struck. The impact point was along a suture, a natural boundary between two of the cerebral plates that fuse together and make the skull. But this skull also had a series of fractures that radiated out from the wound.

"When the bullet impacts the skull, it creates a vacuum just inside the skull wall and that vacuum immediately starts to fill," she explained. "So the bone around the hole actually gets pulled in and causes it to create a concentric fracture."

Wilson asked, "Could you tell what the condition of the body was when the gunshot wound was inflicted?"

"The bone was fresh and I interpret that to mean it was at the time of death."

Sorg said a .22 lead bullet to the skull would leave a hole anywhere between five and eleven millimeters. The size of this hole was nine millimeters. Based on the keyhole-type fracture and the beveled edge, it had the characteristics of an entrance wound. Sorg said a missing fragment could account for the lack of a corresponding exit wound, but a small-caliber projectile like a .22 just as often lodged within the soft tissue of the brain.

Mark Sisti tapped his pen on his legal pad before rising to do his cross-examination. "I want to talk about that particular gunshot evidence there. You're unable to determine the caliber of the round that would have caused that particular defect, correct?"

"The precise caliber? Yes, that is correct."

"In fact, your range is anywhere from five to eleven millimeters. You haven't eliminated, for instance, a nine-millimeter projectile? Or a thirty-two caliber round? Nor a thirty-eight caliber?"

Sorg agreed each time.

"In fact, you're unable to determine whether or not the individual would have been alive, would have been dead, when that particular defect would have been created, right?"

"We can't pinpoint the exact moment, that's true."

"In fact, you haven't come to an opinion from your examination with regard to cause of death?"

"Forensic anthropology does not determine cause of death," Sorg replied. "The medical examiner does that."

"I have nothing further."

Wilson passed Sisti on her way back to the podium. "What role did the destruction of the remains play in your ability to come to a more precise determination about the biological profile?"

"It was very meaningful," said the witness. "If we had more of the remains, we would likely have been able to determine ancestry and be more specific about age and sex."

"So the person who burned, mixed, and pounded these bones prevented you from reaching a more precise determination of a biological profile?"

Sorg turned to the jury and said, "Yes."

Ken Carpenter wrung his folded fingers on the table as he watched Deputy Medical Examiner Jennie Duval take the stand. Kirsten Wilson, in the dark suit she'd been saving for this day, approached the podium and took a deep breath. For months, the AG's office had pestered the medical examiner to issue a death certificate for Pen Meyer. Wilson privately worried that Duval's previous hesitation would be revealed on the stand, and knew that could have a devastating effect on the jury's level of doubt.

"Homicidal violence is how I ruled the cause of death," Duval declared. She said Dr. Sorg's discovery of the bullet hole in the skull had been a key factor in her decision.

"Did you reach a conclusion as to the identification of the remains you examined in this case?" Wilson asked.

Dr. Duval said these were the remains of Edith Pen Meyer. She said the combination of the dental exam and skeletal reconstruction, along with the unique jewelry discovered with the remains, had led to her ruling. Duval also made the point that a low-caliber weapon such as a .22 would likely cause little back spatter, resulting in little or no blood at the crime scene.

Wilson turned the witness over for cross-examination and prayed Sisti would be off his game today. He wasn't.

"You can't rule out this is an accidental death, like being struck by a car?" he started.

"No."

"Can you rule out drowning?"

"I cannot rule out drowning."

"Can you rule out heart attack?"

"I don't have a heart to examine, if that's what you mean."

"You couldn't rule out the bullet defect was self-inflicted?"

"Right," said the doctor. "Except it's in a very unusual location to be self-inflicted."

"You're unable to testify today that this defect created via projectile had anything to do with the cause of death, correct?"

Duval explained the bullet hole did not look like an old wound, nor did it look like it was created postmortem. Sisti waved the response aside and repeated the question.

"Correct," Duval conceded. "She may have survived that wound."

Sisti's voice began to rise. Wilson recognized the building crescendo as he worked his way to a coup de grâce, a finishing blow.

"In fact, you cannot positively identify those remains as being the remains of Edith Pen Meyer for your examination, correct?"

"From my examination alone, no," Duval responded coolly. "I took a lot of different factors into consideration to make this identification."

"That's your *assumption* based on what you know, right?"

"This isn't an assumption," she volleyed. "This is dental records that fit, anthropologic profile that fits. She's missing. Her jewelry is with the remains. This is Pen Meyer."

Wilson sat back in her chair and smiled.

The State recalled Kira Campbell and Jessie Meyer-Eisendrath to wrap up their case. Each identified the charred jewelry as belonging to Pen. To make one final point, Will Delker had Jessie reread the letter in Pen's handwriting about the "incredible day" she had with Carpenter.

"'I have freely spent a day together traveling in harmony. God bless you, Ken. Pen Meyer.'"

"Is there something about the writing that's not characteristic of your sister's writing?" he asked.

"Pen didn't use the word 'God,'" she replied. Pen wouldn't use it in the Pledge of Allegiance, say "Amen" at grace, or even say "Bless you" when someone sneezed. Also, Jessie added, everyone knew she had negative feelings about Ken Carpenter.

"The State rests, Your Honor."

* * *

Before presenting his case, Mark Sisti made a motion to dismiss the prosecution's case, saying they had failed to prove the victim was Pen Meyer, was the victim of a homicide, or that the alleged crime occurred within the state of New Hampshire. Judge Mangones entertained arguments for an hour before dismissing the motion and urging the defense to present its case.

The defense was short and sweet. Mark Sisti called the state trooper who interviewed Lucy Seabrooke and tried to get him to say she was drunk and never provided a description of the man she saw waiting outside Pen Meyer's house. The second witness was an elderly neighbor who wrote in his journal that he saw Pen walking her dog around 8:30 that morning, an hour after Carpenter was supposed to have surprised her inside her home. On cross, Kirsten Wilson pointed out that the man had a habit of forgetting things, which was why he kept the journal. She asked whether he could be mistaken about the day or time, but the old man didn't think he was.

The defense rested on October 10, 2007, with closing arguments slated for the following day.

TWENTY-SIX

Story

Mark Sisti stood up from the defense table and paced toward the jury. He loved closing arguments, and especially savored the moment just before they began. Closing in trial was just like closing a sale, worth doing well, even if it took a while.

"Good afternoon." Sisti gave the jury a broad, open smile. "I'll be a little bit, just so you know, so you can kind of pace yourself." Sisti liked playing the role of friend to the jury. It was a role he played often, and played well.

"This case is not about us. This case is about you. It's a lot bigger than Ken Carpenter or Mark Sisti or Will Delker or Kirsten Wilson. You guys are doing something real important here and I can't emphasize that enough."

Sisti took a breath and appraised the men and women in the jury box.

"If this case, folks, is about whether Ken Carpenter was a good person, okay, then we would be finished. If this case was about whether or not Ken Carpenter lied, then this case would be finished. If this case was about whether or not Ken Carpenter was an adulterer, then this case would be finished. If this case was about Ken Carpenter being a stalker, then this case would be finished. I can go on and on, but that's not what this case is about. You folks have not been drawn from the population of Sullivan County to decide those particular issues.

"You've been drawn here for a much more important, much more significant reason, and that reason is for you to determine whether or not the prosecution in your state, in *your state*, has met its burden of proof by proving your *fellow citizen*, Ken Carpenter, guilty *beyond a reasonable doubt* . . . not whether or not he's a *good* guy, not whether or not he's a piece of *garbage*, but whether or not he's a *murderer*." All trace of good humor had left Sisti's face at this point. Carpenter, sitting quietly at the defense table, winced imperceptibly as his attorney conceded that he was—in fact—a piece of garbage.

"You know, the real question here, folks, is they are asking you to buy in to a theory, not a series of facts, but a theory, a *theory*, that Ken Carpenter killed Edith Meyer in Sullivan County in the State of New Hampshire. The circumstances in this case, folks, do not support that particular theory.

"But you know what's kind of interesting is that even though you heard it over and over and over again, not one of them, not Joanne Dufour, not Jonathan Purick, not Fred Evans, not Richard Dow, nobody, nobody that came forward to say that Ken Carpenter didn't like Edith Meyer, ever said that even in his worst moment, his worst emotional outburst, ever said, 'I'm going to kill her. I'm going to physically hurt her.' Nothing. No physical contact. Nothing. But we're in a situation where they want every one of these people to build some kind of tower to show you that hatred or not liking somebody equals murder. And I've always been told that when the prosecution has no facts, they will emphasize hatred and motive. When they have no facts, they will emphasize the emotion that got the heart.

"The problem that the prosecution is facing is that they have human remains over at the Quimby Farm Road residence of Ken Carpenter that were deposited there at an unknown time between the twenty-third of February 2005 and the twenty-eighth of February 2005 and they also have an additional amount of remains that was deposited there at an unknown time well beyond that.

"Dr. Duval, chief medical . . ." Sisti paused to grin and shrug apologetically. "Not chief, but *assistant* medical examiner for the State of New Hampshire, Dr. Duval took the stand and she agreed that this did not look like all of the remains of a human body. In other words, there was possibly and probably other locations of human remains that could include locations outside of the county and outside of the state. And when there are multiple locations of human remains, then the body has not been found all right. I don't know at this moment what the State's theory is as to how, when, and where this murder took place, but we know from a film at T-Bird's convenience store on Route 12 heading south into another state that Ken Carpenter was in a car and Ken Carpenter was heading *out of New Hampshire*."

Sisti sighed to express his exasperation. He said that speculation had been the backbone of the prosecution's case.

"What's happening here is that not only has the State lost control of placing where this event would have taken place, they continue to delve into theories that are inconsistent with each other. Well, this has got to be it, folks. This has got to be it. Keep throwing it up against the wall, maybe one of them will stick.

"That's not what proof beyond a reasonable doubt is all about. Proof beyond a reasonable doubt is when it links together, when it meshes, when it's comfortable, when you're comfortable, when you look in the mirror the day after your verdict and you say, 'Hey, man, no problem.' When ten years from now you're thinking about this day and you look in the mirror and say, 'Hey, I did the right thing. I followed the law, I followed the facts. I came to the right conclusion.'"

The jurors' eyes were following the charismatic attorney. "You know, they've got to hit a bull's-eye on this target in order for there to be proof beyond a reasonable doubt and they don't have one. They don't have one in the reconstructed skull, they don't have one in any scientific test, they don't have one in any theory, no ballistics, no chemistry, no serology, no fingerprints, no DNA, no eyewitness, no nothing. Nothing but a hope, a hope that you'll hate this guy's guts so that you'll think, 'Oh, because he's so full of bull, he must be guilty.' Full of bull, guilty of murder."

Sisti had been pacing for the better part of his closing argument. Now he stood stock-still and faced the jury square on.

"It's been a long case. Take care of each other back there. Don't do us any special favors. But for God sakes, don't do *them* any special favors, either." He pointed at the prosecution. "At the end of this case, do yourself a special favor, follow the law no matter how difficult the verdict's going to be. Come back through that door and tell the State they just didn't cut it. Thank you."

Will Delker had rewritten his close after his practice run in front of his wife, Annmarie, and Wilson fell flat. They were completely unmoved by the dry recap of the forensic evidence, so with less than twelve hours to go, Delker threw his arguments out and started over from scratch.

"Just tell them a story," his wife advised. No lawyer, but she was an accomplished journalist and knew how to weave a narrative. When Wilson awoke at dawn for her morning run, she passed Delker climbing the stairs to his room. He'd been up all night and now had to pull it together.

Now the senior assistant attorney general pushed his body up from the table and approached the jury. A set of easels with photographs of evidence had been set up in front of the courtroom. For Delker, preparation was key to winning cases. Using an unrehearsed close wasn't exactly his MO, and new territory wasn't something he liked treading into during a murder trial.

"Ladies and gentlemen, for the last hour, Attorney Sisti has thrown out question after question about this case: where, when, why, how, who committed the murder in this case. Well, when the police lifted the cushion from the red chair in the defendant's home at Quimby Hill Road, they found the answers to all of those questions in those journals, the journals written in the defendant's own handwriting. 'In and out. Simple.' Those pages detailed his plans and outlined exactly how he committed the murder."

Delker walked over to a blown-up photo of a page from Carpenter's journal and read it to the jury.

"'House, barn, visit, put down, ground frozen, big fire, outside stove, sticks and limbs. Where did she go? Travel? Visit someone sick. Just disappear. Found.' And on the left margin of that page, he drew a picture of exactly what happened in this case. As crude as that sketch is, there is no doubt about what it depicts. A man wearing a hat walking out with a rifle, shooting Pen Meyer in the head. 'Big fire, outside stove, sticks and limbs.' That's what that man wrote in those journals. That answers every question in this case."

In his mind, Delker heard the advice of his wife: *Tell a story.*

"In this world, there are people just like the defendant who are so twisted and so desperate that they will go to any lengths to cover up their crimes, and the law recognizes that people just like the defendant will mutilate and obliterate the victim's body so that there's nothing recognizable. The defendant should *not* be given the benefit for his horrific actions because he prevented science from determining exactly how the victim died. But what the evidence in this case shows beyond a reasonable doubt is that the defendant killed Pen Meyer."

Tell a story, Delker's mind echoed. As he spoke, the story he wove for the jurors went something like this:

Ken Carpenter slumped in the front seat of Harv's Escort at 6:15 on the morning of February 23, 2005. He had a line of sight down Center Road in front of him, and could see several hundred yards behind the car in his driver's side mirror. He didn't think Pen had left the house for her walk yet, but just in case she had, he wanted to see her coming. He'd thought briefly about driving off when that nosy neighbor had slowed down next to his car, but figured that in this dim light, she probably hadn't really seen him. This far from Pen's house, he was just a guy parked in a nondescript car next to the tree line. He could easily be a hunter, or simply waiting for someone to jump his car battery.

Carpenter perked up when he saw the porch light flick on next to Pen's front door. Right on schedule, the door opened and Fluff burst out of the house, Pen following him in a down coat and heavy, tall boots. Turning out of her driveway, she headed down Center Road in the opposite direction, just like he'd known she would. Fluff romped in front of her, cutting tracks through the snowpack.

Slipping out of his car, Carpenter walked toward Pen's house, and when he reached the driveway, planted his boots in the footprints she'd just made, making no new tracks to her front door. There was no need to break and enter. Pen always left the door unlocked.

After searching the house and finding what he needed, Carpenter waited in the corner of the kitchen out of view of anyone who might come in the door. He knew only one person would. And at 7 a.m. he heard the door open, and felt the rush of cold air sweep into the house, along with the cheerful sound of stomping boots and jingling dog tags. Carpenter emerged from the shadows as Pen was taking off her jacket.

"What the hell are you doing here?" She was too mad to be terrified at his sudden appearance in her kitchen.

"Waiting for you," Carpenter replied. It was then that Pen noticed the rifle in his hands.

"It's almost impossible to imagine what Pen Meyer felt when she found the defendant in her home," Delker said to the jury. "Pen didn't have an opportunity to call the police because the defendant had other plans for her. We know that the defendant was in Pen Meyer's house because at seven thirty-five, Pen Meyer placed a call to Sandy Merritt's answering machine at her home." He held up a document. "Here's the caller ID. Only Sandy wasn't home. She was at work and so the defendant called Sandy Merritt and repeated those same words."

Pen couldn't believe this was happening to her. She was sitting at her own kitchen table in her own house, with a rifle pressed to the back of her head. The whole scene was a perversion. Her hands were shaking as she dialed the phone for a second time. She prayed that Sandy would hear through the script she was about to read and realize she was in trouble. Pen's heart sank when she heard her friend's irritated voice, barely audible over the braying dogs in the kennel where she worked.

Pen read through the script, tears streaming down her cheeks as she realized there was no chance Sandy would understand the code of emotion beneath the words.

"I never meant for it to go this far," Pen recited, prodded by the cold metal pressing on her scalp. "Go to the courthouse and remove the order."

Every bone in Pen's body screamed for her to run, but she couldn't help but hope Carpenter simply wanted her to play this role to add another layer of drama to the situation with Sandy. But when she got a glimpse of the other pages in the notebook, she realized that her chances of escaping had been greatly diminished by the man holding the gun. He'd planned it all out for her. The ending of this story had already been written.

"There's no way anyone will believe any of this, Ken," Pen said through her sobs as she realized the meaning of the papers, "especially not my children." She desperately hoped reminding him that she was someone's mother might humanize her in his eyes. Wasn't that a strategy of self-defense?

"Shut up, bitch. They'll believe it, because you're going to write it all down."

Carpenter then forced Pen to write a long letter, one that explained how she'd spent the day with him voluntarily, and that she had made plans to run off, and wished that he and Sandy would share her home as a couple. Carpenter had Pen copy the letter from one he'd already scripted, in which she also sympathized with his battle against mental illness. As she wrote, Pen hoped that he would snap out of his trance and realize the absurdity of the situation.

"Ken, you'll never get away with this. It's not too late for you to just leave, just walk out the door. I won't tell anyone you were here . . ."

"Shut. UP." Carpenter growled and pushed the muzzle of the rifle against the back of Pen's head. "Write."

When the letter was finished, Carpenter leaned over and scrawled something on the bottom of it. Then he produced one final document. He handed her the property transfer form, which she took with her right hand. "Sign," he ordered.

Pen knew at that moment she was going to die. The

document was blank except for lines for signatures, but Pen understood what they were for. He would fill in afterwards that Pen had signed over her house, the house he knew she loved more than any place in the world. She made a decision to draw the line. He was going to take her life, but he would never live in these walls. He would never eat in this kitchen. He would never walk through the garden she'd planted. He could take her life, but not this.

Pen Meyer turned around and faced the man who was now pointing a rifle directly at her face. She locked eyes with him and took a deep breath.

"Go to hell, Ken."

And then Pen Meyer tried to run.

Delker's eyes went to each juror's face, one by one. "We know that Ken Carpenter made Pen Meyer do all these things because of the journals in which he describes the plan for Pen. And after the defendant made Pen do these things, he knew he couldn't just let Pen go."

Kenneth Carpenter knew that Pen didn't weigh much, but he hadn't expected carrying her out to the Escort would be quite this easy. Of course, the plan hadn't called for having to carry her just then . . . he'd truly hoped to convince her to go somewhere with him, somewhere he could take care of things with less risk. But the bitch had decided to run, and that meant he had to think on his feet.

This time he didn't bother with stepping inside Pen's tracks. It was snowing so hard that even the ones she'd made earlier in the morning had disappeared, and the impression of her body, and the few drops of blood that had spilled on the snow after he shot her, were fast vanishing as well. To make sure, he scooped up the stained snow and packed it into a firm snowball that he threw far into the woods. His single shot had killed her instantly. Easy to clean up, he thought. One of the many benefits of a .22.

He wrapped Pen in a blanket he'd found in her house and placed her in the Escort, slamming the hatchback with the WWJD *bumper sticker. Carpenter then went back to the house to clean up any sign that he'd been there, copying what he'd learned from watching hundreds of episodes of* CSI. *He straightened up the boots in the foyer, wiped down any surface he thought he might have touched. Before leaving the house, he took one last look around, making sure he had everything he'd planned to take. He had her house key, which had been hanging on a hook in the kitchen. He'd also taken the ring that held her car key and her safe-deposit key. He had her AA medallion.*

Fluff had been surprisingly calm the entire time he'd been in the house. The dog was now lying on the kitchen floor near the stove. "Bye, Fluff," Carpenter said before closing the door behind him.

Climbing into the Escort, Carpenter turned around to look at the bundle in the hatchback. Pen was so tiny that the blankets fully obscured her form as a human being. He needed to get gas. Would he try to dispose of the body in

*Greenfield, Massachusetts, or would he do it in Lempster?
Burn the blankets, burn his clothes, burn the remains. She
was too big to lay across his fire pit. Perhaps if he put her in
the barrel first . . .*

*Starting the car, Carpenter checked both ways to make
sure no more nosy neighbors were on their way down the
road. He was alone, and as he pulled out and drove down
Center Road toward civilization, he marveled at the still-
ness of New Hampshire's winter woods.*

Delker pounded the podium. "Pen Meyer stood in Ken
Carpenter's way. She ruined his life in his mind and he
scripted out word for word what he needed her to do. He
typed it on the word processor and then he made Pen
Meyer almost completely disappear by incinerating her
body in order to carry out his plan to reunite with Sandy.
Those actions are as ruthless and calculating and premedi-
tated as the human mind can imagine."

Throughout the trial, Will Delker had been thoughtful, soft-spoken. Now he was speaking emphatically, his
voice raised to a pitch and volume the jury hadn't yet
heard. He wasn't delivering his close; he was preaching
it. He turned to face Kenneth Carpenter.

"That man right there left a trail of human wreckage
in this case that didn't end with the murder of Pen Meyer.
He manipulated witness after witness. Sandy Merritt,
Dale Carpenter. He used his own son to lie to the police
and cover up evidence. He drove his wife to the brink of

suicide with his lies and manipulation. These actions show you that man is willing to do anything to get what he wants.

"It's only a matter of common sense that he would step to the level of committing an almost unimaginable, gruesome murder to get what he wanted. Don't let the defendant manipulate you like he tried to manipulate everyone else in this case. Don't believe his lies."

Delker strode to the jury box and waited a beat to make sure he had their full attention.

"The evidence proves *beyond a reasonable doubt* that the defendant murdered Pen Meyer and that he is guilty of first-degree murder and that is the only just verdict you can render in this case."

TWENTY-SEVEN

Justice

After closings were done, Judge Mangones drew lots to determine which three members of the panel would serve as alternates and who would be the jury foreman. Mangones pulled a plastic numbered ball from a little jug selecting juror number five—the man who kept dozing off during testimony—as foreman.

The panel was dismissed for the afternoon and told to return the following day at 8:00 a.m. to begin deliberations.

On the morning of Friday, October 13, 2007, the jury in the case of *The State of New Hampshire v. Kenneth Carpenter* convened for deliberations in the grand jury room of the Sullivan County Courthouse. After just two hours, notice was sent to Judge Mangones and the attorneys on both sides that a verdict had been reached.

The courtroom was packed to capacity. Behind Wilson and Delker at the prosecution's table, Pen's children sat with their spouses and some of her siblings, including her sister Jessie. Behind them, Jonathan Purick sat with several of his and Pen's friends from AA. There was no one in the courtroom to support Carpenter except for his cousin, Allen Long.

Judge Mangones banged his gavel and the courtroom fell silent. He then nodded to his clerk, who addressed the jury.

"Will the foreperson of the jury please stand. Mr. Foreman, in case 05-S-251, has the jury reached a verdict?"

The foreman nodded. "Yes, we have."

"Mr. Foreman, in Indictment 05-S-251, first-degree murder alleging that Kenneth Carpenter did purposely cause the death of Edith 'Pen' Meyer and incinerate her body, how say you? Is the defendant, guilty or not guilty?"

"Guilty."

The courtroom suddenly came alive with sound as Pen's family began hugging one another. Jessie was crying. Jonathan Purick was shaking hands all around, his back slapped repeatedly by the friends flanking him in support of Pen.

Judge Mangones again banged his gavel, calling the room to order.

"You say he is guilty, Mr. Foreman?" Mangones asked.

"Yes."

"So say you all, ladies and gentlemen of the jury?"

The members of the jury responded in chorus, "Yes, we do."

Mangones turned to the defense table, where Carpenter sat next to Mark Sisti, looking stunned.

"All right," he said. "Do you wish to have the jury polled?"

"We would, Your Honor," Sisti replied quietly.

The clerk then addressed the jury.

"Juror number one, would you please stand? In case 05-S-251, first-degree murder, alleging that Kenneth Carpenter did purposely cause the death of Edith 'Pen' Meyer, how say you? Is the defendant, guilty or not guilty?"

"Guilty."

Ken Carpenter sat silently, staring at his hands. He was trembling slightly, but as each juror declared his guilt, even those in the back of the courtroom could see him shudder violently as he felt the impact of twelve blows of judgment.

"Juror number two . . ."

Sentencing is a hasty matter in New Hampshire, taking place directly after the jury's verdict. In this case, Judge Mangones ordered a short recess, reconvening the court after lunch. The entire jury, officially dismissed from their duties, went to the Salt Hill Pub together for a celebratory meal.

Before exiting for the recess, Will Delker and Kirsten

Wilson went to the gallery to greet Pen's family. There were handshakes and hugs from the grateful relatives. Jessie Meyer-Eisendrath pulled Wilson close and whispered in her ear.

"I believe Pen chose you to be her voice in this case," the sister said.

With that, tears streamed freely down Wilson's face. All she had wanted to do from the beginning was honor Pen Meyer. Even more than the verdict, those words from Pen's sister made her feel that she had accomplished what she'd set out to do.

When the judge returned for sentencing, Delker stood up from the prosecution's table.

"The State has consulted with the victim's family, and they choose not to address the Court at this point. The State's request is the Court impose the statutory mandatory sentence of life imprisonment without the possibility of parole."

Judge Mangones then turned to Sisti. He stood, looking somber.

"Your Honor, there is no option that the Court presently has with regard to that sentence and both I and Mr. Carpenter understand that. Because of that, we will not be commenting concerning the sentence."

"All right. Thank you." Mangones paused and studied his hands for a moment. "Mr. Carpenter, if you'd stand please."

Carpenter shuffled to his feet. Sisti placed a hand on his client's arm as if to steel him for the inevitable.

"Upon a finding of guilty of first-degree murder entered by the jury, Kenneth Carpenter is sentenced to life imprisonment at the New Hampshire State Prison and shall not be eligible for parole at any time."

The courtroom again sprang to life as cameras flashed and the tears of Pen's family and friends flowed.

Mangones banged his gavel one last time and addressed Carpenter.

"You're remanded to the custody of the sheriff, sir."

Outside the courthouse, a crush of reporters waited as Pen's family emerged from the building. Refusing to comment, they waived the press off and walked quickly to their cars. Jonathan Purick, however, had no such reluctance about talking to the press.

"This verdict is bittersweet," he told one reporter. "She always looked for the best in people, and at the same time, was able to not give herself and her dignity away."

"Do you hate Kenneth Carpenter?" another reporter shouted.

Jonathan shook his head. "I understand that he's a sick man," he said, "and because his human frailties are very severe, that's why he did what he did. It's not that I forgive him, but by hating him, I gain nothing. I don't hate him anymore. I feel sorry for him."

Epilogue

Jonathan Purick limped along emotionally for many months after the conviction of Kenneth Carpenter. He settled into his little cabin on Center Road in Goshen, a mile from Pen's old home overlooking the Goshen Ocean. He kept several photos of Pen (who despite her fairylike good looks did not enjoy being photographed) in frames tucked in various corners of the house.

Purick continued to go to Millie's Place and interacted with many of the people who were central to this drama. One day he spoke to Cynthia "Harv" Harvey about how she was getting along since the end of the trial. She had completed her schooling and was now working as a nurse at the VA Hospital in White River Junction, Vermont.

"It's tough," she admitted. "Ken is fighting me about the divorce."

Jonathan offered to go to court with her to speak on her behalf. He thought Harv was surprised that anyone at Millie's would help her with anything to do with Carpenter. Jonathan didn't want to harbor feelings of anger toward Harv, and he thought this could be some form of peace offering.

When Carpenter saw Jonathan enter the courtroom, he stood in his chair and yelled at the judge. "Your Honor, this man is a drunk and a liar and should be thrown out of this courtroom immediately." The judge declined to do so.

Jonathan was taken aback by the outburst, but then he leaned back on the bench and thought, *You know what? Fuck you, Ken. I'm glad my presence here makes you a little uncomfortable.* The divorce was granted, and Carpenter was taken back to the state prison for men in Concord to serve out the rest of his life term.

Joanne Dufour remarried and continues to work at the Newport Town Hall. She says she believes in angels and that her friend Pen is always with her.

Russell Lamson retired from the New Hampshire State Police in 2010, trying to stay ahead of budget cuts and threats by lawmakers to his pension. He took a job as the single patrolman for the Goshen Police Department. Each day, he answers the very phone where that anonymous call came in.

Detective Shawn Skahan was promoted to sergeant and is a patrol supervisor for Troop C. Detective Eric Berube transferred out of the NH State Police and is now an investigator for the NH Fire Marshal's Office. Both say the Pen Meyer case was one of the most challenging they ever had.

Trooper John Encarnacao was promoted to sergeant and continues to work in evidence collection. The lessons learned in the Pen Meyer case regarding the recovery and sifting of obliterated bones helped state police teams a year later when investigating a female serial killer who dismembered her victims and burned their remains. The case is the basis for the author's book *Wicked Intentions*.

Sandy Merritt still lives in Sullivan County, working day to day to keep herself healthy. She said she often reflects on her time with Carpenter and Pen, but remains confused by all that happened to her. She said that she and Pen were just casual friends outside of AA, and didn't see much of each other after Christmas 2004, when Pen and Jonathan's relationship grew more serious.

In a letter Sandy wrote to the authors, she said Pen was always very supportive of her, and she hoped Pen felt the same way about her.

"I am still trying to process the murder and how it transpired," Sandy wrote. "I think of it often, it seems to just intrude on my thoughts at the oddest moments."

The family of Pen Meyer declined requests to be interviewed for this book. Colin Campbell, Pen's first husband, continues his career as a banker and a community leader. Richard Rankin, Pen's second husband, died in August 2011 in Texas. He donated a small footbridge along a walking trail in Goshen, which was dedicated as the "Pen Meyer Bridge" on her birthday, July 4, 2005. Pen's children still live in New Hampshire.

In March 2012, a judge ruled that the remains of Pen Meyer, no longer needed for further legal appeals, could be released to Pen's elderly parents for a family burial.

Mark Sisti remains the highest regarded criminal defense attorney in New Hampshire. His hair is still in a ponytail; his wardrobe is still somewhat ragged. One of Sisti's proudest accomplishments is that his daughter completed law school and is now serving as a public defender.

Defense attorney Aime Cook underwent gender reassignment surgery and now practices at his own firm in Peterborough, New Hampshire, the Adam Cook Law Firm.

As a reporter for the *Concord Monitor*, Will Delker's wife, Annmarie Timmons, had many occasions to return to the aging Sullivan County Courthouse. On one such visit, after interviewing the county attorney on an unrelated matter, he turned to the bailiffs and court staff to announce, "This is Will's wife."

The eyes of all the court personnel grew wide with admiration. "You weren't here for that closing argument, were you?" they asked.

"I wasn't," she said. "I don't get to cover cases that my husband prosecutes."

The bailiffs ushered her into the courtroom and pointed. "He stood right there when he gave it," they said with great reverence. The closing in the Carpenter case was legendary in this building. All who had been there agreed it was the best closing argument they'd ever heard.

Saying he promised Pen's family he would not publicly discuss the case, Will Delker respectfully declined to contribute to this book.

Delker continued on at the Attorney General's Office and won several more homicide convictions for the state of New Hampshire. In 2009, he transferred to work as the full-time prosecutor for the State's newly formed Cold

Case Unit. The unit was established in part after the successful resolution of a twenty-year-old unsolved murder of a child molester and a group of friends who protected the teenage shooter. The case was the basis for the authors' book *Our Little Secret*.

In June 2011, Delker was nominated by Governor John Lynch to become a district court judge. He keeps a letter of thanks written to him by Pen's family on his personal desk.

After the verdict, some of the jurors spoke to the press. One woman said she had fallen in love with the person that Pen Meyer was. Another juror said he was unsure the State had made its case until the very end. He told a reporter that it wasn't until Will Delker's closing argument that he saw all the connections between the evidence he'd been shown, and that's why he voted to convict.

Perhaps most personally changed by the Pen Meyer case was Kirsten Wilson. The assistant AG became the lead prosecutor in a 2005 murder-for-hire case. Wealthy John Brooks had handyman Jack Reid killed for a theft he didn't commit. The attorney general felt so strongly about the case, her office sought a death penalty conviction. It was the first capital crime pursued in the state since the 1930s. (To this day, New Hampshire doesn't have a modern death chamber.)

Wilson spent months embroiled in preparations for the 2008 trial and suffered a crisis of conscience. One night, fighting back tears, she spoke to her husband about it.

"Brooks spent two years planning the death of another man and had two men carry it out for him. Now, I'm doing the exact same thing to him." Wilson, recalling this conversation with the authors, said to her husband in a small voice, "I really feel like I'm going to go to Hell."

Her husband instead asked her just how long she was going to be away for this trial, leaving him alone with the kids.

Kirsten Wilson is now Kirsten Bell. She says she drew on inspiration from Pen Meyer to transform her life. Now divorced, she's no longer working at the Attorney General's Office. For a time, she practiced at a small firm, but now works as a legal consultant and commentator for Fox News. In her spare time, Wilson has returned to painting, and takes photos of scenes she encounters while walking near her New Hampshire home.

When she's asked about her experiences trying the Kenneth Carpenter case, Wilson is emphatic in her belief that what made him stand apart from other defendants she's prosecuted was his frightening ability to identify the vulnerabilities of the women around him, and to exploit those women through sheer manipulation. She's also sure of something else, that there's no way the Pen Meyer she came to know would have ever allowed Kenneth Carpenter to manipulate her in the same way.

"Pen was an unbelievable woman," she says, "I know it sounds strange, but I still feel connected to her."

Another addition to Kirsten Bell's life is a Swiss Mountain Dog mix named Chaos. He got the name his first day home by sticking his head in an open dishwasher and getting his collar wrapped around the drawer, pulling the entire clanging load out with him. Chaos doesn't go with Bell to court or wait in the car while she does her grocery shopping. But when Kirsten attaches his lead as she prepares to take him running in the morning, she's reminded of the friend she never met, but who so changed her life. As she wraps the nylon tether around her wrist and they head out the door, the soft jingle of dog tags sings to her, and she knows that, at least some of the time, things are as they should be.